Presented pursuant to the GRA Act 2000

# Ministry of Defence
# Annual Report and Accounts
# Volume II

including the Annual Performance Report and
Consolidated Departmental Resource Accounts

## 2007-08

(For the year ended 31 March 2008)

Laid in accordance with the Government Resources and Accounts Act 2000

Ordered by the House of Commons to be printed
21 July 2008

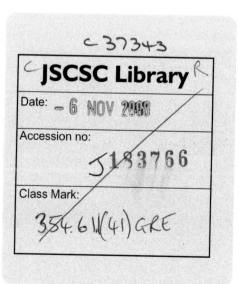

London: The Stationery Office
HC 850-II

21 July 2008
£51.45 Not to be sold separately

# Departmental Resource Accounts 2007-08

# Notes to the accounts

# The Annual Report

## History and Background

The present Ministry of Defence (MoD), the Department, was formed by the amalgamation in 1964 of the Ministry of Defence, the Admiralty, the War Office and the Air Ministry, and the inclusion in 1971 of the Ministry of Aviation Supply. In 1973, the operations of the Atomic Weapons Establishment were transferred from the UK Atomic Energy Authority to the MoD.

## Principal Activity

The principal activity of the Department is to deliver security for the people of the United Kingdom and the Overseas Territories by defending them, including against terrorism, and act as a force for good by strengthening international peace and stability. This is achieved by working together to produce battle-winning people and equipment that are:

- fit for the challenge of today,

- ready for the tasks of tomorrow, and

- capable of building for the future.

Further definition of the Departmental Objectives in terms of outputs is given in the Statement of Operating Costs by Departmental Aim and Objectives and in its supporting Note to the Accounts – Note 24.

## Departmental Boundary[1]

As at 31 March 2008, the Department consisted of 9 (2006-07: 12) Top Level Budget (TLB) Holders. Merging the RAF's Strike and Personnel & Training Commands to form Air Command, and the Defence Procurement Agency with the Defence Logistics Organisation to form Defence Equipment and Support reduced the number of TLBs by two. The reduction in TLBs also reflects the fact that General Officer Commanding (Northern Ireland) (GOC(NI)) ceased to be a TLB when it became part of Land Command on 1 April 2007. The TLBs are responsible for providing forces and support services required for a modern defence force and are detailed in Note 2 to the accounts – Analysis of Net Resource Outturn. Within the TLBs, there were 49 (2006-07: 57) reporting entities, known as management groupings, recording accounting balances and transactions and producing detailed management accounting information as part of in-year financial management and planning and budgeting processes. One of the aims of the Department's Simplify and Improve initiative is to reduce the workload on finance staff. Consequently, whilst accounting transactions are still attributed to the management group level for in-year management purposes, reporting for the annual financial accounts is now normally completed only at TLB level.

There are 8 on-vote Defence Agencies (listed in Note 35), a reduction of 9 from 2006-07 following the removal of agency status on 1 April 2007 from the following: British Forces Post Office, Defence Bills Agency, Defence Communication Services Agency, Defence Estates, Defence Procurement Agency, Defence Transport and Movements Agency, Disposal Services Agency and Duke of York's Royal Military School and the merger of the Armed Forces Personnel Administration Agency and the Veterans Agency, also on 1 April 2007, to form the Service Personnel and Veterans Agency. Defence agencies publish their own accounts. All on-vote agencies are also management groupings, except for the Defence Storage and Distribution Agency which forms part of a larger management grouping. Further information relating to the Defence Agencies can be found at Annex E to the Annual Report and Accounts.

---

1 The Departmental Boundary in this context relates to the boundary of the Departmental Resource Accounts.

Also included within the Departmental Boundary are Advisory Non-Departmental Public Bodies (NDPBs) sponsored by the Department; these are listed at Note 35 – Entities within the Departmental Boundary.

There are 5 (2006-07: 5) Executive Defence Agencies established as Trading Funds, and owned by the Secretary of State for Defence, at 31 March 2008. These Trading Funds produce their own accounts and fall outside the Departmental Boundary. Further details are at: Note 15 – Investments, Note 32 – Related Party Transactions and at Annex E.

The Department also sponsors 5 Executive Non-Departmental Public Bodies, which publish their own accounts. They receive Grants-in-Aid from the MoD and fall outside the Departmental Boundary. Further details are at Note 32 – Related Party Transactions.

The Oil and Pipelines Agency, NAAFI and the Fleet Air Arm Museum are Public Corporations sponsored by the Department. They also fall outside the Departmental Boundary.

## Pension Liabilities

The transactions and balances of the Armed Forces Pension Scheme (AFPS) (including the Gurkha Pension Scheme, the Non-Regular Permanent Staff Pension Scheme and the Reserve Forces Pension Scheme) and the Armed Forces Compensation Scheme are not consolidated in these financial statements. The report and accounts of the AFPS are prepared separately; further information is available on the website: http://www.mod.uk/DefenceInternet/AboutDefence/WhatWeDo/Personnel/Pensions/ArmedForcesPensions/

The Department's share of the transactions and balances of other pension schemes to which employees belong (e.g. under Civil Service Pension (CSP) arrangements, the NHS Superannuation Scheme and the Teachers' Pension Scheme) is also not consolidated in these accounts; separate accounts are prepared for the schemes and details can be found on the following websites:
http://www.civilservice-pensions.gov.uk/facts_and_figures.aspx
www.dfes.gov.uk/aboutus/reports/
www.nhspa.gov.uk/site/index.cfm

Further information on the various pension schemes can be found in the Remuneration Report and at Note 9 – Staff Numbers and Costs.

## Future Developments

The Department has comprehensive efficiency and change programmes that extend right across the Department and affect every employee. The details of many of these programmes are set out in the section on Efficiency and Change in the Annual Performance Report, which forms the first part of the MoD Annual Report and Accounts.

MoD's programme of efficiency and business change includes extensive organisational restructuring and rationalisation that is likely to reduce further the number of on-vote Agencies; the Defence Analytical Services Agency and the Defence Medical Education and Training Agency ceased to have agency status with effect from 1 April 2008.

One of the principal areas of change, being taken forward in response to the Capability Review of the MoD, is being managed under the Streamlining programme. The programme will simplify the Department's organisation and work, ensuring the MoD is focused on strategic tasks and better able to respond to priorities. Streamlining will release more resources to the front line by reducing MoD's Head Office in London, in cost and number of staff, by 25%. Further information on the MoD's actions in response to the Capability Review can be found in the Annual Performance Report which forms the first part of the Annual Report and Accounts.

Project Hyperion continues work to integrate the headquarters of Commander-in-Chief Land Command and the Adjutant General to form a single, integrated headquarters to be known as Headquarters Land Forces (HQ LF). Land Forces became a single Command and TLB with effect from 1 April 2008 and the collocation to the new HQ LF is expected to take place in the first half of 2010.

In May 2007, the MoD announced the creation of a new organisation to provide a maintenance, repair, overhaul and upgrade capability in support of the Armed Forces. Formed by merging ABRO with the retained Defence Aviation Repair Agency business units and some other defence engineering activities, the Defence Support Group began operating as a Trading Fund with effect from 1 April 2008.

## Management

The Ministers who had responsibility for the Department and the composition of the Defence Board (the Defence Management Board was reconstituted as the Defence Board in January 2008) during the year ended 31 March 2008 are shown on pages 252 and 253 in the Remuneration Report.

## Fixed Assets

Intangible and tangible fixed assets are accounted for by Single Balance Sheet Owners based on the category of asset managed:

● Land and Buildings – Defence Estates

● Single Use Military Equipment – Defence Equipment and Support

● Plant & Machinery – Defence Equipment and Support

● Transport – Defence Equipment and Support

● IT & Communications – Defence Equipment and Support

Changes in fixed asset values during the year are summarised at Notes 13, 14 and 15 (Intangible Assets, Tangible Fixed Assets and Investments) to the accounts. Note 1 – Statement of Accounting Policies provides details of the accounting policies relating to fixed assets.

## Research and Development

Research and development expenditure is incurred mainly for the future benefit of the Department. Such expenditure is primarily incurred on the development of new single use military equipment and on the improvement of the effectiveness and capability of existing single use military equipment.

In accordance with Statement of Standard Accounting Practice (SSAP)13, "Accounting for Research and Development" (as adapted for the public sector by HM Treasury's Financial Reporting Manual (FReM), paragraphs 5.3.6 to 5.3.8), amounts spent on research are not capitalised, and certain development expenditure is expensed. The amounts are included at Note 10 – Other Operating Costs.

Capitalised development expenditure is included in Intangible Assets, where appropriate, and shown in Note 13.

## Net Expenditure

The Operating Cost Statement shows net expenditure of £36,223,006,000 which has been charged to the General Fund. Cash voted by Parliament for the Provision of Defence Capability (RfR 1), Operations and Peace Keeping (RfR 2) and War Pensions Benefits (RfR 3) amounting to £33,851,588,000 has been credited to the General Fund (Note 21).

## Dividends

Details of dividends and loan interest received on investments can be found at Notes 11, 12 and 15 (Income, Net Interest Payable and Investments) to the accounts.

## Payments to Suppliers

The Department's bills, with the exception of some payments to suppliers by units locally, are paid through the Financial Management Shared Service Centre (FMSSC), which took over the responsibilities of the Defence Bills Agency. In the period 1 April 2007 to 31 March 2008, the FMSSC paid 99.76% of all correctly submitted bills within eleven calendar days, ensuring that the Department is in compliance with its statutory obligation under the Late Payment of Commercial Debts (Interest) Act 1998. Commercial debt interest paid during this period amounted to £9,956 (2006-07: £8,603) and included interest paid by units locally of £5,228 (2006-07: £23).

## Departmental Reporting Cycle

The MoD's main Departmental Report presented to Parliament each year is the *Ministry of Defence Annual Performance Report* which forms the first section of the Annual Report and Accounts and sets out the MoD's performance over the year, and developments since the year end where appropriate, against the objectives stated in the Statement of Operating Costs by Departmental Aim and Objectives as set out in the *Defence Plan*. In addition *The Government's Expenditure Plans: Ministry of Defence*, sets out planned expenditure over the following year. From 2008-09 these two have been combined into a single document, *Defence Plan 2008 Including the Government's Expenditure Plans 2008-2012*, published in the Spring. The MoD's financial performance is also reported to Parliament in the explanatory memoranda to the Main and Supplementary Estimates, and in the *Public Expenditure Outturn White Paper*. In-year performance against Public Service Agreement and Efficiency targets and Departmental Strategic Objectives is formally reported to Parliament during the year in the Autumn and Spring Performance Reports. Copies of *The Government's Expenditure Plans: Ministry of Defence* can be found at the website:
http://www.mod.uk/DefenceInternet/AboutDefence/CorporatePublications/BusinessPlans/GovernmentExpenditurePlans/
Copies of the Defence Plan can be found at the website:
http://www.mod.uk/DefenceInternet/AboutDefence/CorporatePublications/BusinessPlans/DefencePlans/

## Financial Instruments

The Department does not trade or enter into any speculative transactions in foreign currencies. Forward contract commitments entered into to cover future expenditure in foreign currencies are stated at Note 28 – Financial Instruments.

## Provision of Information and Consultation with Employees

The MoD has a strong Whitley committee structure through which employees' representatives, in the form of recognised industrial and non industrial trades unions (TUs), are consulted on and informed of all matters likely to affect our civilian personnel. This structure is supported by formal policy and procedures for consulting and informing TUs. We also advocate the development of informal relationships with the TUs to discuss ideas together. Our policy makes clear that consulting the TUs is not a substitute for dealing with personnel direct, and vice versa. Managers and project leaders, for example, are encouraged to use all media available, including cascade briefings, newsletters and intranet websites/email. In respect of Service personnel, the process operates through the chain of command, with no formal representation through the TUs.

# Management Commentary

## Performance

The Annual Performance Report forms the first part of the MoD Annual Report and Accounts and provides the detailed information set out, as best practice, in the Accounting Standards Board's (ASB's) Reporting Statement: Operating and Financial Review.

The Performance Report uses the Defence Balanced Scorecard structure to:

● describe Defence strategies, objectives and activities, and how they are managed and delivered in the legislative, regulatory and external environments in which we operate, in particular in the sections on Current Operations, Readiness, Policy, Defence in the Wider Community, Safety, Security and Business Continuity, and Estate;

● provide a forward looking view of performance and development for the reporting year, with sections on Future Personnel, Change, and Future Capabilities;

● set out information on the availability and use of resources, covering: Equipment and Support, Finance and Efficiency (including the Wider Markets Initiative), People, Estate, and Reputation.

The Annual Performance Report also describes some of the risks and uncertainties which might affect performance.

The Statement on Internal Control describes the Department's risk and control framework and its relationship to the Performance Management System. The Department's annual Corporate Governance Report is contained in Annex B to the Annual Report and Accounts, and the Departmental approach to Performance Management is detailed in Annex D.

## Environmental, Social, Community, Employee and Other Matters

The preface to the Annual Report and Accounts summarises senior managers' views of how the Department's work will realise the Defence Vision, highlighting all relevant matters. Some specific aspects mentioned in the ASB's Reporting Statement that are covered by the Performance Report are:

● **Social and Community Issues** – included in the sections: Current Operations e.g. Crisis Response Operations and Military Aid to the Civil Authorities and Defence in the Wider Community, e.g. Sustainable Communities, and in the essay on the Defence Educational Outreach programme.

● **Environmental** – included in the Sustainable Development and Environmental part of the section on Defence in the Wider Community. The MoD owns a large, varied and complex estate, with most of the UK's indigenous habitat types, exceptional biodiversity and some of the finest archaeology in the country. Further information on how the MoD is undertaking its responsibility for stewardship of the estate in the UK and overseas including links to, *Sanctuary*, the annual MoD Conservation magazine can be found at the MoD Conservation Office website: http://www.defence-estates.mod.uk/conservation/index.php

● **Employees** – information is provided in the following sections: People, Future Personnel, and Safety, Security and Business Continuity, and in the essays on the Support to Operations programme and on Civilians in Defence. Information on policy and numbers of disabled staff can be found in the People section and at Annex F – Government Standards.

- **Performance Indicators** – these are included at the start of each section of the Performance Report where the Objective, Public Service Targets, Performance Measures and the Assessment against the measures are set out. Additional information can be found in *Defence Plans* available on the website:
  http://www.mod.uk/DefenceInternet/AboutDefence/CorporatePublications/BusinessPlans/
  DefencePlans/ and in the Summary Assessment and Performance against SR2004 Public Service Agreement Objectives and Targets at the beginning of the Performance Report.

- **Contractual Arrangements** – some of the Department's major contractual commitments are detailed in Note 27 to the accounts – Private Finance Initiative (PFI) Commitments, and in the sections in the Performance Report on Finance and Efficiency, Equipment and Support, and Estate. In 2007-08 the Defence Science and Technology Laboratory, the UK Hydrographic Office, the Met Office, the Defence Aviation Repair Agency and ABRO were Executive Defence Agencies financed by Trading Fund; they provided essential services to the Department. Further information on Trading Funds is at Annex E to the Annual Report and Accounts. Details of significant contracts relating to the management of the Defence Estate are included in the Estate section of the Performance Report.

- **Spending Review** – the financing implications of significant changes following the Department's Comprehensive Spending Review settlement are set out in *Defence Plan 2008 Including the Government's Expenditure Plans 2008-2012*, which, with the MoD Annual Report and Accounts, comprise the MoD's Departmental Report. These reports and other business plans are available on the following website.
  www.mod.uk/DefenceInternet/AboutDefence/CorporatePublications/

- **Contingent Liabilities** – Details of Contingent Liabilities disclosed under Financial Reporting Standard (FRS) 12 and additional liabilities included for Parliamentary Reporting and Accountability are at Notes 29 and 30 to these accounts.

## Personal Data Related Incidents

The following tables set out details of the Department's personal data related incidents during 2007-08 and, in the case of Table 3, the previous three financial years. An incident is defined as a loss, unauthorised disclosure or insecure disposal. Protected personal data is information that links an identifiable living person with information about them which, if released, would put the individual at significant risk of harm or distress; the definition includes sources of information that because of the nature of the individuals or the nature, source or extent of the information, is treated as protected personal data by the Department.

Incidents, the disclosure of which would create an unacceptable risk of harm, have been excluded or limited, in accordance with exemptions contained in the Freedom of Information Act 2000 and other UK information legislation.

## Table 1: Summary of Protected Personal Data Related Incidents Formally Reported to the Information Commissioner's Office in 2007-08

| Month of Incident | Nature of Incident | Nature of Data Involved | Number of People Potentially Affected | Notification Steps |
|---|---|---|---|---|
| January | Loss of a non-encrypted laptop from a hire car outside secured Government premises. | Name, date of birth, address, passport number, next of kin, bank account details, National Insurance number. | Estimated at 620,000 personal records which also contain limited details of approximately 450,000 referees and next of kin. | Individuals notified by post. Police notified. Media releases and a statement to Parliament on 21 January 2008 |
| February | Loss of a non-encrypted laptop from outside secured Government premises. | Name, date of birth, address, next of kin. | Estimated at 250. | Individuals notified by post. Police notified. Media releases. |
| Further action on information risk. | | The Department will continue to monitor and assess its information risks, in light of the events noted above, in order to identify and address any weaknesses and ensure continuous improvement of its systems. The Secretary of State for Defence instigated an independent review, to be conducted by Sir Edmund Burton, in response to the first loss. The recommendations of the Burton review will be acted on in 2008-09. | | |

## Table 2: Summary of Other Protected Personal Data Related Incidents in 2007-08

Incidents deemed by the Data Controller not to fall within the criteria for report to the Information Commissioner's Office but recorded centrally within the Department are set in the table below. Small, localised incidents are not recorded centrally and are not cited in these figures.

| Category | Nature of Incident | Total |
|---|---|---|
| I | Loss of inadequately protected electronic equipment, devices or paper documents from secured Government premises. | - |
| II | Loss of inadequately protected electronic equipment, devices or paper documents from outside secured Government premises. | 2 |
| III | Insecure disposal of inadequately protected paper documents. | 1 |
| IV | Unauthorised disclosure. | - |
| V | Other. | - |

## Table 3: Year-on-Year Total Numbers of Protected Personal data Related Incidents Prior to 2007-08

Total number of protected personal data related incidents formally reported to the Information Commissioner's Office, by category number.

| | I | II | III | IV | V | Total |
|---|---|---|---|---|---|---|
| 2006-07 | - | - | - | - | - | - |
| 2005-06 | - | - | - | 1 | - | 1 |
| 2004-05 | - | - | - | - | - | - |

Total number of other protected personal data related incidents, by category number.

| | I | II | III | IV | V | Total |
|---|---|---|---|---|---|---|
| 2006-07 | 1 | 1 | - | - | - | 2 |
| 2005-06 | - | 1 | - | - | - | 1 |
| 2004-05 | - | 1 | - | - | - | 1 |

## Reconciliation of Resource Expenditure Between Estimates, Accounts and Budgets

| | Estimate | 2007-08 £M Outturn | Estimate | 2006-07 £M Outturn |
|---|---|---|---|---|
| **Net Resources Outturn (Estimates)** | **38,042** | **36,286** | 34,824 | **34,005** |
| *Adjustments to include:* | | | | |
| Consolidated Fund Extra Receipts in the OCS | - | (63) | - | (56) |
| Other adjustments | | | | |
| **Net Operating Cost (Accounts)** | **38,042** | **36,223** | 34,824 | **33,949** |
| *Adjustments to remove:* | | | | |
| voted expenditure outside the budget | (4) | (4) | (4) | 12 |
| *Adjustments to include:* | | | | |
| other Consolidated Fund Extra Receipts | - | 63 | - | 56 |
| resource consumption of non departmental public bodies | 15 | 15 | 16 | 16 |
| Unallocated Resource Provision | - | - | 220 | - |
| **Resource Budget Outturn (Budget)** | **38,053** | **36,297** | 35,056 | **34,033** |
| *of which* | | | | |
| Departmental Expenditure Limits (DEL) | 36,940 | 35,787 | 34,104 | 33,451 |
| Annually Managed Expenditure (AME) | 1,113 | 510 | 952 | 582 |

## Financial Position

The Statement of Parliamentary Supply – Summary of Resource Outturn compares Estimates and Outturn (net total resources). A detailed explanation of the variances against the Departmental Expenditure Limits is set out in the Finance section of the Performance Report.

Request for Resources (RfR) 1, Provision of Defence Capability, provides for expenditure primarily to meet the MoD's operational support and logistics services costs and the costs of providing the equipment capability required by defence policy. Within RfR1, Appropriations in Aid are shown as the lower of actual Outturn or the Estimate. Any Appropriations in Aid in excess of the Estimate are shown at Note 5, and these will be surrendered to the Consolidated Fund. RfR1 is made up of three different controls:

● Resource Departmental Expenditure Limit (DEL), which consists of items such as pay, equipment support costs, fuel and administrative expenses, as well as non cash items such as depreciation, cost of capital and movements in the level of provisions;

● Annually Managed Expenditure (AME), which covers programmes that are demand-led, or exceptionally volatile in a way that could not be controlled by the Department, and where the programmes are so large that the Department could not be expected to absorb the effects of volatility in its programme, such as movements in nuclear provisions; and

● Non Budget costs, items of expenditure which are subject to Parliamentary but not Treasury control, and therefore outside DEL and AME. The majority of the costs relate to changes in the discount rates for pensions and other long term liabilities.

The net outturn for Total Resources is £36,286,316,000 against an Estimate of £38,041,570,000; an underspend of £1,755,254,000.

The net outturn for RfR1, Provision of Defence Capability is £33,076,149,000 against an Estimate of £34,629,760,000; an underspend of £1,553,611,000.

RfR2, Operations and Peace Keeping, shows a net outturn of £2,196,037,000 against an Estimate of £2,381,803,000; an underspend of £185,766,000.

RfR3, War Pensions Benefits shows a net outturn of £1,014,130,000 against an Estimate of £1,030,007,000; an underspend of £15,877,000. This RfR provides for the payment of war disablement and war widows' pensions in accordance with relevant legislation; this is all AME. The costs of administering war pensions are borne by RfR1.

The non-operating Appropriations in Aid were £1,201,329,000; £42,671,000 lower than the Estimate of £1,244,000,000.

The Net Cash Requirement shows a net outturn of £33,504,916,000 against an Estimate of £34,730,098,000; savings of £1,225,182,000.

## Other Areas

The Department's Accounts include a note (Note 31) on Losses and Special Payments. The nature of the losses and special payments, as defined in Managing Public Money, varies from year to year depending on the circumstances arising and decisions made by the Department during the year. Cases brought forward from last year are shown separately in order properly to identify the cases arising during the year. Further details are included in the Resources Section of the Departmental Performance Report.

The Department undertakes a professional revaluation of its land and building fixed assets every five years. The process is managed as a five year rolling programme; further details of the revaluation programme are at Note 14.1 to the accounts.

Details of directorships and other significant interests held by Ministers are set out in The Register of Lords' Interests and The Register of Members' Interests which are available on the UK Parliament website: http://www.publications.parliament.uk/pa/cm/cmregmem/memi02.htm

Details of directorships and other significant interests held by Defence Board members are included at Note 32 – Related Party Transactions.

## Auditor

The financial statements for the Department are audited by the Comptroller and Auditor General under the Government Resources and Accounts Act 2000. The Certificate and Report of the Comptroller and Auditor General on the financial statements are set out on pages 267 to 276. The audit fee is disclosed in Note 10 – Other Operating Costs.

## Statement as to Disclosure of Information to Auditors

So far as I, the Accounting Officer, am aware, there is no relevant audit information of which the Department's auditors are unaware, and I have taken all the steps that I ought to have taken to make myself aware of any relevant audit information and to establish that the Department's auditors are aware of that information.

*Sir Bill Jeffrey*
**Accounting Officer**                                                                 **14 July 2008**

# Remuneration Report

## Remuneration Policy

The Review Body on Senior Salaries provides independent advice to the Prime Minister and the Secretary of State for Defence on the remuneration of senior civil servants and senior officers of the Armed Forces.

The Review Body also advises the Prime Minister from time to time on the pay, pensions and allowances of Members of Parliament; on Peers' allowances; and on the pay, pensions and allowances of Ministers and others, whose pay is determined by the Ministerial and Other Salaries Act 1975 (as amended).

In reaching its recommendations, the Review Body has regard to the following considerations:

- the need to recruit, retain and motivate suitably able and qualified people to exercise their different responsibilities;

- regional/local variations in labour markets and their effects on the recruitment and retention of staff;

- Government policies for improving the public services including the requirement on departments to meet the output targets for the delivery of departmental services;

- the funds available to departments as set out in the Government's departmental expenditure limits; and

- the Government's inflation target.

The Review Body takes account of the evidence it receives about wider economic considerations and the affordability of its recommendations.

Further information about the work of the Review Body can be found at www.ome.uk.com .

There is an established departmental procedure for the appointment of all Non-Executive Directors (NEDs). This requires a visibly fair and open recruitment and selection process with appointment on merit, thus mirroring the Civil Service Commissioners' Recruitment Code for permanent employees to the Civil Service. NEDs appointed to the Defence Board receive a Letter of Appointment setting out, amongst other things, details of the agreed remuneration.

## Performance and Reward

The basic salary and annual increases of the civilian members of the Defence Board, which could include a bonus payment, are performance-related and are set by the Permanent Secretaries' Remuneration Committee and the MoD's Main Pay Committee.

Pay and management arrangements for members of the Senior Civil Service (SCS) reward individuals for delivery and personal achievement. These arrangements include an objective-setting regime complementary to the Department's performance management system and a performance-related incremental pay system.

Up to seventy percent of the SCS population will receive a performance bonus. Bonuses will be awarded to those judged to have made the highest in-year contribution to the MoD's business objectives taking into account, in addition, personal capability objectives (based on Professional Skills for Government (PSG) and leadership frameworks) and evidence of how individuals may have applied and supported diversity in their work. The ceiling for the bonus payments is 7.6% (2006-07 6.5%) of the SCS paybill.

All senior military officers (except for the Chief of the Defence Staff (CDS), Legal Branch 2-star officers, medical and dental officers and those in the Chaplaincy branches) are paid under the Performance Management and Pay System (PMPS). Depending on their performance and position on the pay scale, individuals can be awarded a double increment, a single increment or no increment and progress accordingly up the incremental pay range for their rank. The average value of one incremental rise under the PMPS is 2.6% of salary (2006-07: 2.4%). The award of increments is recommended by the Senior Officers' Remuneration Committee, chaired by the Department's Permanent Under-Secretary.

Whilst Non-Executive remuneration is not directly linked to performance, in part to avoid any suggestion that an employee/employer relationship exists, NED performance is reviewed annually. The aim of the reviews is to consider the impact of the NED on the performance of the board, recognise the contribution of the NED and identify ways this could be improved, and provide feedback.

## Senior Managers' Contracts

Civil Service appointments are made in accordance with the Civil Service Commissioners' Recruitment Code, which requires appointments to be on merit on the basis of fair and open competition but also includes the circumstances when appointments may otherwise be made. Further information about the work of the Civil Service Commissioners can be found at www. civilservicecommissioners.org.

Unless otherwise stated below, the officials covered by this report hold appointments which are open-ended. Early termination, other than for misconduct, would result in the individual receiving compensation as set out in the Civil Service Compensation Scheme.

For the NEDs appointed to the Defence Board, the Department has employed recruitment consultants to search for suitable candidates based upon a specification drawn up by senior officials. Short-listed candidates are then interviewed by a selection panel (Permanent Under-Secretary and Chief of the Defence Staff) with the successful candidate chosen on merit and appointed to the Board for a period of three years.

NEDs are not employees and, therefore, do not have a contractual relationship with the Department but rather are appointees who receive a Letter of Appointment setting out: their role, period of appointment, standards and details of remuneration.

The Chief Scientific Adviser was recruited on a three year fixed term appointment. Conditions covering termination of employment are set out in the contract document.

The Chief of the Defence Staff, Vice Chief of the Defence Staff and Single-Service Chiefs of Staff are appointed on the recommendation of the Secretary of State for Defence to the Prime Minister. The final approval of the appointee lies with Her Majesty The Queen.

Senior Military members of the Defence Board hold appointments which are competed for by the 3 Services. Once selected for the appointment, they will usually hold the post for between 3 and 4 years.

## Management

**Ministers who had responsibility for the Department during the year were:**

*Secretary of State for Defence*
The Right Honourable Des Browne MP
(appointed 6 May 2006).

*Minister of State for the Armed Forces*
The Right Honourable Bob Ainsworth MP
(appointed 30 June 2007, replacing The Right Honourable Adam Ingram MP).

*Parliamentary Under-Secretary of State for Defence (Minister for Defence Equipment and Support)*
The Right Honourable the Baroness Ann Taylor of Bolton
(appointed 8 November 2007, replacing Lord Drayson).

*Parliamentary Under-Secretary of State for Defence (Minister for Veterans)*
Derek Twigg MP
(appointed 7 September 2006).

**During the year the following served as members of the Defence Board:**

*Permanent Under-Secretary of State*
Sir Bill Jeffrey KCB
(appointed 21 November 2005).

*Chief of the Defence Staff*
Air Chief Marshal Sir Jock Stirrup GCB AFC ADC DSc FRAeS FCMI RAF
(appointed 28 April 2006).

*First Sea Lord and Chief of the Naval Staff*
Admiral Sir Jonathon Band GCB ADC
(appointed 7 February 2006).

*Chief of the General Staff*
General Sir Richard Dannatt KCB CBE MC ADC Gen
(appointed 29 August 2006).

*Chief of the Air Staff*
Air Chief Marshal Sir Glenn Torpy GCB CBE DSO ADC BSc(Eng) FRAeS RAF
(appointed 13 April 2006).

*Vice Chief of the Defence Staff*
General Sir Timothy Granville-Chapman GBE KCB ADC Gen
(appointed 22 July 2005).

*Second Permanent Under-Secretary of State*
Sir Ian Andrews CBE TD
(appointed 4 March 2002).

*Chief of Defence Materiel*
General Sir Kevin O'Donoghue KCB CBE
(appointed 1 January 2005).

*Chief Scientific Adviser*
Professor Sir Roy Anderson FRS*
(appointed 1 October 2004; served until 30 September 2007).

*Finance Director*
Trevor Woolley CB
(appointed to the Defence Board 24 June 2004).

*Non-Executive Directors*

Charles Miller Smith, Chairman of Scottish Power
(appointed 20 May 2002; served until 18 July 2007).

Philippa Foster Back OBE, Director of the Institute of Business Ethics**
(appointed 24 July 2002; served until 31 July 2007).

Paul Skinner, Chairman of Rio Tinto plc and Rio Tinto Limited
(appointed 1 June 2006).

Ian Rushby, Chair of the Defence Audit Committee from 1 August 2007.
(appointed 29 January 2007).

Priscilla Vacassin, Group Human Resources Director, Prudential plc
(appointed 1 September 2007).

*Sir Roy Anderson's Fixed Term Appointment as Chief Scientific Adviser (CSA) ended on
30 September 2007. The new CSA with effect from 7 April 2008 will be Professor Mark Welland
FRS FREng.

**Chair of the Defence Audit Committee for the period 1 April 2007 to 31 July 2007.

## Ministerial Salaries, Allowances and Taxable Benefits

*(This section has been subject to audit)*

| | 2007 – 08 Salary* £ | 2007 – 08 Benefits-in-kind (to nearest £100)* | 2006 – 07 Salary* £ | 2006 – 07 Benefits-in-kind (to nearest £100)* |
|---|---|---|---|---|
| **Secretary of State for Defence:** The Rt Hon Des Browne MP (from 6 May 2006) *Full year equivalent salary* | 76,904 *75,963* | Nil | 68,642 | Nil |
| **Minister of State for the Armed Forces:** The Rt Hon Bob Ainsworth MP (from 30 June 2007) *Full year equivalent salary* | 30,031 *39,893* | Nil | Nil | Nil |
| The Rt Hon Adam Ingram MP (to 29 June 2007) *Full year equivalent salary* | 9,862 *39,893* | Nil | 39,405 | Nil |
| **Parliamentary Under-Secretary of State for Defence (Minister for Defence Equipment and Support):** The Rt Hon the Baroness Ann Taylor of Bolton (from 8 November 2007) *Full year equivalent salary* | 28,197 *70,986* | Nil | Nil | Nil |
| **Minister of State for Defence Equipment and Support:** Lord Drayson † (to 7 November 2007) | Nil | Nil | Nil | Nil |
| **Parliamentary Under-Secretary of State for Defence (Minister for Veterans):** Derek Twigg MP (from 7 September 2006) *Full year equivalent salary* | 30,280 | Nil | 17,002 *29,909* | Nil |

*Disclosures cover the period during which individuals served as Ministers in the MoD.
† Lord Drayson did not receive the Ministerial salary of £81,504 to which he was entitled.

Ministers who, on leaving office, have not attained the age of 65 and are not appointed to a relevant Ministerial or other paid office within three weeks, are eligible for a severance payment of one quarter of the annual Ministerial salary being paid. One payment was made in 2007-08 (2006-07 – two).

## Ministerial Salary

'Salary' includes: gross salary; performance pay or bonuses; overtime; London weighting or London allowances; recruitment and retention allowances; private office allowances; ex-gratia payments and any other allowance to the extent that it is subject to UK taxation.

The figures above are based on payments made by the Department and thus recorded in these accounts. In respect of Ministers in the House of Commons, the Department bears only the cost of the additional Ministerial remuneration; the salary for their services as an MP – £60,675 pa with effect from 1 April 2007 (£60,277 pa with effect from 1 November 2006; £59,686 pa with effect from 1 April 2006) and various allowances to which they are entitled, are borne centrally. The arrangements for Ministers in the House of Lords are different in that they do not receive a salary but rather an additional remuneration, which cannot be quantified separately from their Ministerial salaries. This total remuneration, as well as the allowances to which they are entitled, is normally paid by the Department and is therefore shown in full above.

## Benefits-in-Kind for Ministers

Ministers' private use of official cars is exempt under the rules governing the definition of taxable benefits-in-kind. Where Ministers are provided with living accommodation and a taxable benefit-in-kind arises, its value is calculated in accordance with HM Revenue & Customs regulations.

## Ministerial Pensions

*(This section has been subject to audit)*

Figures for **2007-08** in bold. The real increase in the value of the accrued pension compared to the 2006-07 value, is shown in italics (in bands of £2,500).

| | Total Accrued Pension at Retirement as at 31 Mar 08 £000 | CETV* at 31 Mar 07 or Date of Appointment if Later £000 | CETV at 31 Mar 08 or on Cessation of Appointment if Earlier £000 | Real Increase in CETV £000 |
|---|---|---|---|---|
| **Secretary of State for Defence:** | | | | |
| The Rt Hon Des Browne MP | **5-10** | 63 | 79 | 8 |
| | *0-2.5* | | | |
| **Minister of State for the Armed Forces:** | | | | |
| The Rt Hon Bob Ainsworth MP | **5-10** | 87 | 97 | 4 |
| (from 30 June 2007) | *0-2.5* | | | |
| The Rt Hon Adam Ingram MP | **5-10** | 146 | 153 | 4 |
| (to 29 June 2007) | *0-2.5* | | | |
| **Parliamentary Under-Secretary of State for Defence (Minister for Defence Equipment and Support):** | | | | |
| The Rt Hon the Baroness Ann Taylor of Bolton | **0-5** | Nil | 4 | 2 |
| (from 8 November 2007) | *0-2.5* | | | |
| **Minister of State for Defence Equipment and Support:** | **Nil** | Nil | Nil | Nil |
| Lord Drayson † | | | | |
| (to 7 November 2007) | | | | |
| **Parliamentary Under-Secretary of State for Defence and Minister for Veterans:** | **0-5** | 24 | 31 | 3 |
| Derek Twigg MP | *0-2.5* | | | |

† Lord Drayson is not a member of the Parliamentary Contributory Pension Fund.
* CETV – Cash Equivalent Transfer Value.

Pension benefits for Ministers are provided by the Parliamentary Contributory Pension Fund (PCPF). The scheme is made under statute (the regulations are set out in Statutory Instrument SI 1993 No 3253, as amended). Ministers who are Members of Parliament may also accrue an MP's pension under the PCPF; this pension is not included in the table above. The accrued pension quoted is the pension the Minister is entitled to receive when they reach the age of 65, or immediately on ceasing to be an active member of the scheme if they are already 65.

The arrangements for Ministers provide benefits on an 'average salary' basis, taking account of all service as a Minister. The accrual rate has been 1/40th since 15 July 2002 (or 5 July 2001 for those that chose to backdate the change). Ministers, in common with all other members of the PCPF, can opt for a 1/50th accrual rate and a lower rate of employee contribution.

Benefits for Ministers are payable at the same time as MPs' benefits become payable under the PCPF or, for those who are not MPs, on retirement from Ministerial office from age 65. Pensions are increased annually in line with changes in the Retail Prices Index. Members pay contributions of 6% of their Ministerial salary if they have opted for the 1/50th accrual rate or 10% if they have opted for the 1/40th accrual rate. There is also an employer contribution paid by the Exchequer representing the balance of cost as advised by the Government Actuary. This is currently 26.8% of the Ministerial salary.

## The Cash Equivalent Transfer Value (CETV)

This is the actuarially assessed capitalised value of the pension scheme benefits accrued by a member at a particular point in time. The benefits valued are the member's accrued benefits and any contingent spouse's pension payable from the scheme. It is a payment made by a pension scheme or arrangement to secure pension benefits in another pension scheme or arrangement when the member leaves a scheme and chooses to transfer the pension benefits they have accrued in their former scheme. The pension figures shown relate to the benefits that the individual has accrued as a consequence of their total Ministerial service, not just their current appointment as a Minister. CETVs are calculated within the guidelines and framework prescribed by the Institute and Faculty of Actuaries.

## The Real Increase in the Value of the CETV

This is effectively the element of the increase in accrued pension funded by the Exchequer. It excludes increases due to inflation and contributions paid by the Minister and is calculated using common market valuation factors for the start and end of the period.

# Defence Board – Salaries, Allowances and Taxable Benefits-in-Kind

*(This section has been subject to audit)*

| | 2007 – 08 Salary* £000 | 2007 – 08 Benefits-in-Kind (to nearest £100)** | 2006 – 07 Salary* £000 | 2006 – 07 Benefits-in-Kind (to nearest £100)** |
|---|---|---|---|---|
| **Permanent Under-Secretary of State**<br>Sir Bill Jeffrey KCB | 180-185 | 29,700 | 175-180 | 29,600 |
| **Chief of the Defence Staff**<br>Air Chief Marshal Sir Jock Stirrup GCB AFC ADC DSc FRAeS FCMI RAF<br>(from 28 April 2006)<br>*Full year equivalent salary* | 220-225 | 37,000 | 190-195<br><br>205-210 | 32,200 |
| **First Sea Lord and Chief of the Naval Staff**<br>Admiral Sir Jonathon Band GCB ADC | 165-170 | 27,900 | 155-160 | 26,000 |
| **Chief of the General Staff**<br>General Sir Richard Dannatt KCB CBE MC ADC Gen<br>(from 29 August 2006)<br>*Full year equivalent salary* | 170-175 | 26,800 | 100-105<br><br>170-175 | 10,900 |
| **Chief of the Air Staff**<br>Air Chief Marshal Sir Glenn Torpy GCB CBE DSO ADC BSc(Eng) FRAeS RAF<br>(from 13 April 2006)<br>*Full year equivalent salary* | 160-165 | 26,800 | 140-145<br><br>145-150 | 24,100 |
| **Vice Chief of the Defence Staff**<br>General Sir Timothy Granville-Chapman GBE KCB ADC Gen | 160-165 | 27,300 | 150-155 | 25,500 |
| **Second Permanent Under-Secretary of State**<br>Sir Ian Andrews CBE TD | 145-150 | 8,100 | 145-150 | 9,800*** |
| **Chief of Defence Materiel**<br>General Sir Kevin O'Donoghue KCB CBE | 160-165 | Nil | 145-150 | Nil |
| **Chief Scientific Adviser**<br>Professor Sir Roy Anderson FRS<br>(to 30 September 2007)<br>*Full year equivalent* | 75-80<br><br>145-150 | 10,800 | 145-150 | 22,100 |
| **Finance Director**<br>Trevor Woolley CB | 130-135 | Nil | 130-135 | Nil |
| **Non-Executive Directors** | Fees | | Fees | |
| Charles Miller Smith<br>(to 18 July 2007)<br>*Full year equivalent* | 5-10<br><br>25-30 | Nil | 25-30 | Nil |
| Philippa Foster Back OBE<br>(to 31 July 2007)<br>*Full year equivalent)* | 5-10<br><br>25-30 | Nil | 25-30 | Nil |
| Paul Skinner<br>(from 1 June 2006)<br>*Full year equivalent* | 20-25 | Nil | 20-25<br><br>20-25*** | Nil |
| Ian Rushby<br>(from 29 January 2007)<br>*Full year equivalent* | 25-30 | Nil | 0-5<br><br>25-30 | Nil |
| Priscilla Vacassin<br>(from 1 September 2007)<br>*Full year equivalent* | 10-15<br><br>20-25 | Nil | Nil | Nil |

\* Salary includes gross salary, performance pay (paid in 2007-08 but based on performance in an assessment period ended prior to the start of the financial year) and taxable allowances paid.
\*\* Benefits-in-kind figures for civilian members of the Defence Board represent the taxable benefit attributed to individuals where an official car is available for private use (the benefit accrues even if the individual chooses not to make use of the car). For Service members of the Board, the benefits-in-kind are the taxable benefits relating to the occupation of Official Service Residences. The Department has an arrangement with HM Revenue and Customs where MoD pays the tax liability that would normally be paid by the individual on the benefits-in-kind; this tax liability is included in the figures in the table.
\*\*\* Restated. The Benefits-in-Kind figure was restated, from Nil, following an HMRC ruling (in September 2007) that the benefit accrues even if (as in this case) no private use is made of the car.

# Defence Board – Pension Benefits

*(This section has been subject to audit)*

2007-08 figures are in **bold**. The real increase in the pension, from 2006-07, and where applicable the real increase in the lump sum payment, are shown in *italics*.

| | Total Accrued Pension at Retirement as at 31 Mar 08<br>£000 | CETV at 31 Mar 07 or Date of Appointment if Later<br>£000 | CETV at 31 Mar 08 or on Cessation of Appointment if Earlier<br>£000 | Real Increase or (Decrease) in CETV<br>£000 |
|---|---|---|---|---|
| **Permanent Under-Secretary of State**<br>Sir Bill Jeffrey KCB | Pension<br>**75-80**<br>*0-2.5*<br>Lump Sum<br>**230-235**<br>*5-7.5* | 1,725 | 2,007 | 62 |
| **Chief of the Defence Staff**<br>Air Chief Marshal Sir Jock Stirrup GCB AFC ADC DSc FRAeS FCMI RAF | Pension<br>**115-120**<br>*7.5-10*<br>Lump Sum<br>**350-355**<br>*22.5-25* | 2,244* | 2,438 | 167 |
| **First Sea Lord and Chief of the Naval Staff**<br>Admiral Sir Jonathon Band GCB ADC | Pension<br>**85-90**<br>*5-7.5*<br>Lump Sum<br>**260-265**<br>*15-17.5* | 1,707* | 1,836 | 110 |
| **Chief of the General Staff**<br>General Sir Richard Dannatt KCB CBE MC ADC Gen | Pension<br>**80-85**<br>*2.5-5*<br>Lump Sum<br>**240-245**<br>*10-12.5* | 1,620* | 1,668 | 72 |
| **Chief of the Air Staff**<br>Air Chief Marshal Sir Glenn Torpy GCB CBE DSO ADC BSc(Eng) FRAeS RAF | Pension<br>**75-80**<br>*5-7.5*<br>Lump Sum<br>**230-235**<br>*17.5-20* | 842* | 970 | 75 |
| **Vice Chief of the Defence Staff**<br>General Sir Timothy Granville-Chapman GBE KCB ADC Gen | Pension<br>**85-90**<br>*2.5-5*<br>Lump Sum<br>**255-260**<br>*12.5-15* | 1,438* | 1,548 | 89 |
| **Second Permanent Under-Secretary of State**<br>Sir Ian Andrews CBE TD | Pension<br>**55-60**<br>*10-12.5*<br>Lump Sum<br>**135-140**<br>*(2.5-5)* | 1,025 | 1,188 | 13 |
| **Chief of Defence Materiel**<br>General Sir Kevin O'Donoghue KCB CBE | Pension<br>**80-85**<br>*5-7.5*<br>Lump Sum<br>**250-255**<br>*15-17.5* | 1,448* | 1,554 | 78 |
| **Chief Scientific Adviser**<br>Professor Sir Roy Anderson FRS | Pension<br>**5-10**<br>*0-2.5*<br>Lump Sum<br>**N/A** | 93 | 116 | 18 |

| | Total Accrued Pension at Retirement as at 31 Mar 08 £000 | CETV at 31 Mar 07 or Date of Appointment if Later £000 | CETV at 31 Mar 08 or on Cessation of Appointment if Earlier £000 | Real Increase or (Decrease) in CETV £000 |
|---|---|---|---|---|
| **Finance Director** Trevor Woolley CB | Pension **45-50** 0-2.5 Lump Sum **145-150** 2.5-5 | 854* | 1,006 | 27 |
| **Non-Executive Directors** | | | | |
| Charles Miller Smith | N/A | N/A | N/A | N/A |
| Philippa Foster Back OBE | N/A | N/A | N/A | N/A |
| Paul Skinner | N/A | N/A | N/A | N/A |
| Ian Rushby | N/A | N/A | N/A | N/A |
| Priscilla Vacassin | N/A | N/A | N/A | N/A |

*The factors used to calculate the 2007-08 CETV for members of the Armed Forces Pension and Civil Service Pension Schemes were revised, to include the value of providing dependents' benefits. The figures for 31 March 2007 have been recalculated using the new factors and this has led to changes to the figures published last year.

## Civil Service Pensions

Pension benefits are provided through the Civil Service pension arrangements. From 30 July 2007, civil servants may be in one of four defined benefit schemes; either a 'final salary' scheme (classic, premium, or classic plus) or a 'whole career' scheme (nuvos). Classic, premium and classic plus are now closed to new members. These statutory arrangements are unfunded with the cost of benefits met by monies voted by Parliament each year. Pensions payable under nuvos, classic, premium, and classic plus are increased annually in line with changes in the Retail Prices Index (RPI). Recent entrants to premium (after 1 October 2002) and nuvos (from 30 July 2007) may choose between membership of the scheme or joining a good quality 'money purchase' stakeholder pension with a significant employer contribution (partnership pension account). The accrued pensions quoted above are the pensions the members are entitled to receive when they reach 60 (nuvos 65), or immediately on ceasing to be an active member of the scheme if they are already 60 (nuvos 65).

Employee contributions are set at the rate of 1.5% of pensionable earnings for classic and 3.5% for premium, classic plus and nuvos. Benefits in classic accrue at the rate of 1/80th of final pensionable earnings for each year of service; in addition, a lump sum equivalent to three years' pension is payable on retirement. For premium, benefits accrue at the rate of 1/60th of final pensionable earnings for each year of service; unlike classic, there is no automatic lump sum. Classic plus is essentially a hybrid with benefits in respect of service before 1 October 2002 calculated broadly as per classic and benefits for service from October 2002 calculated as in Premium. In nuvos a member builds up a pension based on pensionable earnings during their period of scheme membership. At the end of the scheme year (31 March) the member's earned pension account is credited with 2.3% of their pensionable earnings in that scheme year and the accrued pension is uprated in line with RPI. In all cases members may opt to give up (commute) pension for a lump sum up to the limits set by the Finance Act 2004.

The partnership pension account is a stakeholder pension arrangement. The employer makes a basic contribution of between 3% and 12.5% (depending on the age of the member) into a stakeholder pension product chosen by the employee. The employee does not have to contribute but, where they do make contributions, the employer will match these up to a limit of 3% of pensionable salary (in addition to the employer's basic contribution). Employers also contribute a further 0.8% of pensionable salary to cover the cost of centrally-provided risk benefit cover (death in service and ill health retirement).

Further details about the Civil Service pension arrangements can be found at the website www.civilservice-pensions.gov.uk.

## Armed Forces Pension Scheme (AFPS)

From 6 April 2005, a new Armed Forces Pension Scheme (known as AFPS 05) was introduced for all new members of the Armed Forces; those in service before this date have been given the opportunity to transfer, from AFPS 75, to the new scheme. Both schemes are defined benefit, salary-related, contracted out, occupational pension schemes. The AFPS is non-contributory for members; the cost of accruing benefits are met by the employer at rates approximately equivalent to 36.3% (Officers) and 21.8% (Other Ranks) of pensionable pay for regular personnel. Members are entitled to a taxable pension for life and a tax-free pension lump sum if they leave the Armed Forces at or beyond either the Early Departure Point or the Immediate Pension Point. If a scheme member leaves before these points, they will be entitled to a preserved pension and related lump sum.

Further details about Armed Forces Pensions can be found at the website www.mod.uk/DefenceInternet/AboutDefence/WhatWeDo/Personnel/SPVA/Pensions.htm

## Cash Equivalent Transfer Value

A Cash Equivalent Transfer Value (CETV) is the actuarially assessed capitalised value of the pension scheme benefits accrued by a member at a particular point in time. The benefits valued are the member's accrued benefits and any contingent spouse's pension payable from the scheme. A CETV is a payment made by a pension scheme or arrangement to secure pension benefits in another pension scheme or arrangement when the member leaves a scheme and chooses to transfer the benefits accrued in their former scheme. The pension figures shown relate to the benefits that the individual has accrued as a consequence of their total membership of the pension scheme, not just their service in a senior capacity to which disclosure applies. The figures include the value of any pension benefit in another scheme or arrangement which the individual has transferred to the AFPS or Civil Service pension arrangements. They also include any additional pension benefit accrued to the member as a result of their purchasing additional pension benefits at their own cost. CETVs are calculated within the guidelines and framework prescribed by the Institute and Faculty of Actuaries.

## Real Increase in CETV

This reflects the increase in CETV effectively funded by the employer. It does not include the increase in accrued pension due to inflation or contributions paid by the employee (including the value of any benefits transferred from another pension scheme or arrangement) and uses common market valuation factors for the start and end of the period.

*Sir Bill Jeffrey*
**Accounting Officer**

**14 July 2008**

# Statement of Accounting Officer's Responsibilities

Under the Government Resources and Accounts Act 2000, HM Treasury has directed the Ministry of Defence to prepare for each financial year resource accounts detailing the resources acquired, held or disposed of during the year and the use of resources by the Department during the year.

The accounts are prepared on an accruals basis and must give a true and fair view of the state of affairs of the Department and of its net resource outturn, resources applied to objectives, recognised gains and losses, and cash flows for the financial year.

In preparing the accounts, the Accounting Officer is required to comply with the requirements of the *Government Financial Reporting Manual* and in particular to:

- observe the Accounts Direction issued by HM Treasury, including the relevant accounting and disclosure requirements, and apply suitable accounting policies on a consistent basis;

- make judgements and estimates on a reasonable basis;

- state whether applicable accounting standards, as set out in the *Government Financial Reporting Manual*, have been followed, and disclose and explain any material departures in the accounts; and

- prepare the accounts on a going-concern basis.

HM Treasury has appointed the Permanent Head of Department as Accounting Officer of the Department. The responsibilities of an Accounting Officer, including responsibility for the propriety and regularity of the public finances for which the Accounting Officer is answerable, for keeping proper records and for safeguarding the Department's assets, are set out in the Accounting Officers' Memorandum issued by HM Treasury and published in *Managing Public Money*.

# Statement on Internal Control

## 1. Scope of responsibility

As Accounting Officer, I have responsibility for maintaining a sound system of internal control that supports the achievement of Defence policies, aims and objectives, whilst safeguarding the public funds and Departmental assets for which I am personally responsible, in accordance with the responsibilities assigned to me in *Managing Public Money*.

During the Financial Year 2007-08, the Department's outputs were delivered through 9 Top Level Budget areas (8 from 1 April 2008), each managed by a military or civilian Top Level Budget (TLB) Holder, together with 5 Trading Fund Agencies (4 from 1 April 2008). The Department also has 5 executive Non-Departmental Public Bodies (NDPBs) and 2 Public Corporations with delegated responsibilities. Included within the TLBs are 8 on-vote Defence Agencies whose Chief Executives are responsible for producing annual accounts which are laid before Parliament but which also form part of the Departmental Resource Accounts. TLB Holders operate within a framework of responsibilities delegated by me. To assist me in assessing the adequacy of control arrangements across the Department, TLB Holders submit to me an Annual Statement of Assurance, endorsed by their Audit Committee and Management Board, also covering the Agencies for which they are responsible.

Armed Forces Pension Scheme (AFPS) and Armed Forces Compensation Scheme (AFCS) administration is undertaken by the Service Personnel and Veterans Agency (SPVA) which is part of the Central TLB. AFPS and AFCS services are delivered through a combination of MoD Civilian and Service Personnel and EDS (Defence) Ltd via a commercial partnering agreement. A further contract is in place between the SPVA and Xafinity Paymaster Ltd for the payment of Armed Forces pensions. The arrangement for joint working with EDS is managed via the Agency Management Group (AMG) chaired by the Chief Executive. The Agency Chief Executive is directly accountable for the delivery of all these services.

The 5 MoD Trading Funds (the Defence Aviation Repair Agency, ABRO, the Defence Science and Technology Laboratory (Dstl), the UK Hydrographic Office, and the Met Office) fall outside the Departmental Accounting Boundary and their Chief Executives are Accounting Officers in their own right. They therefore publish their own Statements on Internal Control together with their Annual Accounts. Given their close integration into the Department's business, and their extensive use of Departmental personnel and assets, their Chief Executives also provide to me the Statement on Internal Control prepared for their Annual Accounts. Although sponsored by the Department, the 5 Non-Departmental Public Bodies and 2 Public Corporations also fall outside the Departmental Boundary and their accounts are also published separately. The NDPBs and one Public Corporation (the Fleet Air Arm Museum) each operate within a financial memorandum agreed between their respective Boards of Trustees and the Department. The other Public Corporation (Oil and Pipelines Agency) has a Board of Directors on which the Department is represented.

Ministers are involved in the delivery of outputs, including the management of risks to delivery, through their routine oversight of the Department. They also chair a variety of internal Boards which review the performance of the Trading Funds and the primary on-vote Agencies. In particular, all Trading Fund Agencies report to Advisory Boards chaired by MoD Ministers. Ministers are consulted on all key decisions affecting Defence, including major investment decisions and on operational matters. A Defence Ministerial Committee was established in April 2008, which brings together Ministers with the Department's most senior officials, to ensure that Ministers collectively are regularly engaged in the business of the Department.

Command and administration of the Armed Forces is vested in the Defence Council by Letters Patent, chaired by the Secretary of State for Defence, and beneath that in the Service Boards, chaired by a Minister. Membership of the Defence Council comprises all Defence Ministers and the executive members of the Defence Board. The Chief of the Defence Staff is the Government's and the Secretary of State's principal advisor on military operations and is responsible for the maintenance of military operational capability and for the preparation and conduct of military operations, including managing the risks to successful outcomes. The Chiefs of Staff Committee is chaired by the Chief of the Defence Staff and is the main forum in which the collective military advice of the Chiefs is obtained on operational issues. The individual Service Chiefs also advise the Chief of the Defence Staff, the Secretary of State and, when required, the Prime Minister on the operational employment of their Service.

## 2. The purpose of the system of internal control

The system of internal control is designed to manage risk to a reasonable level rather than to eliminate all risk of failure to achieve policies, aims and objectives; it can therefore provide only reasonable and not absolute assurance of effectiveness. The system of internal control is based on an ongoing process designed to identify and prioritise the risks to the achievement of Departmental policies, aims and objectives, to evaluate the likelihood of those risks being realised and the impact should they be realised, and to manage them efficiently, effectively and economically. The system of internal control has been in place in the Ministry of Defence for the year ended 31 March 2008 and up to the date of approval of the annual report and accounts, and accords with Treasury guidance.

## 3. Capacity to handle risk

Active management of risk is fundamental to the effective achievement of Defence objectives, and is central to the way business is conducted within the Department. It informs operational decision making, contingency planning, investment decisions and the financial planning process. The major strategic risks are regularly considered by the Defence Board and risk forms an integral element of the quarterly performance reviews. Guidance on the Department's approach to risk is detailed in a Joint Service Publication, which is periodically reviewed and updated. This sets out the Department's corporate governance and risk management policy statement and strategy to be cascaded down through Top Level Budget Holders, and provides extensive guidance to staff on definitions, criteria and methods available for risk assessment and management. It is made available to all personnel in either hard copy or via the Department's intranet. Individual training, at both awareness and practitioner level, is available to all staff via the Department's in-house training provider.

## 4. The risk and control framework

The Defence Board manages the top level risks to the Department through a structured series of discussions of the major risks through the course of the year. The Department's Performance Management System provides the overall framework for the consideration of risks within the Defence Balanced Scorecard and lower level scorecards, providing a means for the identification, evaluation, control and reporting of risk against a balanced assessment of Departmental objectives. Key Departmental objectives, performance indicators and targets are defined by the Defence Board for each year in the Defence Plan and cascaded to Top Level Budget Holders. Performance is monitored and discussed quarterly at Defence Board and lower level management board meetings, including explicit consideration of key risks.

The Department's risk appetite varies according to the area of business. In particular it has a high tolerance of risk in regard to its purpose, preparedness and willingness to undertake military operations with potentially fatal consequences for both our opponents and UK Service personnel. Risk appetite is determined through the advice given to Ministers on operations, through the decisions taken as part of the Department's planning process including assessing any gaps against Planning Assumptions, and demonstrated through the limits and controls placed on individual investment projects as part of the Department's Investment Approval process and the total number of projects.

Risks to information management are being managed and controlled, and steps have been taken to mitigate them. The Department is fully engaged with the Cabinet Office led programme to improve Information Assurance, so that information within the Defence community, including personal information covered by the Data Protection Act, is maintained reliably, accurately, securely, in accordance with the law and is available when required. Information Risk Management (IRM) processes includes letters of delegation for IRM and Integration of Information Architecture risks in the Defence Balanced Scorecard.

## 5. Review of effectiveness

As Accounting Officer, I have responsibility for reviewing the effectiveness of the system of internal control. My review of the effectiveness of the system of internal control is informed by the internal auditors and the executive managers within the Department who have responsibility for the development and maintenance of the internal control framework, and comments made by the external auditors in their management letter and other reports. I have been advised on the implications of the result of my review of the effectiveness of the system of internal control by the Defence Board and the Defence Audit Committee. Plans to address weaknesses and ensure continuous improvement of the system are in place.

The following processes are in operation in order to maintain and review the effectiveness of the system of internal control:

- A Defence Board, which meets approximately once a month to manage the plans, performance and strategic direction of the Department, comprising the senior members of the Department and at least two external independent members;

- A Defence Audit Committee, chaired by an external independent member of the Defence Board, which reviews the Department's risk-based approach to internal control. The Committee itself has also adopted a risk-based approach in its assurance work process, co-ordinating the activities of internal audit, and drawing on reports from pan-Departmental process owners and specialist assurance sources, including:

  - The 2nd Permanent Under-Secretary, as the Chair of the Defence Environment and Safety Board (including Scientific risks);

  - the Chief of Defence Materiel for the logistics process;

  - the Finance Director for departmental financial and planning systems;

  - the Surgeon General for Clinical Governance;

  - the Deputy Chief of the Defence Staff (Personnel) for Service personnel processes;

  - the Personnel Director for civilian personnel processes;

  - the Defence Commercial Director for the Department's commercial process;

  - the Director General Information for the Department's Information processes and as the Department's Senior Information Risk Owner for information assurance;

  - the Director General Media and Communication for communications processes;

  - the Director General Security and Safety as the Departmental Security Officer, for security and business continuity;

- the Director General of Defence Acquisition Policy for acquisition processes;

- the Director of Operational Capability;

- Defence Internal Audit, including the Defence Fraud Analysis Unit;

- the Director of Internal Management Consultancy; and

- the National Audit Office.

- A Strategic Risk Register and a Departmental risk register supported by operational-level risk registers, which complement the Defence Balanced Scorecard. Departmental risks are routinely reviewed by the Defence Board in the context of its regular reviews of Departmental programmes. The Departmental risk management process has been reviewed by the Defence Audit Committee;

- Through Top Level Budget Holders, a cascaded system for ensuring compliance with legal and statutory regulations. Each TLB holder is supported by an Audit Committee, chaired by a non-executive director and at which representatives from the internal and external auditors are present. Like the Defence Audit Committee these committees focus their activities to provide advice on wider-business risk and assurance processes;

- A Business Management System, with responsibility for the effective and efficient operation of the key pan-Departmental processes and standards such as Health and Safety, Finance, and Human Resources (military and civilian), including the identification of risks within these processes and the maintenance of effective controls to manage them, assigned to functional heads or process owners. Process Owners are responsible directly to the Defence Board;

- Through Top Level Budget Holders, a cascaded system which has developed further over the year, for ensuring that business continuity plans are in place, and that these plans are tested on a regular basis;

- An annual risk-based programme of internal audit provided by Defence Internal Audit, who are the primary source of independent assurance, which is complemented by the activity of the Directorate of Operational Capability, to provide independent operational audit and assurance to the Secretary of State and the Chief of the Defence Staff. On the basis of the audit work conducted during the year, Defence Internal Audit offered Substantial Assurance that the systems of internal control, risk management and governance reviewed are operating effectively across the Department;

- The Department's external audit function is provided on behalf of Parliament by the Comptroller and Auditor General, supported by staff from the National Audit Office (NAO). NAO staff see all Defence Audit Committee and TLB Audit Committee papers and attend their meetings. There was no relevant audit information which the NAO were not already aware of. Additionally the Accounting Officer held periodic private discussions with Internal Audit and with non-executive members of the Defence Audit Committee;

- Annual Reports providing measurable performance indicators and more subjective assessments on the Health of Financial Systems from all Top Level Budget Holders and key functional specialists. The Department has delivered its outputs within the resources voted by Parliament notwithstanding the pressure generated by the high level of operations, and remained within the Treasury's Total Departmental Expenditure Limit;

- An effective governance structure and performance management system that addresses the risks arising from the introduction of the general right of access to information from January 2005 under the Freedom of Information Act.

## 6. Significant Internal Control Issues

2007-08 was the first full year of live operation of the Joint Personnel Administration system (JPA) following the third and final phase of rollout to the Army in April 2007. Over the year it became clear that the shortfalls identified in 2006-07 in JPA's support to Departmental financial and manpower accounting processes were more deep-seated than we had thought and were of sufficient materiality as to have a continuing impact on the Department's ability to exercise full financial control. Significant progress was made during the year and there is a continuing programme of further work. Owing to the technical nature of some of the issues and the range and scope of the rectification and improvement work required, it is likely that resolving them will take a further 12-18 months.

Following the theft in January 2008 of an MoD laptop containing unencrypted recruiting records the Secretary of State for Defence asked Sir Edmund Burton to conduct an independent review into the circumstances that led to the data loss. Sir Edmund found that the Department's policies and procedures were fit for purpose but that the treatment of information, knowledge and data as key operational and business assets was inadequate in practice. He also concluded that at least some of the Department's information systems were likely for a time to have been in contravention of the Data Protection Act. In combination these factors, and in particular the inadequacies in the handling of personal data, represented a significant failure of internal control. The Department has accepted all Sir Edmund's recommendations and has published an action plan to take them forward. In addition the Defence Board has added Information Security to its strategic risks, and I have appointed a senior dedicated Data Protection Officer to ensure MoD practices and procedures are at the highest possible standard.

*Sir Bill Jeffrey*
**Accounting Officer**

**14 July 2008**

# The Certificate of the Comptroller and Auditor General to the House of Commons

I certify that I have audited the financial statements of the Ministry of Defence for the year ended 31 March 2008 under the Government Resources and Accounts Act 2000. These comprise the Statement of Parliamentary Supply, the Operating Cost Statement and Statement of Recognised Gains and Losses, the Balance Sheet, the Cash Flow Statement and the Statement of Operating Costs by Departmental Aim and Objectives and the related notes. These financial statements have been prepared under the accounting policies set out within them. I have also audited the information in the Remuneration Report that is described in that report as having been audited.

## Respective responsibilities of the Accounting Officer and auditor

The Accounting Officer is responsible for preparing the Annual Report, which includes the Remuneration Report, and the financial statements in accordance with the Government Resources and Accounts Act 2000 and HM Treasury directions made thereunder and for ensuring the regularity of financial transactions. These responsibilities are set out in the Statement of Accounting Officer's Responsibilities.

My responsibility is to audit the financial statements and the part of the Remuneration Report to be audited in accordance with relevant legal and regulatory requirements, and with International Standards on Auditing (UK and Ireland).

I report to you my opinion as to whether the financial statements give a true and fair view and whether the financial statements and the part of the Remuneration Report to be audited have been properly prepared in accordance with HM Treasury directions issued under the Government Resources and Accounts Act 2000. I report to you whether, in my opinion, the information which comprises the management commentary, included in the Annual Report, is consistent with the financial statements. I also report whether in all material respects the expenditure and income have been applied to the purposes intended by Parliament and the financial transactions conform to the authorities which govern them.

In addition, I report to you if the Department has not kept proper accounting records, if I have not received all the information and explanations I require for my audit, or if information specified by HM Treasury regarding remuneration and other transactions is not disclosed.

I review whether the Statement on Internal Control reflects the Department's compliance with HM Treasury's guidance, and I report if it does not. I am not required to consider whether this statement covers all risks and controls, or to form an opinion on the effectiveness of the Department's corporate governance procedures or its risk and control procedures.

I read the other information contained in the Annual Report and consider whether it is consistent with the audited financial statements. This other information comprises the Foreword, the unaudited part of the Remuneration Report and the Performance Report, including commentary on Purpose, Future, Enabling Processes and Resources. I consider the implications for my certificate if I become aware of any apparent misstatements or material inconsistencies with the financial statements. My responsibilities do not extend to any other information.

## Basis of audit opinions

I conducted my audit in accordance with International Standards on Auditing (UK and Ireland) issued by the Auditing Practices Board, except that the scope of our work was limited as explained below. My audit includes examination, on a test basis, of evidence relevant to the amounts, disclosures and regularity of financial transactions included in the financial statements and the part of the

Remuneration Report to be audited. It also includes an assessment of the significant estimates and judgments made by the Accounting Officer in the preparation of the financial statements, and of whether the accounting policies are most appropriate to the Department's circumstances, consistently applied and adequately disclosed.

I planned my audit so as to obtain all the information and explanations which I considered necessary in order to provide me with sufficient evidence to give reasonable assurance that the financial statements and the part of the Remuneration Report to be audited are free from material misstatement, whether caused by fraud or error, and that in all material respects the expenditure and income have been applied to the purposes intended by Parliament and the financial transactions conform to the authorities which govern them. However, the evidence available to me to confirm whether expenditure is accurate was limited in that it was not possible to obtain sufficient supporting evidence over allowances paid to military personnel totalling £920 million.

In forming my opinion I also evaluated the overall adequacy of the presentation of information in the financial statements.

## Votes A

The Ministry of Defence's Votes A is presented annually to Parliament to seek statutory authority for the maximum numbers of personnel to be maintained for service with the armed forces. Note 36 to the Accounts shows that the maximum numbers maintained during 2007-08 for the Naval, Army and Air Force Services in all active and reserve categories were within the numbers voted by Parliament. My role is to inform Parliament whether or not the approved Estimates (Votes A) have been exceeded. My staff have reviewed the information supporting actual numbers provided in the note to the financial statements and I am content that the numbers provided for in the Estimates have not been exceeded.

## Qualified opinion arising from a limitation in audit scope

In my opinion:

● Except for any adjustments which might have been found to be necessary had I been able to obtain sufficient evidence concerning allowances paid to military personnel, the financial statements give a true and fair view, in accordance with the Government Resources and Accounts Act 2000 and directions made thereunder by HM Treasury, of the state of the Department's affairs as at 31 March 2008, and the net cash requirement, net resource outturn, net operating cost, operating costs applied to objectives, recognised gains and losses and cashflows for the year then ended;

● the financial statements and the part of the Remuneration Report to be audited have been properly prepared in accordance with HM Treasury directions issued under the Government Resources and Accounts Act 2000; and

● information given within the Annual Report, which comprises a Management Commentary, is consistent with the financial statements.

In respect alone of the limitation on my work relating to allowances paid to military personnel:

- I have not obtained all the information and explanations that I considered necessary for the purposes of my audit; and

- proper accounting records had not been maintained.

## Opinion on Regularity

- In my opinion, in all material respects, the expenditure and income have been applied to the purposes intended by Parliament and the financial transactions conform to the authorities which govern them.

## Report

My report on pages 270 to 276 provides further details of my qualified audit opinion on the financial statements.

T J Burr
Comptroller and Auditor General
July 2008

National Audit Office
151 Buckingham Palace Road
Victoria
London SWIW 9SS

# Comptroller and Auditor General's Report on the 2007-08 Resource Accounts of the Ministry of Defence

## Introduction

**1.** The Ministry of Defence Resource Accounts for 2007-08 include payroll costs of £8.6 billion for the Armed Forces reported under Request for Resources 1 and 2. This expenditure is administered via the Joint Personnel Administration (JPA) project which was rolled out in three tranches across the RAF, Royal Navy and Army (in March 2006, October 2006 and March–July 2007 respectively), in order to modernise their human resources administration, including all aspects of pay and allowances.

## The purpose of my report

**2.** This Report explains the basis for the qualification of my audit opinion due to a limitation of scope. It also describes the problems encountered in implementing the JPA system; the action taken and planned by the Department to address these weaknesses; and my recommendations for further improvements. My Report does not focus on the wider objectives of the JPA beyond the administration of payroll.

**3.** The Department is actively working to address the weaknesses identified in this Report, but there remains significant further work to be done to ensure that a robust control environment is established. Some of the issues identified will take a considerable amount of effort and time to address effectively.

## My obligations as Auditor

**4.** Under the Government and Resources Act 2000 (the Act) I am required to examine and certify all Departmental Resource Accounts. International Standards on Auditing (UK and Ireland) require me to obtain evidence to give reasonable assurance that the Department's financial statements are free from material misstatement. In forming my opinion I examine, on a test basis, evidence supporting the disclosures in the financial statements and assess the significant estimates and judgements made in preparing them. I also consider whether the accounting policies are appropriate, consistently applied and adequately disclosed. I have qualified my opinion on the Ministry of Defence's 2007-08 financial statements due to a limitation in the scope of my audit and because the Department was unable to supply sufficient evidence to support payments of £920 million in relation to allowances paid to military personnel.

## Audit opinion

**Qualified opinion owing to a limitation in scope due to the inadequacy of evidence available in respect of amounts paid as allowances to military personnel.**

**5.** I have limited the scope of my opinion on this expenditure because of the lack of evidence available to me to substantiate, in particular:

- whether the amounts paid in relation to allowances to service personnel are correctly stated;

- the level of error caused by known issues within the JPA payroll system;

- whether selected payments on allowances and for expenses paid through JPA are valid due to the lack of supporting documentation.

There were no other procedures available to me to carry out an audit of this expenditure and I have therefore limited the scope of my opinion in this regard.

## Initiation of the Joint Personnel Administration project

**6.** The Joint Personnel Administration (JPA) project is designed to modernise administrative support to approximately 190,000 regular and 90,000 reserve members of the Armed Forces. The JPA project depends on a software package that manages a wide range of administrative processes including the payroll function, centralised records of service and the management of assignments and training. During 2007-08, the JPA payroll system was used to administer around £8.6 billion of staff costs for service personnel and this expenditure is reported in the Resource Accounts. The system is managed by the Service Personnel and Veterans Agency (SPVA) with the major elements delivered by its commercial partner, Electronic Data Systems (Defence) Ltd (EDS).

**7.** Prior to implementation of the JPA, the individual services operated their own pay and personnel administration systems including bespoke IT systems and associated business processes which then fed into a payroll delivery system operated by SPVA. The services' IT software and hardware were becoming increasingly old and costly to support and were unable to respond efficiently to changes such as the introduction of flexible employment packages.

**8.** To address these weaknesses, the Defence Board approved the introduction of a new HR and payroll system. Work started on the JPA project in 2000 and, in late 2001, the ORACLE Human Resource Management System (HRMS) a commercial off-the-shelf software package (COTS) was selected as the software application to support JPA.

**9.** In implementing JPA, the Department wanted to:

● harmonise conditions of service and associated allowances and payments across the services, including removing anomalies where service personnel could be doing the same tasks in the same location but depending on their service could be paid differently;

● allow personnel direct self-service access to certain personnel functions such as the ability to update bank details on-line;

● improve management information available both to operational and strategic levels of management; and

● make cash savings of £605 million over 10 years which would largely be achieved by reducing the number of staff involved in the operation of personnel administration systems by 1,439 by 2008-09.

## Implementation of the JPA project

**10.** The JPA has now been rolled out across all three services. Substantial improvements have been achieved for example:

● Where appropriate, allowances (eg annual leave) across the services have been harmonised as well as other conditions of service. This work continues.

● Many individuals now have access to their own personal data and can update this more easily than previously and this has been widely welcomed.

● Efficiency savings have been delivered which the Department put at £63 million up to 31 March 2008 mainly through Service and Civilian HR reductions.

**11.** However, there have also been significant problems with certain financial control and reporting aspects of the JPA project. A key reason for the difficulties experienced with the implementation of the JPA was that insufficient focus was given to the need for internal financial controls. In some cases, where the software application originally had the facility for data entry checks or exception reporting to be performed as part of the process, these controls were not used as they were considered to be inefficient and cumbersome. This decision, coupled with other gaps in key controls, undermined the robustness of the JPA control framework and mean that, in my view, it is not yet sufficiently robust to support a process which delivers pay and allowances for the armed services.

**12.**   In addition, insufficient emphasis was placed on the requirements for management information and financial reporting. User requirements for this information were not originally adequately specified. Because of the lack of adequate specification of user requirements and the size of the JPA systems and volume of data, a key decision was made to post transactions to the general ledger in aggregate, rather than in detail. This reduced the flow of information to the general ledger making the transfer of such information more efficient but had the consequence of detracting from the visibility of the transactions themselves. While reports are available from JPA itself these have proved difficult to obtain and use although improvements are being made all the time. As a result, the quality of management information has been undermined.

**13.**   The Armed Forces' personnel policies, rules and processes and the resultant pay structures are very complex, especially in the areas of specialist pay and allowances. While some progress has been made on the harmonisation and simplification of policies, rules and processes, it has been slower than intended. As at 31 March 2008, there were still some 2,800 separate pay elements including around 780 different elements of allowances for which the pay software application must cater. As a result, the software is more complex than originally envisaged with around 400 "extensions" to the application package.

**14.**   With the significant issues arising from the implementation of the JPA, the Accounting Officer commissioned a specific internal review of the reasons for the lack of adequate financial controls within JPA and their report was made in May 2008. The review reached the following conclusions:

- In paying close attention to project timescale and the costs and benefits to be delivered, the Department gave insufficient priority to ensuring that the basic financial control and reporting requirements were delivered.

- The Department saw the JPA primarily as an HR project and did not sufficiently involve finance staff in the specification and design of JPA so that the original specification did not include financial requirements for the system.

- The Department relied overly on EDS to advise it of the controls needed but the contractor had difficulties in understanding what the Department required.

- The Department should have put in place tighter monitoring arrangements to confirm that the contractor was delivering in line with expectations.

**15.**   Although the Department tested certain aspects of the JPA application and the link with its main accounting systems, it did not adequately test its ability to meet the Department's financial requirements. It was only when the system went live for the RAF in March 2006 that the Department started to realise the extent of the problems. Furthermore, under pressure to achieve its efficiency targets, the Department sought to achieve the planned savings in HR personnel at too early a stage in the implementation of the JPA. Around 300 HR staff posts were cut at a time when the difficulties associated with the implementation were, in fact, creating a need for more experienced HR staff support.

## Departmental responses to identified weaknesses

**16.**   The impact of some of these problems on the services as a whole was lessened by the roll-out of the system in stages. The Department made a number of important improvements to their procedures in response to early experience of the system in the RAF. Measures included providing additional staff for the new call centre, better training and delaying some aspects eg self-service until the teething problems of the basic service could be rectified. Where possible, it introduced compensatory controls and added further functionality to address some of the major weaknesses.

**17.** For example, during the latter part of 2006, following several significant overpayments due to individual input errors, the Department introduced a manual check, prior to payment, on all net payments over a set limit (initially set at £15,000 and reduced to £10,000 in July 2008). It has also put in place a specific cap for Long Service Advance of Pay and, for other payments which could potentially be in error, provided advisory warning flags to alert users of possible incorrect data entry, although these can still be overridden.

**18.** The Department has also worked closely with EDS to improve the payroll control accounts reconciliation process. This is an extensive piece of work with significant adjustments often being required to resolve balances. As at 31 March 2008, 14 key control accounts out of 40 were still considered to be at significant risk of continuing error.

## Weaknesses in Financial Control

**19.** We have identified the following main weaknesses in financial control and management information:

- There are insufficient controls within the system to prevent errors which could be made either intentionally or unintentionally and which have led to regular instances of significant over and under payments.

- The levels of mis-postings between cost centres were higher than originally anticipated and the lack of traceability and the inability to obtain reports easily meant that Top Level Budget Holders (and lower levels of accountability), where responsibility for budgetary oversight lay, were unable to confirm that their service personnel were paid the correct amount or that costs were charged to the correct account codes, restricting the ability to make corrections.

- A substantial number of individual personnel records (the Department believe some 5-10 per cent of personnel may be affected) may not include correct information and need investigating to confirm whether under- or over-payments have occurred.

- Payroll control accounts including those for service personnel debt, pay deductions and social security costs could not be adequately reconciled and a backlog quickly developed.

- Debt due from service personnel has grown and has become more difficult to recover. Because of uncertainty about the amount of debt owed by individuals and delays in initiating recovery, debt recovery levels remain lower than under the previous legacy system and the level of debt overall is therefore higher. At present £28.9 million is outstanding with recovery rates at 76% compared with 91% under the previous system. A substantial amount may now need to be written off but the amounts involved can not yet be estimated with certainty.

- While individuals or Units may cause errors which can have an impact on the performance of SPVA (for example through incomplete or inaccurate input of data and failure to provide the information necessary to manage control accounts) the Agency has limited control over such errors.

- There is a lack of up-to-date and accurate information on pay expenditure, debt and liabilities and the financial information due to the lack of reconciliations, which has been inadequate for the purposes of the Department in terms of budget monitoring.

- Other management information is considered inadequate and not sufficiently reliable. For example, the Defence Analysis and Statistics Agency (DASA) has qualified its reports on manning numbers since the introduction of the JPA.

- Limitations in the systems have been exacerbated by inadequate training for service users, Unit HR staff and business users (for example, budget holders) and the helplines set up to support users did not initially perform adequately.

## Inability to provide evidence in support of payments

**20.** The difficulties experienced with JPA mean that I have limited the scope of my opinion on part of military pay and allowances expenditure because of the lack of evidence available to me to substantiate the following:

- amounts spent on individual types of allowances for the current and prior years;

- the level of error caused by known issues within the JPA payroll system;

- whether selected payments on allowances and for expenses paid through JPA are valid given the lack of supporting documentation;

- the overall reconciliation of the general ledger to JPA to ensure the accounts reflect all expenditure;

- individual TLBs' reconciliations of elements of pay, allowances and expenses, for which they hold budgetary responsibility, back to JPA to enable correction of mis-postings;

- control accounts have not been reconciled to individual elements and corrective action taken to clear these. There is a lack of understanding of the interaction of some control accounts.

There were no other procedures available to me to carry out an audit of this expenditure and I have therefore limited the scope of my opinion in this regard.

**21.** In some cases where paper evidence is no longer required, electronic data can provide sufficient evidence in support of expenditure provided that system controls exist and are sufficiently strong, for example, to provide evidence of the identity and location of the relevant individuals. However, as indicated above, it is my opinion that the framework of system controls is currently insufficient to provide appropriate assurances about the authorisation of payments.

## Further Actions by the Department to improve financial controls

**22.** The Department has already devoted significant resource to improving the robustness of the JPA payroll systems. They are currently taking forward further improvements in the following key areas:

- Development of a detailed systems map in order to assess whether all necessary controls exist and whether some are duplicated. This will also enable the Department to consider the appropriate balance of system and clerical checks to ensure that all significant risks are efficiently mitigated. At the time of my report, this work has not yet been completed.

- Establishment of a working group of stakeholders to ensure that issues at Top Level Budget Holder and lower accountability levels can be escalated and resolved.

- Formation of a targeted team of accountants to identify the financial implication of known weaknesses, such as the need for reconciliation of control accounts, and to monitor EDS progress on clearing these.

- In some areas TLBs have recognised that the reduction in local support staff to assist service personnel with JPA-related issues was taken too far. For example the RAF are planning to introduce JPA specialists in each of their Units to assist staff and be a local repository of expertise.

- To improve the management information being provided by the JPA, training in the production of regular and ad-hoc reports has been improved and on-line access has been widened to help with solving problems.

**23.** The Department faces difficulties in the speed with which it can effect improvements. It can only implement software changes as part of the formal roll-out phases of the project. It is worth noting that EDS estimate that the upgrade to the next database version could take one year. There can therefore be considerable delays between the time that the need for a control is identified and the time it is in place and operating.

## Recommendations for further action

**24.** Against this background, we recommend that the Department should take the following additional actions which are already in hand:

- As described at paragraph 22 above, the detailed systems map of the end-to-end personnel and pay processes which the Department is currently preparing should enable it to form a complete picture of the current control environment. This exercise needs to be completed urgently to allow the Department to instigate the necessary mitigating controls which would allow it to provide assurance to the system users.

- This same system map should also enable the Department to identify, for the medium-term, which controls should be built into the JPA automated system and which should be retained as supporting clerical controls.

- For each of these two stages, the Department should produce an overall plan which prioritises the significant issues, with timescales set by which actions should be completed and adequate resources allocated to achieve the plans. The cost involved of implementing such controls should be weighed against the risks associated with not introducing a system of input controls. The controls put in place need to be fully tested and Internal Audit could be directed to provide independent assurance that the framework is appropriate.

- In the immediate short term, more will need to be done to prevent , and if necessary detect, input and processing errors. Interim output controls should be continued at least until appropriate input controls are in place and management should consider whether the limit above which payments are clerically checked prior to issue should be reduced further below the revised limit of £10,000.

- The Department should revisit its working relationship with EDS. It is essential for the contractor to have a sufficiently in-depth understanding of the Department's requirements including its expectations of the contractor. With greater clarity about its expectation of EDS, the Department should be able to monitor EDS's delivery better.

- Given the current systems constraints and the lack of familiarity of some users with JPA, the Department should investigate the potential to increase the range of standard reports produced by the system which would cover the majority of standard user's key requirements.

- Payroll control account reconciliations now need to concentrate on making corrections in sufficient time for departmental processing timetables and action needs to be taken to devise system fixes to halt further errors occurring.

- The Department is reviewing corporate governance arrangements as part of its Streamlining initiative and it should consider whether the oversight arrangements of the JPA project as part of the military pay process are sufficient to drive the necessary improvements given the diverse spread of responsibilities between the Process Owner, SPVA, the Services and Top Level Budget holders.

- The Department should carry out an evaluation of the JPA project with a view to the future direction of JPA including whether the Department's financial information needs can be met effectively and whether the customisation of the JPA software has limited its future capability including the ability to cope with future Oracle updates.

**25.**   I shall continue to work with the Department as it seeks to resolve the significant problems it is experiencing with the implementation of the JPA system and will provide an update on the progress made in my Report on the 2008-09 Resource Accounts.

# Statement of Parliamentary Supply

## Summary of Resource Outturn 2007-08

| Request for Resources | Note | Estimate | | | Outturn | | | 2007-08 Net Total Outturn compared to Estimate Savings/ (Excess) | 2006-07 Total Outturn |
|---|---|---|---|---|---|---|---|---|---|
| | | Gross Expenditure £000 | A in A* £000 | Net Total £000 | Gross Expenditure £000 | A in A* £000 | Net Total £000 | £000 | £000 |
| 1 | 2 | 36,105,264 | 1,475,504 | 34,629,760 | 34,458,832 | 1,382,683 | 33,076,149 | 1,553,611 | 31,518,502 |
| 2 | 2 | 2,405,837 | 24,034 | 2,381,803 | 2,218,138 | 22,101 | 2,196,037 | 185,766 | 1,448,420 |
| 3 | 2 | 1,030,007 | - | 1,030,007 | 1,014,130 | - | 1,014,130 | 15,877 | 1,038,073 |
| Total resources | 3 | 39,541,108 | 1,499,538 | 38,041,570 | 37,691,100 | 1,404,784 | 36,286,316 | 1,755,254 | 34,004,995 |
| Non operating cost A in A | | | | 1,244,000 | | | 1,201,329 | 42,671 | 498,287 |

* Appropriation in Aid (A in A)

## Net Cash Requirement 2007-08

| | Note | Estimate £000 | Outturn £000 | 2007-08 Net Total Outturn compared to Estimate Savings/ (Excess) £000 | 2006-07 Total Outturn £000 |
|---|---|---|---|---|---|
| Net Cash Requirement | 4 | 34,730,098 | 33,504,916 | 1,225,182 | 31,454,292 |

## Summary of Income Payable to the Consolidated Fund

(In addition to appropriations in aid, the following income relates to the Department and is payable to the Consolidated Fund (cash receipts being shown in *italics*)).

| | Note | Forecast 2007-08 | | Outturn 2007-08 | |
|---|---|---|---|---|---|
| | | Income £000 | *Receipts* £000 | Income £000 | *Receipts* £000 |
| Total | 5 | 55,000 | *55,000* | 63,310 | *750,810* |

The notes on pages 282 to 335 form part of these accounts

Further analysis of the variances between Estimate and Outturn is at Note 2 and a summary of the overall financial position, including an explanation of the main variances identified above, is provided in the Management Commentary and the following paragraphs. A detailed explanation of the Department's financial performance in relation to HM Treasury's Departmental Expenditure Limits is included in the Finance section of the Annual Performance Report which forms the first part of this Annual Report and Accounts.

The net outturn for Total Resources is £36,286,316,000 against an Estimate of £38,041,570,000; an underspend of £1,755,254,000. The variance against the Supply Estimate results from an underspend of £1,093,592,000 against Resource DEL; an underspend of £661,662,000 in Annually Managed Expenditure (AME).

Request for Resources (RfR) 1, Provision of Defence Capability, provides for expenditure primarily to meet the MoD's operational support and logistics services costs and the costs of providing the equipment capability required by Defence policy. Any Appropriations in Aid in excess of the Estimate are shown at Note 5, and these will be surrendered to the Consolidated Fund.

The net outturn for RfR1 is £33,076,149,000 against an Estimate of £34,629,760,000 an underspend of £1,553,611,000. The main reason for the underspend is depreciation charges and provisions, included in the Spring Supplementary Estimate, that did not materialise.

RfR2, Operations and Peace-Keeping, shows a net outturn of £2,196,037,000 against an Estimate of £2,381,803,000; an underspend of £185,766,000. The underspend principally relates to an over-stated request for indirect DEL in the Spring Supplementary Estimate which has not materialised at the year end. Further detail is provided in the RfR2 analysis at Note 2 to the accounts.

RfR3, War Pensions Benefits shows a net outturn of £1,014,130,000 against an Estimate of £1,030,007,000; an underspend of £15,877,000. This RfR provides for the payment of war disablement and war widows' pensions in accordance with relevant legislation; this is all AME. The costs of administering war pensions are borne by RfR1.

The non-operating Appropriations in Aid total £1,201,329,000 against an Estimate of £1,244,000,000; a shortfall of £42,671,000 against expected receipts.

The Net Cash Requirement shows a net outturn of £33,504,916,000, against an Estimate of £34,730,098,000; an underspend of £1,225,182,000. This results from planned working assumptions made in the Spring Supplementary Estimates that did not materialise.

# Operating Cost Statement

for the year ended 31 March 2008

| | Note | 2007-08 £000 | 2006-07 £000 |
|---|---|---|---|
| Staff costs | 9 | 11,484,909 | 11,204,262 |
| Other operating costs | 10 | 22,595,155 | 20,764,796 |
| Gross operating costs | | 34,080,064 | 31,969,058 |
| Operating income | 11 | (1,395,770) | (1,429,392) |
| **Net operating cost before interest** | | 32,684,294 | 30,539,666 |
| Net interest payable | 12 | 167,804 | 167,096 |
| Cost of capital charge | 21 | 3,370,908 | 3,241,907 |
| **Net operating cost** | | 36,223,006 | 33,948,669 |
| **Net resource outturn** | 3 | 36,286,316 | 34,004,995 |

## Statement of Recognised Gains and Losses

for the year ended 31 March 2008

| | Note | 2007-08 £000 | 2006-07 £000 |
|---|---|---|---|
| Net gain on revaluation of intangible fixed assets | 22 | (1,653,255) | (602,077) |
| Net gain on revaluation of tangible fixed assets | 22 | (2,852,140) | (2,629,943) |
| Net (gain) / loss on revaluation of stock | 22 | (83,884) | 385,024 |
| Net (gain) / loss on revaluation of investments | 22 | (7,181) | 9,991 |
| Receipts of donated assets and gain on revaluation | 22 | (453,461) | (59,233) |
| Net loss/(gain) on the change in the discount rate of pension schemes | 21 | 41,815 | (50,600) |
| **Recognised gains for the financial year** | | (5,008,106) | (2,946,838) |

The notes on pages 282 to 335 form part of these accounts

# Balance Sheet

as at 31 March 2008

| | Note | 31 March 2008 £000 | 31 March 2008 £000 | 31 March 2007 £000 | 31 March 2007 £000 |
|---|---|---|---|---|---|
| **Fixed Assets** | | | | | |
| Intangible assets | 13 | 26,692,246 | | 24,162,622 | |
| Tangible fixed assets | 14 | 77,930,278 | | 74,600,538 | |
| Investments | 15 | 497,294 | | 500,062 | |
| Debtors: due after more than one year | 17 | 1,977,080 | | 1,723,400 | |
| | | | 107,096,898 | | 100,986,622 |
| **Current Assets** | | | | | |
| Stocks and work-in-progress | 16 | 5,288,755 | | 5,321,394 | |
| Debtors: due within one year | 17 | 1,945,139 | | 1,514,019 | |
| Cash at bank and in hand | 18 | 513,852 | | 473,676 | |
| | | 7,747,746 | | 7,309,089 | |
| Creditors: amounts falling due within one year | 19 | (8,111,184) | | (6,738,594) | |
| **Net current assets** | | | (363,438) | | 570,495 |
| **Total assets less current liabilities** | | | 106,733,460 | | 101,557,117 |
| Creditors: amounts falling due after more than one year | 19 | (1,143,332) | | (975,146) | |
| Provisions for liabilities and charges | 20 | (5,753,771) | | (5,771,881) | |
| | | | (6,897,103) | | (6,747,027) |
| **Net assets** | | | 99,836,357 | | 94,810,090 |
| **Taxpayers' equity** | | | | | |
| General fund | 21 | | 76,647,800 | | 75,434,183 |
| Revaluation reserve | 22 | | 20,452,461 | | 17,129,769 |
| Donated assets reserve | 22 | | 2,496,316 | | 2,013,539 |
| Investment reserve | 22 | | 239,780 | | 232,599 |
| | | | 99,836,357 | | 94,810,090 |

*Sir Bill Jeffrey*
**Accounting Officer**

**14 July 2008**

The notes on pages 282 to 335 form part of these accounts

# Cash Flow Statement

for the year ended 31 March 2008

| | Note | 2007-08 £000 | 2006-07 £000 |
|---|---|---|---|
| Net cash outflow from operating activities | 23.1 | (25,689,124) | (24,671,233) |
| Capital expenditure and financial investment | 23.2 | (6,990,157) | (6,767,865) |
| Payments of amounts due to the Consolidated Fund | | (790,465) | (119,654) |
| Financing | 23.4 | 33,509,922 | 31,014,183 |
| Increase/(decrease) in cash at bank and in hand | 23.5 | 40,176 | (544,569) |

# Statement of Operating Costs by Departmental Aim and Objectives

for the year ended 31 March 2008

## Aim

The principal activity of the Department is to deliver security for the people of the United Kingdom and the Overseas Territories by defending them, including against terrorism; and to act as a force for good by strengthening international peace and stability.

In pursuance of this aim, the Department has the following objectives:

| | 2007-08 | | | 2006-07 | | |
|---|---|---|---|---|---|---|
| | Gross £000 | Income £000 | Net £000 | Gross £000 | Income £000 | Net £000 |
| **Objective 1:** Achieving success in the tasks we undertake | 4,361,822 | (311,571) | 4,050,251 | 4,014,273 | (303,275) | 3,710,998 |
| **Objective 2:** Being ready to respond to the tasks that might arise | 29,375,411 | (1,055,206) | 28,320,205 | 27,373,390 | (1,081,131) | 26,292,259 |
| **Objective 3:** Building for the future | 2,867,413 | (28,993) | 2,838,420 | 2,952,325 | (44,986) | 2,907,339 |
| | 36,604,646 | (1,395,770) | 35,208,876 | 34,339,988 | (1,429,392) | 32,910,596 |
| Paying war pensions benefits | 1,014,130 | | 1,014,130 | 1,038,073 | - | 1,038,073 |
| **Total** | 37,618,776 | (1,395,770) | 36,223,006 | 35,378,061 | (1,429,392) | 33,948,669 |

See additional details in Note 24.

The notes on pages 282 to 335 form part of these accounts

# Notes to the Accounts

### 1. Statement of Accounting Policies

## Introduction

**1.1** These financial statements have been prepared in accordance with the generic Accounts Direction issued by HM Treasury under reference DAO(GEN)06/07. They comply with the requirements of HM Treasury's Financial Reporting Manual (FReM) except where HM Treasury has approved the following departures to enable the Department to reflect its own particular circumstances:

- The Operating Cost Statement is not currently segmented into programme and non-programme costs. However, as a result of the Comprehensive Spending Review Settlement 2007, which introduced the requirement for an administration budget, separate disclosure of administration costs will be made from 1 April 2008.

- The FReM's requirement for Departments to prepare accounts that present the transactions and flows for the financial year and the balances at the year end between "core" Department and the consolidated group in respect of the Operating Cost Statement (and supporting notes) and Balance Sheet (and supporting notes) has not been applied. Since agencies falling within the Departmental Boundary are on-vote and embedded within the Departmental chain of command, HM Treasury permits them to be treated as an integral part of the "core" Department. Throughout these accounts, the consolidated figures for the Ministry of Defence (including its on-vote agencies) are deemed to represent those of the "core" Department;

- The Department has not fully complied with the FReM emissions cap and trade scheme accounting requirements on the grounds of materiality. Rather than registering an asset and a liability to reflect its holding of allowances and its obligation to pay for emissions discharged, the Department has reflected the purchase and sale of allowances as expenditure and income within the Operating Cost Statement. All other costs associated with the scheme, such as compliance checking, are also charged to the Operating Cost Statement. On the grounds of materiality, HM Treasury has also agreed that the information normally required by the FReM on Fees and Charges disclosures (paragraph 7.4.32) is not required and the disclosure provided at Note 11.1 is sufficient.

**1.2** As directed by HM Treasury, for Financial Year 2008/09, the Department will prepare both UK GAAP compliant accounts and 'shadow' financial statements based on International Financial Reporting Standards (IFRS) as adapted and interpreted by HM Treasury in the IFRS based FReM. The latter will be subject to NAO review but not published. The UK GAAP based accounts for 2008-09 will adopt Financial Reporting Standards 25, 26 and 29 – implementing the financial instrument accounting requirements. From Financial Year 2009/10, the Department will prepare only IFRS based accounts.

## Accounting Convention

**1.3** These financial statements have been prepared on an accruals basis under the historical cost convention, modified to include the revaluation of certain fixed assets and stocks.

## Basis of Preparation of Departmental Resource Accounts

**1.4** These financial statements comprise the consolidation of the Department, its Defence Supply Financed Agencies and those Advisory Non-Departmental Public Bodies (NDPBs) sponsored by the Department, which are not self-accounting. The Defence Agencies and the Advisory NDPBs sponsored by the Department are listed in Note 35.

**1.5** Five of the Department's agencies are established as Trading Funds. As such, they fall outside Voted Supply and are subject to a different control framework. The Department's interests in the Trading Funds are included in the financial statements as fixed asset investments. Executive NDPBs operate on a self-accounting basis and are not included within the consolidated accounts. They receive grant-in-aid funding from the Department, which is treated as an expense in the Operating Cost Statement.

**1.6** The Department's interest in QinetiQ Group plc, formerly a Self-Financing Public Corporation, is included in the financial statements as a fixed asset investment.

**1.7** The Armed Forces Pension Scheme (AFPS) is not consolidated within these financial statements. Separate accounts are prepared for the AFPS.

**1.8** Machinery of Government changes which involve the merger of two or more Departments into one new Department, or the transfer of functions or responsibility of one part of the public service sector to another, are accounted for using merger accounting in accordance with Financial Reporting Standard (FRS) 6.

## Net Operating Costs

**1.9** Costs are charged to the Operating Cost Statement in the period in which they are incurred and are matched to any related income. Costs of contracted-out services are included net of recoverable VAT. Other costs are VAT inclusive, although a proportion of this VAT is recovered via a formula agreed with HM Revenue and Customs. Surpluses and deficits on disposal of fixed assets and stock are included within Note 10 – Other Operating Costs.

**1.10** Income from services provided to third parties is included within operating income, net of related VAT. In accordance with FRS 21, as interpreted by the FReM, Trading Fund dividends are recognised as operating income on an accruals basis, whilst other dividends are recognised in the year in which they are declared.

## Fixed Assets

**1.11** The Department's fixed assets are expressed at their current value through the application of the Modified Historical Cost Accounting Convention (MHCA). Prospective indices, which are produced by the Defence Analytical Services Agency, are applied at the start of each financial year to the fixed assets which fall within the categories listed below. These indices, which look ahead to the subsequent balance sheet date, are also adjusted to reflect the difference between the actual change in prices in the prior year and the earlier prediction.

– Land (by region and type);

– Buildings – Dwellings (UK and specific overseas indices);

– Buildings – Non Dwellings (UK and specific overseas indices);

– Single Use Military Equipment – Sea Systems;

– Single Use Military Equipment – Air Systems;

– Single Use Military Equipment – Land Systems;

– Plant and Machinery;

– Transport – Fighting Equipment;

- Transport – Other;

- IT and Communications Equipment – Office Machinery and Computers; and

- IT and Communications Equipment – Communications Equipment.

**1.12** Property fixed assets are also subject to a quinquennial revaluation by external professional valuers in accordance with FRS 15, as interpreted by the FReM.

**1.13** Assets under construction are valued at cost and are subject to indexation. On completion, they are released from the project account into the appropriate asset category.

**1.14** The Department's policy on the capitalisation of subsequent expenditure under FRS15 is to account separately for material major refits and overhauls, when their value is consumed by the Department over a period which differs from that of the overall life of the corresponding core asset and where this is deemed to have a material effect on the carrying values of a fixed asset and the depreciation charge.

**1.15** Subsequent expenditure is also capitalised, where it is deemed to enhance significantly the operational capability of the equipment, including extension of life, likewise when it is incurred to replace or restore a component of an asset that has been treated separately for depreciation purposes.

## Intangible Fixed Assets

**1.16** Pure and applied research costs are charged to the Operating Cost Statement in the period in which they are incurred.

**1.17** Development costs are capitalised where they contribute towards defining the specification of an asset that will enter production. Those not capitalised are charged to the Operating Cost Statement. Capitalised development costs are amortised, on a straight line basis, over the planned operational life of that asset type, e.g. class of ship or aircraft. Amortisation commences when the asset type first enters operational service within the Department. If it is decided to withdraw the whole class of an asset type early, then any residual unamortised development costs relating to that class are written off to the OCS, along with the value of the underlying tangible fixed assets.

## Tangible Fixed Assets

**1.18** The useful economic lives of tangible fixed assets are reviewed annually and adjusted where necessary. The Departmental capitalisation threshold is generally £10,000 and it is this which determines whether or not an asset is recorded on the Department's Fixed Asset Register (FAR). An exception to this is the Managed Equipment FAR where a capitalisation threshold of £5,400 is applied to the assets which are managed by DE&S Integrated Project Teams on behalf of the three services. Agencies may also apply a lower capitalisation threshold to those assets which form part of their Agency accounts balance sheet. The decision to record an asset on the FAR normally takes place at the point of initial acquisition.

**1.19** The Departmental threshold of £10,000 for single fixed assets is not applied to Capital Spares and assembled Guided Weapons Missiles and Bombs (GWMB). For accounting purposes, these items are treated as pooled assets and included within the Single Use Military Equipment category of tangible fixed assets.

**1.20** GWMB and Capital Spares are categorised as tangible fixed assets and subject to depreciation. The depreciation charge in the OCS also includes the cost of GWMB fired to destruction. The principal asset categories and their useful economic lives, depreciated on a straight line basis, are:

| | Category | Years |
|---|---|---|
| Land and Buildings | Land | Indefinite, not depreciated |
| | Buildings, permanent | 40 – 50 |
| | Buildings, temporary | 5 – 20 |
| | Leasehold | Shorter of expected life and lease period |
| Single Use Military Equipment (including GWMB) | Air Systems – Fixed Wing | 13 – 35 |
| | Air Systems – Rotary Wing | 25 – 30 |
| | Sea Systems – Surface Ships | 24 – 30 |
| | Sea Systems – Submarines | 28 – 32 |
| | Land Systems – Armoured Vehicles | 25 – 30 |
| | Land Systems – Small Arms | 10 – 15 |
| Plant and Machinery | Equipment | 10 – 25 |
| | Plant and Machinery | 5 – 25 |
| Transport | Air Systems – Fixed Wing | 25 – 35 |
| | Air Systems – Rotary Wing | 15 – 32 |
| | Sea Systems – Surface Ships | 20 – 30 |
| | Land Systems – Specialised Vehicles | 15 – 30 |
| | Land Systems – Other Standard Vehicles | 3 – 5 |
| IT and Communications Equipment | Office Machinery | 3 – 10 |
| | Communications Equipment | 3 – 30 |
| Capital Spares | Items of repairable material retained for the purpose of replacing parts of an asset undergoing repair, refurbishment, maintenance, servicing, modification, enhancement or conversion. | As life of prime equipment supported |
| Operational Heritage Assets * | | As other tangible fixed assets |

*Operational Heritage Assets are included within the principal asset category to which they relate.

## Donated Assets

**1.21**     Donated assets (i.e. those assets that have been donated to the Department or assets for which the Department has continuing and exclusive use, but does not own legal title, and for which it has not given consideration in return) are capitalised at their current valuation on receipt and are revalued/depreciated on the same basis as purchased assets.

**1.22**     The Donated Assets Reserve represents the value of the original donation, additions and any subsequent professional revaluation and indexation (Modified Historic Cost Accounting). Amounts equal to the donated asset depreciation charge, impairment costs and any in-year surplus/deficit on disposal are released from this reserve to the Operating Cost Statement.

## Impairment

**1.23**     Impairment charges to the Operating Cost Statement occur in circumstances which include a decision to retire a fixed asset from service and dispose of it at below net book value; on transfer of a fixed asset into stock; on reduction in service potential or where the application of MHCA indices causes a downward revaluation below the depreciated historical cost, which is deemed to be permanent. For example, there will be a reduction in service potential if a specialist building is subsequently used for non-specialist purposes. Any reversal of an impairment charge is recognised in the Operating Cost Statement to the extent that the original charge, adjusted for subsequent depreciation, was previously recognised in the Operating Cost Statement. The remaining amount is recognised in the Revaluation Reserve.

## Disposal of Tangible Fixed Assets

**1.24**    Disposal of assets is handled principally by two specialist internal organisations: Defence Estates for property assets and the Disposal Services Authority for non-property assets.

**1.25**    Property assets identified for disposal are included at the open market value, with any write down in value to the net recoverable amount (NRA) charged to the Operating Cost Statement against impairment. Any increase in value to the NRA is credited to the Revaluation Reserve. On subsequent sale, the surplus or deficit is included in the Operating Cost Statement under surplus/deficit on disposal of fixed assets.

**1.26**    Non-property assets are subject to regular impairment reviews. An impairment review is also carried out when a decision is made to dispose of an asset and take it out of service. Any write down in value to the NRA is charged to the Operating Cost Statement against impairment whilst any increase in value to the NRA is credited to the Revaluation Reserve. The surplus or deficit at the point of disposal is included in the Operating Cost Statement under surplus/deficit on disposal of fixed assets. Non-property assets, where the receipts on sale are anticipated not to be separately identifiable, are transferred to stock at their NRA and shown under assets declared for disposal. Any write down on transfer is included in the Operating Cost Statement under impairment.

## Leased Assets

**1.27**    Assets held under finance leases are capitalised as tangible fixed assets and depreciated over the shorter of the lease term or their estimated useful economic lives. Rentals paid are apportioned between reductions in the capital obligations included in creditors, and finance costs charged to the Operating Cost Statement. Expenditure under operating leases is charged to the Operating Cost Statement in the period in which it is incurred. In circumstances where the Department is the lessor of a finance lease, amounts due under a finance lease are treated as amounts receivable and reported within Debtors.

## Private Finance Initiative (PFI) Transactions

**1.28**    Where the substance of the transaction is such that the risks and rewards of ownership remain with the Department, the assets and liabilities are reported on the Department's Balance Sheet. Unitary charges in respect of on-balance sheet PFI deals are apportioned between reduction in the capital obligation and charges to the Operating Cost Statement for service performance and finance cost. Where the risks and rewards are transferred to the private sector, the transaction is accounted for in the Operating Cost Statement in accordance with FRS 5 and HM Treasury Guidance.

**1.29**    Where assets are transferred to the Private Sector Provider, and the consideration received by the Department is in the form of reduced unitary payments, the sales value is accounted for as a prepayment. This prepayment is then reduced (charged to the Operating Cost Statement) over the course of the contract, as the benefits of the prepaid element are utilised.

## Investments

**1.30**    Investments represent holdings that the Department intends to retain for the foreseeable future. Fixed asset investments are stated at market value where available; otherwise they are stated at cost. In the case of Trading Funds (which are not consolidated into the Department's Resource Accounts), the value of loans and public dividend capital held by the Department is recorded at historic cost. In February 2006, QinetiQ Group plc became a listed company. The MoD's investment in QinetiQ Group plc is now recorded at market value. Details of the QinetiQ Group plc investment are given in Note 15. Investments may either be equity investments, held in the name of the Secretary of State for Defence, or medium or long-term loans made with the intention of providing working capital or commercial support.

## Stocks and Work-in-Progress

**1.31** Stock is recognised on the Department's Balance Sheet from the point of acquisition to the point of issue for use, consumption, sale, write-off or disposal. The point of consumption for Land stocks is the point at which stock is issued from depots. For Air stocks, the point of consumption is when stocks are issued from final depots such as an air base, and for Naval stocks it is when the stock item is used.

**1.32** Stock is valued at current replacement cost, or historic cost if not materially different. Provision is made to reduce cost to net realisable value (NRV) where there is no expectation of consumption or sale in the ordinary course of the business. Stock provision is released to the Operating Cost Statement on consumption, disposal and write-off.

**1.33** Internal work in progress represents the ongoing work on the manufacture, modification, enhancement or conversion of stock items and is valued on the same basis as stocks. External work in progress represents ongoing work on production or repair contracts for external customers and is valued at the lower of current replacement cost and NRV.

**1.34** Assets declared for disposal include stock held for disposal and those non-property fixed assets identified for disposal where receipts are not anticipated to be separately identifiable.

**1.35** Stocks written-off, included within Other Operating Costs, represent the book value of stock which has been scrapped, destroyed or lost during the year, and also adjustments to bring the book values into line with the figures recorded on the supply systems.

## Provisions for Liabilities and Charges

**1.36** Provisions for liabilities and charges have been established under the criteria of FRS 12 and are based on realistic and prudent estimates of the expenditure required to settle future legal or constructive obligations that exist at the Balance Sheet date.

**1.37** Provisions are charged to the Operating Cost Statement unless the expenditure provides access to current and future economic benefits, in which case the provision is capitalised as part of the cost of the underlying facility. In such cases, the capitalised provision will be depreciated and charged to the Operating Cost Statement over the remaining estimated useful economic life of the underlying asset. All long-term provisions are discounted to current prices using the rate advised by HM Treasury. The rate for financial year 2007-08 is 2.2% (2.2% for 2006-07). The discount is unwound over the remaining life of the provision and shown as an interest charge in the Operating Cost Statement.

## Reserves

**1.38** The Revaluation Reserve reflects the unrealised element of the cumulative balance of revaluation and indexation adjustments on fixed assets and stocks (excluding donated assets). The Donated Asset Reserve reflects the net book value of assets that have been donated to the Department.

**1.39** The Investment Reserve represents the value of the Departmental investment in QinetiQ Group plc on flotation, and the subsequent movement in market valuation as at 31 March 2008.

**1.40** The General Fund represents the balance of the Taxpayers' Equity.

## Pensions

**1.41**　Present and past employees are mainly covered by the Civil Service pension arrangements for civilian personnel and the AFPS for Service personnel. There are separate scheme statements for the AFPS and Civil Service pensions as a whole.

**1.42**　Both the AFPS and the main Civil Service pension schemes are unfunded defined benefit pension schemes, although, in accordance with the HM Treasury FReM, the Department accounts for the schemes in its accounts as if they were defined contribution schemes. The employer's charge is met by payment of a Superannuation Contribution Adjusted for Past Experience (SCAPE), which represents an estimate of the cost of providing future superannuation protection for all personnel currently in pensionable employment. In addition, civilian personnel contribute 1.5% of salary to fund a widow/widower's pension if they are members of classic, and 3.5% if they are members of premium, classic plus and nuvos. The Department's Balance Sheet will only include a creditor in respect of pensions to the extent that the contributions paid to the pension funds in the year fall short of the SCAPE and widow/widower's pension charges due. Money purchase pensions delivered through employer-sponsored stakeholder pensions have been available as an alternative to all new Civil Service entrants since October 2002.

**1.43**　The pension schemes undergo a reassessment of the SCAPE contribution rates by the Government Actuary at four-yearly intervals. Provisions are made for costs of early retirement programmes and redundancies up to the minimum retirement age and are charged to the Operating Cost Statement.

**1.44**　The Department operates a number of small pension schemes for civilians engaged at overseas locations. Since 1 April 2003, they have been accounted for in accordance with FRS 17 – *Retirement Benefits*. The pension scheme liability is included within the total provisions reported at Note 20 – Provisions for Liabilities and Charges, and, following a change in policy by HM Treasury, the gain on the change in the discount rate from 31 March 2007 is shown in the General Fund and the Statement of Recognised Gains and Losses. Gains or losses arising from discount rate changes prior to 2006-07 have been charged to the Operating Cost Statement.

**1.45**　The disclosures required under FRS 17 for the main pension schemes are included in: the Remuneration Report, Note 9 – Staff Numbers and Costs, and on the websites of the Civil Service Pension Scheme and the Armed Forces Pension Scheme (see Note 9 paragraphs 9.3 and 9.4).

## Early Departure Costs

**1.46**　The Department has previously provided in full for the cost of meeting pensions up to the minimum retirement age in respect of military and civilian personnel early retirement programmes. Pensions payable after the minimum retirement age are met by the Armed Forces Pension Scheme for military personnel and the Civil Service pension arrangements for civilian personnel. No provisions have been made for the current year for early retirement programmes. Redundancies are provided for in full.

## Cost of Capital Charge

**1.47**  A charge, reflecting the cost of capital utilised by the Department, is included in the Operating Cost Statement and credited to the General Fund. The charge is calculated using the HM Treasury standard rate for Financial Year 2007-08 of 3.5% (2006-07: 3.5%) in real terms on all assets less liabilities except for the following, where the charge is nil:

- Donated assets and cash balances with the Office of HM Paymaster General (OPG).

- Liabilities for the amounts to be surrendered to the Consolidated Fund and for amounts due from the Consolidated Fund.

- Assets financed by grants.

- Additions to heritage collections where the existing collection has not been capitalised.

**1.48**  The cost of capital charge on the fixed asset investments in the Trading Funds is calculated at a specific rate applicable to those entities, and is based on their underlying net assets.

## Foreign Exchange

**1.49**  Transactions that are denominated in a foreign currency are translated into Sterling using the General Accounting Rate ruling at the date of each transaction. In the past US$ and Euros were purchased forward from the Bank of England, details of existing contracts are at Note 28 to the accounts. Monetary assets and liabilities are translated at the mid-market closing rate applicable at the Balance Sheet date and the exchange differences are reported in the Operating Cost Statement.

**1.50**  Overseas non-monetary assets and liabilities are subject to annual revaluation and are translated at the mid-market closing rate applicable at the Balance Sheet date. The exchange differences are taken to the Revaluation Reserve for owned assets, or the Donated Asset Reserve for donated assets.

## 2. Analysis of Net Resource Outturn

| Request for Resources 1: Provision of Defence Capability | 2007-08 | | | | | | 2006-07 |
|---|---|---|---|---|---|---|---|
| | Other Current Expenditure £000 | Grants £000 | Operating Appropriation in Aid £000 | Total Net Resource Outturn £000 | Total Net Resource Estimate £000 | Total Net Outturn Compared With Estimate £000 | Re-stated Total Net Resource Outturn £000 |
| TLB HOLDER/TLB | | | | | | | |
| Commander-in-Chief Fleet | 2,215,527 | 11,217 | (42,118) | 2,184,626 | 2,204,982 | 20,356 | 2,147,878 |
| Commander-in-Chief Land Command | 5,690,472 | 57,647 | (110,376) | 5,637,743 | 5,729,900 | 92,157 | 5,333,289 |
| Commander-in-Chief Air Command | 2,776,472 | 7,115 | (148,267) | 2,635,320 | 2,647,231 | 11,911 | 2,686,140 |
| Chief of Joint Operations | 500,503 | - | (25,604) | 474,899 | 379,355 | (95,544) | 400,460 |
| Defence Equipment & Support | 16,796,154 | 463 | (339,014) | 16,457,603 | 17,382,369 | 924,766 | 14,611,153 |
| Adjutant General's Command | 866,286 | 16,742 | (16,191) | 866,837 | 800,719 | (66,118) | 963,217 |
| Central | 2,444,193 | 184,011 | (310,167) | 2,318,037 | 2,297,535 | (20,502) | 2,156,941 |
| Defence Estates | 2,349,513 | - | (390,718) | 1,958,795 | 2,643,360 | 684,565 | 2,695,277 |
| SIT (Science, Innovation, Technology) | 538,781 | 3,736 | (228) | 542,289 | 544,309 | 2,020 | 524,147 |
| Total (RFR 1) | 34,177,901 | 280,931 | (1,382,683) | 33,076,149 | 34,629,760 | 1,553,611 | 31,518,502 |

From April 2007: General Officer Commanding (Northern Ireland) TLB became part of Land Command TLB, Commander-in-Chief RAF Strike Command TLB and Commander-in-Chief Personnel & Training Command TLB merged to form Air Command TLB and Chief of Defence Logistics TLB and the Defence Procurement Agency TLB merged to form the Defence Equipment and Support TLB with the Chief of Defence Materiel as the TLB Budget Holder. The Army Recruiting and Training Division transferred from the Adjutant General TLB to the Land Command TLB.

| Request for Resources 2: Operations and Peacekeeping | 2007-08 | | | | | | 2006-07 |
|---|---|---|---|---|---|---|---|
| | Other Current Expenditure £000 | Grants £000 | Operating Appropriation in Aid £000 | Total Net Resource Outturn £000 | Total Net Resource Estimate £000 | Total Net Outturn Compared With Estimate £000 | Total Net Resource Outturn £000 |
| Programme Expenditure: Sub-Saharan Africa | 24,719 | - | - | 24,719 | 29,063 | 4,344 | 29,538 |
| Programme Expenditure: Rest of the World* | 2,193,419 | - | (22,101) | 2,171,318 | 2,352,740 | 181,422 | 68,071 |
| Peace Keeping Rest of the World | - | - | - | - | - | - | 1,350,811 |
| Total (RFR 2) | 2,218,138 | - | (22,101) | 2,196,037 | 2,381,803 | 185,766 | 1,448,420 |

*Programme Expenditure: Rest of the World includes expenditure that, in 2006-07, was shown separately, as Peace Keeping: Rest of the World.

| Request for Resources 3: War Pensions Benefits | Other Current Expenditure £000 | Grants £000 | Operating Appropriation in Aid £000 | Total Net Resource Outturn £000 | Total Net Resource Estimate £000 | Total Net Outturn Compared With Estimate £000 | Total Net Resource Outturn £000 |
|---|---|---|---|---|---|---|---|
| | | | 2007-08 | | | | 2006-07 |
| War Pensions Benefits Programme costs | - | 1,013,740 | - | 1,013,740 | 1,029,507 | 15,767 | 1,036,803 |
| War Pensions Benefits Programme costs – Far Eastern Prisoners of War | - | 390 | - | 390 | 500 | 110 | 1,270 |
| Total (RFR 3) | - | 1,014,130 | - | 1,014,130 | 1,030,007 | 15,877 | 1,038,073 |
| Total Net Resource Outturn | 36,396,039 | 1,295,061 | (1,404,784) | 36,286,316 | 38,041,570 | 1,755,254 | 34,004,995 |

## Provision of Defence Capability (RfR1)

**2.1** The net outturn is £33,076,149,000 against an Estimate of £34,629,760,000, an underspend of £1,553,611,000. The underspend principally relates to an over estimated Indirect Resource request in the Spring Supplementary Estimate relating to depreciation charges and movements on provisions that did not materialise. A detailed explanation of the variances against the Departmental Expenditure Limit (DEL) is shown in Finance and Efficiency section of the Performance Report.

## Operations and Peace Keeping (RfR2)

**2.2** The following table shows net resource outturn and capital expenditure for the three major areas of operation with other activities grouped under either the African or the Global Pools. The table also compares expenditure against the Estimate (voted funding) for the year.

| Operations and Peace Keeping | Net Resource Outturn £000 | Capital Costs £000 | Total £000 | Outturn £000 |
|---|---|---|---|---|
| | | | 2007-08 | 2006-07 |
| Afghanistan | 1,071,014 | 433,089 | 1,504,103 | 742,304* |
| Iraq | 1,054,825 | 402,658 | 1,457,483 | 956,162 |
| Balkans | 25,708 | 131 | 25,839 | 56,421* |
| Global pool | 19,771 | - | 19,771 | 12,193 |
| African pool | 24,719 | - | 24,719 | 29,538 |
| Total RfR2 | 2,196,037 | 835,878 | 3,031,915 | 1,796,618 |
| Total Estimate | 2,381,803 | 992,000 | 3,373,803 | 1,876,526 |
| Difference – savings/ (excess) | 185,766 | 156,122 | 341,888 | 79,908** |

*Excess A-in-A attributed to Operations in Afghanistan and the Balkans in 2006-07 is not included in the figures above. This is the reason for the difference between the Outturn figures and those at Table 2.3 (which include excess A-in-A) for that year.
**In 2006-07 the Department incurred an excess on the Net Resource Outturn. This was more than offset by savings on Capital Costs.

**2.3** A breakdown of the net operating and capital costs for the three main Operations is shown in the following table alongside the Departmental Allocation for the year and the Outturn for 2006-07.

| | Iraq | | | Afghanistan | | | Balkans | | |
|---|---|---|---|---|---|---|---|---|---|
| | Total Departmental Allocation 2007-08 £000 | Total Outturn 2007-08 £000 | Total Outturn 2006-07 £000 | Total Departmental Allocation 2007-08 £000 | Total Outturn 2007-08 £000 | Total Outturn 2006-07 £000 | Total Departmental Allocation 2007-08 £000 | Total Outturn 2007-08 £000 | Total Outturn 2006-07 £000 |
| Direct costs | | | | | | | | | |
| Service manpower | 93,150 | 98,211 | 99,779 | 79,340 | 84,782 | 49,487 | 2,842 | 2,492 | 11,006 |
| Civilian manpower | 14,628 | 13,597 | 14,733 | 7,649 | 8,829 | 4,340 | 2,066 | 2,081 | 5,310 |
| Infrastructure costs | 108,901 | 130,351 | 83,136 | 162,666 | 148,808 | 100,928 | 7,627 | 8,345 | 12,853 |
| Equipment support | 356,569 | 278,166 | 206,065 | 220,026 | 199,745 | 111,739 | 2,846 | 1,135 | 5,557 |
| Other costs and services | 162,060 | 161,985 | 137,273 | 152,754 | 160,286 | 89,215 | 10,200 | 6,713 | 13,977† |
| Income | 5,291 | 4,198 | 4,720 | 17,775 | 11,255 | (2,008) | (732) | (737) | (9,573) |
| Stock consumption | 263,400 | 236,856 | 218,010 | 236,790 | 301,341 | 164,205 | 6,151 | 6,170 | 15,100 |
| Indirect costs | | | | | | | | | |
| Stock write-off / (write-on) | 2,120 | 200 | 238 | 5,670 | 3,727 | - | | 10 | - |
| Provisions | 3,710 | 4,579 | 5,547 | 54 | 71 | 18 | | (726) | 720 |
| Depreciation, amortisation (including UOR‡) and fixed asset write-off | 169,162 | 119,177 | 14,443 | 197,018 | 143,345 | 39,113 | | 6 | 293 |
| Cost of capital | 24,009 | 7,505 | 2,771 | 22,258 | 8,825 | 2,500 | | 219 | 147 |
| **Total Operating Costs*** | **1,203,000** | **1,054,825** | **786,715** | **1,102,000** | **1,071,014** | **559,537** | **31,000** | **25,708** | **55,390** |
| **Capital Cost** | | | | | | | | | |
| Capital addition (including UORs and Recuperation) | 445,000 | 402,658 | 169,447 | 547,000 | 433,089 | 178,208 | - | 131 | 543 |
| **Total by Operation** | **1,648,000** | **1,457,483** | **956,162** | **1,649,000** | **1,504,103** | **737,745*** | **31,000** | **25,839** | **55,933*** |

†Corrected (from £13,997).
‡Urgent Operational Requirements.
*In 2006-07 excess A-in-A was attributed to Operations in Afghanistan and the Balkans. This is the reason for the difference between the outturn for these areas at Table 2.2 (where excess A-in-A is excluded) and the figures in Table 2.3 above.

**2.4** In accordance with the accounting principles agreed with HM Treasury, the Department has identified the costs of operations on the basis of net additional costs. Expenditure such as wages and salaries for permanently employed personnel are not included as these costs would have been incurred in the normal course of business. Costs of activities such as training and exercises which would have been incurred, but which have been cancelled due to operational commitments, have been deducted.

Negative numbers are shown in brackets and usually represent negative expenditure i.e. income but when comparing outturn against Estimate, an excess of expenditure over Estimate is shown in brackets.

Positive figures on the income line represent a cost – the cost of income foregone (loss of receipts) as a result of conducting operations (e.g. food and accommodation receipts in respect of deployed personnel). Negative figures (figures in brackets) on the income line represent income generated on operations (e.g. support to other nations in respect of catering and medical services).

## Major Changes in Operational Costs

**2.5** Between 2006-07 and 2007-08

In Afghanistan costs have doubled as a result of increased operational activity in Helmand Province. The increased tempo of operations resulted in: increases in the number of Service personnel, generating additional personnel related costs; increased use of ammunition and technical and engineering stores. The purchase of Urgent Operational Requirements (UORs) and the increase in the number of forward operating bases and support costs were also factors in the increase in cost.

The effect of manpower reductions in Iraq are reflected in the reduced cost of personnel but these savings are more than offset by costs related to increased force protection measures. Infrastructure has been enhanced in the Central Operating Base with hardened accommodation to protect against mortar attack and improvements to the perimeter walling resulting in increased costs. The cost of UORs has more than doubled; purchases include vehicle protection and sensor and warning systems – reflecting the importance placed on the security of our personnel serving in Iraq.

Following the Comptroller and Auditor General's Report on the 2006-07 accounts the Department reviewed and improved its procedures for identifying indirect resource costs (such as depreciation of, or the cost of capital charge on, assets) incurred on operations. The increased costs this year reflect the improved procedures in place to identify these costs.

**2.6** Between 2007-08 Outturn and Estimate

The Capital Estimate for Iraq and Afghanistan was based on details of UORs that had received financial approval at the time the estimates were prepared – and therefore represented the maximum level of expenditure the Department could expect. Not all the UORs were delivered prior to the end of the financial year resulting in the underspend against capital. New reporting procedures for 2008-09 will enable the Department to refine future capital Estimates. Further details of Capital Additions can be found in the Current Operations section of the Performance Report.

Costs are difficult to forecast, they are sensitive to changes in policy and the tempo of operations. The Department works hard to ensure that the figures presented to Parliament are reliable but there is always likely to be a variation between the forecasts used to inform the Spring Supplementary Estimates (based on information available two-thirds of the way through the year) and the final end of year outturn. The Spring Supplementary Estimates have to be robust enough to cater for the unforeseen requirements of commanders, in-theatre, making decisions on resources to support military objectives.

## War Pensions Benefits – Programme Costs (RfR3)

2.7     The Chief Executive of the Service Personnel and Veterans Agency is not a Top Level Budget Holder, but exercises all the responsibilities for the programme costs. The outturn for 2007-08 is £1,014,130,000 compared with £1,038,073,000 for 2006-07. The reduction (£23,943,000) reflects the ongoing decline in the number of claimants entitled to the pensions and treatment expenses administered through the War Pensions Scheme.

## 3. Reconciliation of Net Resource Outturn to Net Operating Cost

| | | | 2007-08 | 2006-07 |
|---|---|---|---|---|
| | | | Outturn | |
| | | Supply | compared with | |
| | Outturn | Estimate | Estimate | Outturn |
| | £000 | £000 | £000 | £000 |
| Net Resource Outturn (Statement of Parliamentary Supply) | 36,286,316 | 38,041,570 | 1,755,254 | 34,004,995 |
| – Less income scored as Consolidated Fund Extra Receipts and included in operating income and interest (inc. excess operating Appropriation in Aid) (Note 5) | (63,310) | (55,000) | 8,310 | (56,326) |
| Net Operating Cost | 36,223,006 | 37,986,570 | 1,763,564 | 33,948,669 |

Net Resource Outturn is the total of those elements of expenditure and income that are subject to Parliamentary approval and included in the Department's Supply Estimate. Net operating cost is the total of expenditure and income appearing in the Operating Cost Statement. The Outturn against the Estimate is shown in the Statement of Parliamentary Supply.

## 4. Reconciliation of Resources to Cash Requirement

| | Note | Estimate £000 | Outturn £000 | Savings / (Excess) £000 |
|---|---|---|---|---|
| Resource Outturn | 2 | 38,041,570 | 36,286,316 | 1,755,254 |
| Capital: | | | | |
| Purchase of fixed assets: | | | | |
| – RfR 1 | 13/14 | 7,664,530 | 7,626,717 | 37,813 |
| – RfR 2 | 13/14 | 992,000 | 835,878 | 156,122 |
| – RfR 1 Capitalised provisions | 13/14 | | (21,501) | 21,501 |
| Non operating cost A in A: | | | | |
| Proceeds on sale of fixed assets | 10/13/14 | (1,193,071) | (1,174,198) | (18,873) |
| Repayment of loans made to the Trading Funds | 15 | (50,929) | (9,949) | (40,980) |
| Accruals adjustments: | | | | |
| Non-cash transactions- | | | | |
| Included in operating costs | 23.1 | (8,839,180) | (7,453,879) | (1,385,301) |
| Included in net interest payable | 12 | | (123,288) | 123,288 |
| Capitalised provisions shown above | | | 21,501 | (21,501) |
| Cost of capital charge | 23.1 | (3,512,193) | (3,370,908) | (141,285) |
| Changes in working capital other than cash, excluding movements on creditors falling due after one year | | 1,128,227 | (80,744) | 1,208,971 |
| Increase in creditors falling due after one year | | | (168,187) | 168,187 |
| Use of provisions for liabilities and charges | 20 | 499,144 | 486,911 | 12,233 |
| Cash receipts surrenderable to the Consolidated Fund | | | 687,500 | (687,500) |
| Adjustment for movements on cash balances in respect of collaborative projects | 23.5 | | (37,253) | 37,253 |
| Net cash requirement | 23.5 | 34,730,098 | 33,504,916 | 1,225,182 |

## 5. Analysis of income payable to the Consolidated Fund

In addition to Appropriations in Aid, the following income relates to the Department and is payable to the Consolidated Fund (cash receipts being shown in italics).

| | 2007-08 Forecast | | 2007-08 Outturn | |
| --- | --- | --- | --- | --- |
| | Income £000 | Receipts £000 | Income £000 | Receipts £000 |
| Operating income and receipts – excess A in A Request for Resources 1 | - | - | - | - |
| Operating income and receipts – excess A in A Request for Resources 2 | - | - | - | - |
| Other operating income and receipts not classified as A in A | 55,000 | 55,000 | 63,310 | 63,310 |
| Subtotal operating income and receipts payable to the Consolidated Fund | 55,000 | 55,000 | 63,310 | 63,310 |
| Other amounts collectable on behalf of the Consolidated Fund | - | - | - | 687,500 |
| Total income payable to the Consolidated Fund | 55,000 | 55,000 | 63,310 | 750,810 |

## 6. Reconciliation of income recorded within the Operating Cost Statement to operating income payable to the Consolidated Fund

| | Note | 2007-08 £000 | 2006-07 £000 |
| --- | --- | --- | --- |
| Operating Income | 11 | 1,395,770 | 1,429,392 |
| Income included within other operating costs | | | • |
| – Refunds of formula based VAT recovery | | 36,080 | 51,250 |
| – Foreign exchange gains | | 7,937 | 39,230 |
| – Other | | (103) | (71) |
| Interest Receivable | | 28,410 | 30,263 |
| Gross Income | | 1,468,094 | 1,550,064 |
| Income authorised to be appropriated in aid | | (1,404,784) | (1,493,738) |
| Operating Income payable to the Consolidated Fund | 5 | 63,310 | 56,326 |

## 7. Non-Operating income – Excess A in A

| | 2007-08 £000 | 2006-07 £000 |
| --- | --- | --- |
| Principal repayments of voted loans | 9,949 | 8,479 |
| Proceeds on disposal of fixed assets | 1,191,380 | 489,808 |
| Non-operating income – excess A in A | - | - |

## 8. Non-Operating income not classified as A in A

| | Income £000 | Receipts £000 |
| --- | --- | --- |
| Cash receipts surrenderable to the Consolidated Fund | - | 687,500 |

# 9. Staff Numbers and Costs

**9.1**    The average number of full-time equivalent persons employed during the year was: Service 193,610[2] (2006-07: 198,020[3]) and Civilian 83,930[2] (2006-07: 90,520[3]). Source: Defence Analytical Services and Advice (DASA).

| | Permanent Staff | Temporary Staff | Armed Forces | Ministers & Special Advisers | 2007-08 Total | 2006-07 Re-stated Total |
|---|---|---|---|---|---|---|
| Analysis of Staff Numbers | 83,044[2] | 880 | 193,610[2] | 6 | 277,540[2] | 288,540[3] |

In order to align with the total pay costs incurred during the year, shown below, the calculation of the average number of staff uses monthly statistics to identify an average number employed for the year. The staff numbers quoted reflect the number of personnel employed in organisations within the Departmental Boundary for the Annual Accounts (see page 241) and therefore exclude those in the Trading Funds. The staff numbers reported in the Performance Report include employees in the MoD Trading Funds. More information on the Department's staff numbers, and the statistical calculations used, is available on the website: http://www.dasa.mod.uk/index.php?page=47&skipCheck=1.

**9.2**    The aggregate staff costs, including grants and allowances paid, were as follows:

| | 2007-08 £000 | 2006-07 £000 |
|---|---|---|
| Salaries and wages | 8,887,522 | 8,728,349 |
| Social security costs | 643,737 | 641,539 |
| Pension costs | 1,824,800 | 1,761,944 |
| Redundancy and severance payments | 128,850 | 72,430 |
| | **11,484,909** | **11,204,262** |
| Made up of: | | |
| Service | 8,649,051 | 8,422,935 |
| Civilian | 2,835,858 | 2,781,327 |
| | **11,484,909** | **11,204,262** |

## Principal Civil Service Pension Scheme

**9.3**    The Principal Civil Service Pension Scheme (PCSPS) is an unfunded multi-employer defined benefit scheme. The Ministry of Defence is unable to identify its share of the underlying assets and liabilities. The Scheme Actuary (Hewitt Associates) reviewed the scheme as at 31 March 2007; details can be found at www.civilservice-pensions.gov.uk.

For 2007-08, total pension contributions of £362,827,000 were payable in respect of the various schemes in which MoD civilian staff were members. Contributions to the PCSPS in the same period were £321,837,000 (2006-07: £323,481,000) calculated using four percentage rates (17.1%, 19.5%, 23.2% and 25.5%) of pensionable pay, based on four salary bands. The scheme's Actuary reviews employer contributions, usually, every four years following a full scheme valuation. As a result of the latest review the 2007-08 salary bands and the 2008-09 salary bands were revised; the percentage rates remained the same (as stated above). The percentage rates will change with effect from April

2 Figures for civilians are calculated as weighted averages for the financial year, for military personnel the calculation is a thirteen month rolling average.  The civilian figure includes an estimate of the Locally Employed Civilians (LEC) in Land Forces, based on the financial resources bid for LEC in 2008-09; this issue is under investigation and the LEC figure is provisional and subject to review.  The Armed Forces figure uses data from the Joint Personnel Administration system and, due to ongoing validation, Army statistics from 1 April 2007, and Navy and RAF statistics from 1 May 2007 are provisional and subject to change.
3 Following validation of JPA data and a review of the calculation of the average number of civilian personnel the 2006-07 figures have been re-stated (Service – reduced by 60 from 198,080: Civilian – reduced by 130 from 90,650).

2009. The contribution rates are set to meet the cost of the benefits accruing, to be paid when the member retires, not the benefits paid during the period to existing pensioners.

Employees can opt to open a partnership pension account, a stakeholder pension with an employer contribution. Employer contributions are age-related and range from 3% to 12.5% of pensionable pay. Employers also match employee contributions up to 3% of pensionable pay. In addition, employer contributions of 0.8% of pensionable pay were payable to the PCSPS to cover the cost of the future provision of lump sum benefits on death in service and ill health retirement of these employees.

### Armed Forces Pension Scheme

**9.4**    The Armed Forces Pension Scheme (known as AFPS 05) is an unfunded, non-contributory, defined benefit, salary-related, contracted out, occupational pension scheme. A formal valuation of the AFPS was carried out as at 31 March 2005 by the scheme's actuary, the Government Actuary's Department. Scheme members are entitled to a taxable pension for life and a tax-free pension lump sum if they leave the Regular Armed Forces at or beyond normal retirement age; those who have at least two years service who leave before age 55 will have their pensions preserved until age 65. Pensions may be payable to the spouse, civil partner, partner or to eligible children. Death-in-service lump sums are payable subject to nomination. AFPS 05 offers ill-health benefits if a career is cut short by injury or illness, irrespective of cause. Additionally, if the injury or illness is mainly attributable to service, compensation for conditions caused on or after 6 April 2005 will be considered under the Armed Forces Compensation Scheme (AFCS).

AFPS 05 members who leave before the age of 55 may be entitled to an Early Departure Payment, providing they have at least 18 years service and are at least 40 years of age. The Early Departure Payment Scheme pays a tax-free lump sum and income of between 50% and 75% of preserved pension between the date of the individual's departure from the Armed Forces and age 55. The income rises to 75% of preserved pension at age 55 and is index linked. At age 65, the Early Departure Payment stops and the preserved pension and preserved pension lump sum are paid.

For 2007-08, total employer's pension contributions payable were £1,461,985,000. This figure includes £1,461,908,000 payable to the AFPS, (2006-07 £1,419,529,000) based on employer's contribution rates determined by the Government Actuary. For 2007-08, the employer's contribution rates were 36.3% of pensionable pay for Officers and 21.8% of pensionable pay for Other Ranks. The contribution rates reflect benefits as they are accrued, not costs actually incurred in the period, and reflect past experience of the scheme. Further information on the Armed Forces Pension Scheme and the Armed Forces Compensation Scheme can be found at the website: www.mod.uk/DefenceInternet/AboutDefence/WhatWeDo/Personnel/Pensions/ArmedForcesPensions/

### Other Pension Schemes

**9.5**    The Armed Forces Pension Scheme incorporates the following schemes: the Non-Regular Permanent Staff Pension Scheme, the Gurkha Pension Scheme and the Reserve Forces Pension Scheme. The membership of these schemes is approximately 3.08% of the AFPS total membership and the employer's contributions to the schemes are included in the figure payable to the AFPS, at paragraph 9.4.

Certain other employees are covered by schemes such as the National Health Service Pension Scheme and the Teachers' Pension Scheme. The figure for total employers' pension contributions at paragraph 9.3 includes contributions in respect of these schemes.

## 10. Other Operating Costs

| | 2007-08 £000 | 2006-07 £000 |
|---|---|---|
| **Operating expenditure:** | | |
| – Fuel | 537,029 | 415,637 |
| – Stock consumption | 1,071,383 | 1,140,287 |
| – Surplus arising on disposal of stock (net) | (9,638) | 4,078 |
| – Provisions to reduce stocks to net realisable value | 137,193 | 90,771 |
| – Stocks written off (net) | 431,651 | 94,903 |
| – Movements: includes personnel travelling, subsistence/relocation costs and Movement of stores and equipment | 858,095 | 774,031 |
| – Utilities | 306,902 | 319,591 |
| – Property management * | 1,523,191 | 1,258,024 |
| – Hospitality and entertainment | 4,202 | 4,337 |
| – Accommodation charges | 442,850 | 465,946 |
| – Equipment support costs | 4,271,796 | 3,793,183 |
| – Increase in nuclear and other decommissioning provisions | 233,751 | (438,617) |
| – IT and telecommunications | 655,232 | 718,780 |
| – Professional fees | 470,748 | 482,706 |
| – Other expenditure * | 1,616,150 | 1,749,806 |
| – Research expenditure and expensed development expenditure | 951,557 | 987,649 |
| – PFI service charges | | |
|     IT and Telecommunications | 492,581 | 424,930 |
|     Property Management | 425,931 | 348,863 |
|     Transport | 141,388 | 193,806 |
|     Equipment support | 166,084 | 121,454 |
|     Plant and Machinery | 50,147 | 58,607 |
| **Depreciation and amortisation:** | | |
| – Intangible assets (Note 13) | 1,196,571 | 1,152,633 |
| – Tangible owned fixed assets (Note 14) | 5,024,648 | 4,545,251 |
| – Donated assets depreciation – release of reserve | (48,379) | (53,984) |
| – Tangible fixed assets held under finance leases (Note 14) | 165 | 219 |
| **Impairment on fixed assets:** | | |
| – Arising on Quinquennial valuation | (46,207) | 302,843 |
| – Arising on Other items | 43,251 | 4,682 |
| Impairment – release of reserve | 77,302 | (131,820) |
| Surplus arising on disposal of tangible and intangible fixed assets**** | (682,647) | (123,135) |
| Fixed assets written off – net | 869,919 | 730,325 |
| Capital project expenditure write off/(write on) | 19,238 | 58,830 |
| Bad debts written off | 29,607 | 26,557 |
| Increase/(decrease) in bad debts provision | (1,224) | 4,298 |
| Rentals paid under operating leases | | |
| – Plant and Machinery | 27,432 | 11,604 |
| – Other | 124,512 | 126,521 |
| Auditors' remuneration – audit work only ** | 3,600 | 3,600 |
| Grants-in-Aid *** | 128,267 | 61,319 |
| Exchange differences on foreign currencies: net deficit/(surplus) | 36,261 | (2,293) |
| War Pensions Benefits | 1,014,616 | 1,038,574 |
| **Total Other Operating Costs** | **22,595,155** | **20,764,796** |

*The prior year figure for Property Management has been restated by an increase of £61,000,000, and Other Expenditure has been reduced by £61,000,000 to reflect a more accurate disclosure of expenditure.
**Auditors' remuneration: No charge is made for non-audit work carried out by the auditors.
***£66,000,000 of the increase in Grants in Aid is as a result of a new grant to the Marine Society & Sea Cadets and the change in status of the Council of Reserve Forces and Cadets Associations (see Note 32.3).
****The surplus on disposal includes profit on the sale of Chelsea Barracks of £599,600,000. Proceeds from the sale were £959,000,000. £383,600,000 was received in 2007-08 the balance is payable by three annual instalments of £191,800,000. In accordance with Financial Reporting Standard 5 these future receipts have been discounted (at 2.2%) and are recorded in the accounts as debtors: amounts receivable within one year £187,700,000 and amounts receivable in more than one year £363,300,000.

# 11. Income

| | RfR1 £000 | RfR2 £000 | 2007-08 Total £000 | 2006-07 Re-stated Total £000 |
|---|---|---|---|---|
| **Income Source** **External Customers** | | | | |
| Rental income – property | 33,514 | - | **33,514** | 28,752 |
| Receipts – personnel | 61,740 | - | **61,740** | 62,077 |
| Receipts – sale of fuel | 100,963 | - | **100,963** | 105,592 |
| Receipts – personnel related | 119,288 | - | **119,288** | 152,332 |
| Receipts – supplies and services | 119,506 | - | **119,506** | 186,410 |
| Receipts – provision of service Accommodation | 229,223 | - | **229,223** | 214,744 |
| Receipts – NATO/UN/US Forces/Foreign Govts | 345,861 | 22,101 | **367,962** | 314,743 |
| Other** | 149,920 | - | **149,920** | 118,617 |
| **Other Government Departments, Trading Funds and QinetiQ** | | | | |
| Rental income – property | 510 | - | **510** | 618 |
| Receipts – personnel related | 2,451 | - | **2,451** | - |
| Reverse tasking * | 31,663 | - | **31,663** | 29,275 |
| Dividends from Investments (Note 15.4) | 39,555 | - | **39,555** | 49,617 |
| Income from provision of goods and services** | 139,369 | - | **139,369** | 166,158 |
| Other | 106 | - | **106** | 457 |
| | **1,373,669** | **22,101** | **1,395,770** | **1,429,392** |

*Receipts for invoiced goods and/or services supplied to the Trading Funds and QinetiQ Group plc by MoD.
**The 2006-07 figure for External Customers Other has been reduced by £36,086,000 (there is a corresponding increase to the 2006-07 figure for Income from Provision of Goods and Services) to provide a more accurate analysis of receipts.

## Fees and Charges

**11.1** Where the Department has spare capacity, it provides a range of services to external organisations. The majority of these services are in the form of military support to foreign governments and other government departments. Where appropriate, costs are recovered in accordance with HM Treasury's Fees and Charges Guide. On a smaller scale, the Department provides services to support charities, local community initiatives as well as commercial companies where there is a defence interest.

## 12. Net Interest Payable

| | 2007-08 £000 | 2006-07 £000 |
|---|---|---|
| **Interest receivable:*** | | |
| Bank interest | (24,063) | (25,705) |
| Loans to Trading Funds | (4,347) | (4,556) |
| Other interest receivable | - | (2) |
| | **(28,410)** | **(30,263)** |
| **Interest payable:** | | |
| Bank interest | 5,139 | 148 |
| Loan interest | 3,136 | 3,237 |
| Unwinding of discount on provision for liabilities and charges (Note 20) | 123,288 | 126,414 |
| Finance leases and PFI contracts | 64,641 | 67,551 |
| Late payment of Commercial debts | 10 | 9 |
| | **196,214** | **197,359** |
| Net interest payable | **167,804** | **167,096** |

*Interest receivable of which £65,803 is payable to the Consolidated Fund (£831,000 in 2006-07).

## 13. Intangible Assets

Intangible assets include development expenditure in respect of fixed assets in use and assets under construction.

| | Single Use Military Equipment £000 | Others £000 | Total £000 |
|---|---|---|---|
| **Cost or Valuation*** | | | |
| At 1 April 2007 | 30,351,519 | 521,222 | 30,872,741 |
| Additions** | 1,529,640 | 225,918 | 1,755,558 |
| Disposals | (656,676) | (11,488) | (668,164) |
| Revaluation*** | 1,584,905 | 221,405 | 1,806,310 |
| Reclassification**** | (1,504,914) | 1,862,312 | 357,398 |
| **At 31 March 2008** | 31,304,474 | 2,819,369 | **34,123,843** |
| **Amortisation** | | | |
| At 1 April 2007 | (6,534,922) | (175,197) | (6,710,119) |
| Charged in Year | (986,247) | (210,324) | (1,196,571) |
| Disposals | 641,288 | 9,465 | 650,753 |
| Revaluation*** | (154,421) | (7,903) | (162,324) |
| Reclassification**** | 378,987 | (392,323) | (13,336) |
| **At 31 March 2008** | **(6,655,315)** | **(776,282)** | **(7,431,597)** |
| **Net Book Value:** | | | |
| **At 31 March 2008** | **24,649,159** | **2,043,087** | **26,692,246** |
| At 1 April 2007 | 23,816,597 | 346,025 | 24,162,622 |

*Intangible asset valuations are based on the actual costs incurred over time, where available, or derived by applying a ratio to the tangible fixed asset valuations based on the historical relationship between development and production costs.
**Additions of intangible assets include accruals of £395,583,000. In 2006-07 only a combined figure of £2,666,839,000 for intangible and tangible accruals was identifiable; the comparable 2007-08 total is £3,206,126,000.
***Revaluations include changes due to Modified Historic Cost Accounting through indexation, impairment and impairment reversals. Intangible Assets are only impaired when the class of underlying fixed assets is changed e.g. when the assets are destroyed.
****Reclassifications include assets classified to or from tangible fixed assets and transfers to or from operating costs.

## 14. Tangible Fixed Assets

| | Dwellings £000 | Other Land and Buildings £000 | Single Use Military Equipment (SUME) £000 | Plant and Machinery £000 | Transport £000 | IT and Communications Equipment £000 | Assets under Construction (SUME) £000 | Assets under Construction (Others) £000 | Total £000 |
|---|---|---|---|---|---|---|---|---|---|
| **Cost or Valuation** | | | | | | | | | |
| At 1 April 2007 | 3,616,251 | 18,947,776 | 65,711,586 | 4,898,883 | 9,713,086 | 1,808,565 | 12,366,214 | 1,426,667 | 118,489,028 |
| Additions* ** | 90,800 | 34,966 | 657,395 | 35,862 | 54,931 | 361,234 | 2,680,839 | 2,769,509 | 6,685,536 |
| Donations | 63,317 | 4,481 | - | 72 | - | - | - | - | 67,870 |
| Disposals | - | (490,564) | (1,172,696) | (69,140) | (187,032) | (51,492) | - | - | (1,970,924) |
| Re-classifica-tions*** | 150,749 | 313,640 | 2,192,256 | (1,593,977) | 1,068,905 | (110,716) | (3,795,993) | (433,158) | (2,208,294) |
| Revaluations† | 384,702 | 2,486,002 | 1,091,656 | 88,905 | 10,585 | (62,130) | (110,260) | 63,141 | 3,952,601 |
| **At 31 March 2008** | **4,305,819** | **21,296,301** | **68,480,197** | **3,360,605** | **10,660,475** | **1,945,461** | **11,140,800** | **3,826,159** | **125,015,817** |
| **Depreciation** | | | | | | | | | |
| At 1 April 2007 | (645,850) | (3,484,757) | (31,467,782) | (2,249,392) | (5,365,670) | (675,039) | - | - | (43,888,490) |
| Charged in year | (106,416) | (744,557) | (3,229,610) | (234,505) | (441,055) | (268,670) | - | - | (5,024,813) |
| Disposals | - | - | 799,560 | 35,061 | 128,458 | 37,307 | - | - | 1,000,386 |
| Reclassifica-tions*** | 29,692 | 137,295 | 818,246 | 888,011 | (338,628) | (4,594) | - | - | 1,530,022 |
| Revaluations† | (78,877) | (934,273) | 365,995 | (46,930) | (32,966) | 24,407 | - | - | (702,644) |
| **At 31 March 2008** | **(801,451)** | **(5,026,292)** | **(32,713,591)** | **(1,607,755)** | **(6,049,861)** | **(886,589)** | - | - | **(47,085,539)** |
| **Net Book Value: At 31 March 2008** | **3,504,368** | **16,270,009** | **35,766,606** | **1,752,850** | **4,610,614** | **1,058,872** | **11,140,800** | **3,826,159** | **77,930,278** |
| At 1 April 2007 | 2,970,401 | 15,463,019 | 34,243,804 | 2,649,491 | 4,347,416 | 1,133,526 | 12,366,214 | 1,426,667 | 74,600,538 |
| **Asset Financing** | | | | | | | | | |
| Owned | 2,774,020 | 13,656,136 | 35,766,606 | 1,624,054 | 4,561,170 | 1,020,761 | 11,140,800 | 3,826,159 | 74,369,706 |
| Donated**** | 443,187 | 2,012,863 | - | 39,942 | 91 | 233 | - | - | 2,496,316 |
| Long Lease | 174,567 | 95,356 | - | - | - | - | - | - | 269,923 |
| Short Lease | 499 | 54,605 | - | - | - | - | - | - | 55,104 |
| Operating Lease | - | 8,175 | - | - | - | - | - | - | 8,175 |
| Finance Lease | - | - | - | - | 257 | - | - | - | 257 |
| On-Balance Sheet PFI | 112,095 | 412,455 | - | 88,854 | 49,096 | 37,878 | - | - | 700,378 |
| PFI residual interest | - | 30,419 | - | - | - | - | - | - | 30,419 |
| **Net Book Value: At 31 March 2008** | **3,504,368** | **16,270,009** | **35,766,606** | **1,752,850** | **4,610,614** | **1,058,872** | **11,140,800** | **3,826,159** | **77,930,278** |
| In – Year depreciation for assets held under PFI contracts | (3,316) | (11,263) | - | (5,484) | (6,993) | (3,290) | - | - | (30,346) |

*Additions of tangible fixed assets include accruals of £2,810,543,000. In 2006-07 only a combined figure of £2,666,839,000 for tangible and intangible accruals was identifiable; the comparable 2007-08 total is £3,206,126,000.
**Fixed Assets as at 31 March 2008 include capitalised provisions at cost of £177,730,000 (2006-2007: £199,231,000 restated).
***Includes assets reclassified to/from intangible assets and transfers to/from operating costs.
****Donated Assets in use have been valued on the same basis as all other assets used by the Department.
†Revaluations include changes due to Modified Historic Cost Accounting through indexation, impairment and impairment reversals. Assets are impaired for a variety of reasons e.g. changes due to increased wear and tear as a result of operations. Land and buildings are subject to quinquennial revaluation (see note 14.1 below).

## 2007 – 08 Quinquennial Revaluation

**14.1** All Land and Buildings with the exception of Assets Under Construction, are subject to a quinquennial revaluation (QQR), which is being conducted on a rolling programme. During 2007-08, only some 2.7% of Land and Buildings were re-valued to sweep up any residual estate assets not revalued during the previous 4 years. The new rolling programme plans for 25% of assets to be revalued each year across four years and begins in 2008-09. The valuations were performed by two external organisations: the Valuation Office Agency, who dealt with the UK estate, and GVA Grimley, who were responsible for the overseas estate. The valuations were undertaken in accordance with the Royal Institute of Chartered Surveyors Appraisal and Valuation Manual and were completed on the basis of the existing use value to the Department. Due to the specialised nature of the Departmental estate, the majority of assets were valued using the Depreciated Replacement Cost method.

**14.2** Data from the 2006-07 quinquennial review (Land and Buildings) was used to process an estimated increase in the value of Land and Buildings (£137,555,000) in the 2006-07 Annual Accounts, although the change in valuation had not been processed in the Fixed Asset Register (FAR). The data has now been processed in the FAR and this has identified an increase in the net book value to Buildings of £385,265,000 and a decrease in the net book value of Land of £276,088,000 equating to a total net increase of £109,177,000 for the 2006-07 QQR compared to the estimate (£137,555,000) included in the 2006-07 accounts. The required adjustment, a net reduction of £28,378,000 in the value of Land and Buildings, compared to the original 2006-07 increase has been processed in the 2007-08 accounts.

**14.3** The net credit to the OCS in respect of impairments following the processing of the QQR is £46,207,000. This is made up of a debit of £71,318,000 in respect of adjustments to the value of Buildings impairment estimated in the 2006-07 accounts off-set by a credit of £117,525,000 in respect of Land impairment.

## 15. Investments

| | Trading Funds | | QinetiQ Group plc and Other Investments | Total |
|---|---|---|---|---|
| | Public Dividend Capital £000 | Loans £000 | £000 | £000 |
| Balance at 1 April 2007 | 184,254 | 81,960 | 233,848 | 500,062 |
| Additions: | - | - | - | - |
| Loan Repayments: | | | | |
|    UK Hydrographic Office | | (421) | | (421) |
|    Met Office | | (2,533) | | (2,533) |
|    Defence Aviation Repair Agency | | (4,840) | | (4,840) |
|    ABRO | | (2,155) | | (2,155) |
| Revaluations | | | 7,181 | 7,181 |
| **Balance at 31 March 2008** | **184,254** | **72,011** | **241,029** | **497,294** |
| Balance at 1 April 2007 | 184,254 | 81,960 | 233,848 | 500,062 |

Public Dividend Capital and Loans at 31 March 2008 were held in the following Trading Funds:

| | Public Dividend Capital £000 | Loans £000 | Interest Rates % p.a. |
|---|---|---|---|
| Defence Science Technology Laboratory | 50,412 | | |
| UK Hydrographic Office | 13,267 | 10,184 | 8.375 |
| Met Office | 58,867 | 6,769 | 4.45 – 5.65 |
| Defence Aviation Repair Agency | 42,303 | 35,670 | 4.20 – 5.00 |
| ABRO | 19,405 | 19,388 | 5.625 |
| **Balance at 31 March 2008** | **184,254** | **72,011** | |

Analysis of loans repayable by instalments:

| | Due within one year £000 | Due after one year £000 | Total £000 |
|---|---|---|---|
| UK Hydrographic Office | 457 | 9,727 | 10,184 |
| Met Office | 2,663 | 4,106 | 6,769 |
| Defence Aviation Repair Agency* | 35,670 | - | 35,670 |
| ABRO* | 19,388 | - | 19,388 |
| **Balance at 31 March 2008** | **58,178** | **13,833** | **72,011** |

*The scheduling of loan repayments reflects preparation for the formation of the Defence Support Group.

## Investment in QinetiQ Group plc and Other Investments

**15.1**    On 1 April 2007, the Department's shareholding in QinetiQ Group plc, 124,885,445 (19.3%) Ordinary Shares (nominal value 1p each), were valued at 187.25p per share; a total value of £233,847,995.76. The market price of the shares had risen to 193.00p per share on 31 March 2008; an increase in the total market value of £7,180,913.09 to £241,028,908.85.

Holders of Ordinary Shares in QinetiQ Group plc are entitled to receive notice of, attend, speak and vote at general and extraordinary meetings of the company and have one vote for every share owned.

The Department also holds one Special Share in QinetiQ Group plc, and one Special Share in each of two of its subsidiary companies, QinetiQ Holdings Limited and QinetiQ Limited. The Special Shares can only be held by the Crown and give the Government the right to: implement and operate the Compliance System, prohibit or restrict QinetiQ from undertaking activities, which may lead to an unmanageable conflict of interest that would be damaging to the defence or security interests of the United Kingdom, and to veto any transaction, which may lead to unacceptable ownership of the company. The Special Shareholder must receive notice of, and may attend and speak at, general and extraordinary meetings. The Special Shares carry no voting rights, except to enforce certain aspects of the compliance regime. The shareholder has no right to share in the capital or profits of the company other than – in the event of liquidation – to be repaid the capital paid up in respect of the shares before other shareholders receive any payment.

## Other Investments

**15.2**     As at 31 March 2008, investments, including Special Shares, were held in the following:

| | 7.5% Non-cumulative Irredeemable Preference Shares at £1 each |
|---|---|
| Chamber of Shipping Limited | 688 Shares |
| British Shipping Federation Limited | 55,040 Shares |

| | Preferential Special Shares at £1 each |
|---|---|
| Devonport Royal Dockyard Limited | 1 Share |
| Rosyth Royal Dockyard Limited | 1 Share |
| AWE plc | 1 Share |
| AWE Pension Trustees Limited | 1 Share |
| QinetiQ Group plc | 1 Share |
| QinetiQ Holdings Limited | 1 Share |
| QinetiQ Limited | 1 Share |
| BAE Systems Marine (Holdings) Limited | 1 Share |

| | Non Preferential Shares of £1 each |
|---|---|
| International Military Services Limited | 19,999,999 Shares |

The Department has a 100% interest in the non-preferential shares of International Military Services Limited, a company registered in England. International Military Services Limited ceased trading on 31 July 1991. Following settlement of outstanding contracts, the company will be liquidated. The Department has written down the value of the investment to nil.

The 7.5% Non-cumulative Irredeemable Preference Shares in Chamber of Shipping Limited and British Shipping Federation Limited are valued at 1p each reflecting the value at which shares would be recovered by the two companies should membership by the Department be ceded, as laid down in the Articles of Association of the respective companies.

Special Shares confer on the Secretary of State for Defence special rights regarding ownership, influence and control, including voting rights in certain circumstances, under the individual Articles of Association of the relevant companies in which the shares are held. Further detailed information can be obtained from the companies' annual reports and accounts, which can be obtained from:

| Company | Registration Number |
|---|---|
| Devonport Royal Dockyard Limited, Devonport Royal Dockyard, Devonport, Plymouth PL1 4SG | 02077752 |
| Rosyth Royal Dockyard Limited, c/o Babcock BES, Rosyth Business Park, Rosyth, Dunfermline, Fife KY11 2YD | SC101959 |
| AWE plc, AWE Aldermaston, Reading, Berkshire RG7 4PR | 02763902 |
| AWE Pension Trustees Limited, AWE Aldermaston, Reading, Berkshire RG7 4PR | 02784144 |
| QinetiQ Group plc, 85 Buckingham Gate, London SW1E 6PD | 04586941 |
| QinetiQ Holdings Limited, 85 Buckingham Gate, London SW1E 6PD | 04154556 |
| QinetiQ Limited, 85 Buckingham Gate, London SW1E 6PD | 03796233 |
| BAE Systems Marine (Holdings) Limited, Warwick House, PO Box 87, Farnborough Aerospace Centre, Farnborough, Hants, GU14 6YU | 01957765 |

## Net Assets of Trading Funds

**15.3** The reported net assets, after deducting loans due to MoD, of the investments held in Trading Funds at 31 March 2008 and 31 March 2007 were:

| | 31 March 2008 £000 | 31 March 2007 £000 |
|---|---|---|
| Defence Science and Technology Laboratory | 265,100 | 242,600 |
| UK Hydrographic Office | 42,294 | 51,315 |
| Met Office | 205,788 | 198,700 |
| Defence Aviation Repair Agency | 60,264 | 89,085 |
| ABRO | 46,197 | 49,953 |
| **Total** | **619,643** | 631,653 |

## Dividends from Investments

**15.4** The following dividends are shown as income in Note 11.

| | 31 March 2008 £000 | 31 March 2007 £000 |
|---|---|---|
| QinetiQ | 5,724 | 4,309 |
| Defence Science and Technology Laboratory | 3,000 | 6,000 |
| UK Hydrographic Office | 7,854 | 9,171 |
| Met Office* | 11,077 | 18,937 |
| Defence Aviation Repair Agency | 4,200 | 6,000 |
| ABRO | 7,700 | 5,200 |
| **Total** | **39,555** | 49,617 |

\* Dividends paid in 2006-07 were in respect of financial years 2004-05, 2005-06 and 2006-07.

## 16. Stocks and Work in Progress

| | 31 March 2008 £000 | 31 March 2007 £000 |
|---|---|---|
| Work in progress – long term contract | 124,773 | 4,525 |
| Work in progress – other | 4,599 | 7,145 |
| Raw materials and consumables | 5,158,447 | 5,309,724 |
| Assets declared for disposal** | 936 | - |
| | **5,288,755** | 5,321,394 |

**In the prior year, assets had been declared for disposal as part of the DSDA Rationalisation programme, however the Net Book Value of these assets could not easily be identified.

## 17. Debtors

### 17.1　Analysis by type

| | 31 March 2008 £000 | 31 March 2007 £000 |
|---|---|---|
| **Amounts falling due within one year** | | |
| Trade debtors | 388,031 | 233,860 |
| Deposits and advances | 63,312 | 28,207 |
| Value Added Tax | 411,187 | 317,118 |
| Other debtors | 221,381 | 213,501 |
| Staff loans and advances* | 49,823 | 46,072 |
| Prepayments and accrued income | 735,092 | 633,614 |
| Current part of PFI prepayment | 76,313 | 41,647 |
| | **1,945,139** | **1,514,019** |
| **Amounts falling due after one year** | | |
| Trade debtors | 584,933 | 286,160 |
| Other debtors | 41,532 | 3,165 |
| Staff loans and advances* | 53,001 | 51,843 |
| Prepayments and accrued income** | 1,297,614 | 1,382,232 |
| | **1,977,080** | **1,723,400** |
| **Total Debtors** | **3,922,219** | **3,237,419** |

*Staff loans and advances includes loans for house purchase. The number of staff with house purchase loans was 12,781 (2006-07:12,167).

**Prepayments falling due after one year include an amount of £424,000,000 in respect of an adjudication decision where an appeal is pending: the amount represents an amount paid into an Escrow Account in the financial year 2002-03 and interest earned on it since that date.

### 17.2　Intra-Government Balances

| | 2007-08 Amounts falling due within one year £000 | 2006-07 Amounts falling due within one year £000 | 2007-08 Amounts falling due after more than one year £000 | 2006-07 Amounts falling due after more than one year £000 |
|---|---|---|---|---|
| Balances with other central government bodies | 470,202 | 374,454 | 331 | 14,873 |
| Balances with local authorities | 103,431 | 949 | 314 | - |
| Balances with NHS Trusts | 4,188 | 5,770 | 207 | 787 |
| Balances with public corporations and trading funds | 36,530 | 24,040 | 3 | - |
| Subtotal: intra-government balances | **614,351** | 405,213 | **855** | 15,660 |
| Balances with bodies external to government | 1,330,788 | 1,108,806 | 1,976,225 | 1,707,740 |
| **Total debtors at 31 March** | **1,945,139** | **1,514,019** | **1,977,080** | **1,723,400** |

The table above provides an analysis of the balances in Table 17.1 by customer type.

## 18. Cash at Bank and in Hand

| | 2007-08 £000 | 2006-07 £000 |
|---|---|---|
| Balance at 1 April | 473,676 | 1,018,245 |
| Net Cash Inflow/(Outflow): | | |
| Received from Consolidated Fund | 33,622,000 | 31,025,000 |
| Utilised | (33,581,824) | (31,569,569) |
| Increase/(decrease) during year | 40,176 | (544,569) |
| **Balance at 31 March** | **513,852** | **473,676** |
| The following balances at 31 March were held at: | | |
| Office of HM Paymaster General | 339,757 | 157,237 |
| Commercial Banks and Cash in Hand | 174,095 | 316,439 |
| **Balance at 31 March** | **513,852** | **473,676** |

The cash at bank balance includes £167,181,000 (2006-07: £204,434,000) of sums advanced by foreign governments to the Department on various collaborative projects where the United Kingdom is the host nation. Advances made by foreign governments for the procurement of defence equipment on their behalf are also included in this amount. The corresponding liability for these advances is shown under creditors due within one year.

## 19. Creditors

### 19.1    Analysis by type

| | 31 March 2008 £000 | 31 March 2007 £000 |
|---|---|---|
| **Amounts falling due within one year** | | |
| VAT | 55,465 | 47,131 |
| Other taxation and social security | 278,284 | 234,373 |
| Trade creditors | 499,999 | 880,088 |
| Other creditors* | 716,550 | 266,872 |
| Payments received on account | 13,413 | 14,940 |
| Accruals and deferred income | 6,176,337 | 5,003,057 |
| Current part of finance leases | 43 | 2,595 |
| Current part of imputed finance lease element of on-balance sheet PFI contracts | 22,401 | 18,391 |
| Current part of NLF loans** | 2,019 | 1,904 |
| Amounts issued from the Consolidated Fund for supply but not spent *** | 346,673 | 229,588 |
| Consolidated Fund extra receipts due to be paid to the Consolidated Fund – Received | - | 39,655 |
| | **8,111,184** | **6,738,594** |
| **Amounts falling due after more than one year** | | |
| Other creditors | 268,825 | 12,186 |
| Accruals and deferred income | 75,573 | 190,579 |
| Finance leases | - | 43 |
| Imputed finance lease element of on-balance sheet PFI contracts | 754,522 | 640,107 |
| NLF loans** | 44,412 | 46,431 |
| Loans – other | - | 85,800 |
| | **1,143,332** | **975,146** |
| **Total Creditors** | **9,254,516** | **7,713,740** |

*Other creditors includes amounts advanced by foreign governments to the Department in respect of various collaborative projects where the United Kingdom is the host nation and for the procurement of defence equipment on their behalf of £167,181,000 (2006-07 – £204,434,000).
**Under the Armed Forces (Housing Loans) Acts 1949, 1958 and 1965, the Ministry borrowed £94M from the National Loans Fund for the construction of married quarters over the period 1950/51 to 1967/68. These loans are fully repayable between 2012 and 2028, with the last instalment due on 20 February 2028. Interest on the loans is payable at rates ranging from 4% to 7% per annum.
***The amount comprises amounts drawn down and deemed drawn down from the Consolidated Fund less the Net Cash Requirement.

### 19.2 Intra-Government Balances

| | 2007-08 | 2006-07 | 2007-08 | 2006-07 |
|---|---|---|---|---|
| | Amounts falling due within one year | | Amounts falling due after more than one year | |
| | £000 | £000 | £000 | £000 |
| Balances with other central government bodies | 686,264 | 481,008 | 45,772 | 132,231 |
| Balances with local authorities | 332 | 448 | 7 | - |
| Balances with NHS Trusts | 12,924 | 10,782 | 5 | - |
| Balances with public corporations and trading funds | 135,189 | 104,919 | 413 | - |
| Subtotal: intra-government balances | 834,709 | 597,157 | 46,197 | 132,231 |
| Balances with bodies external to government | 7,276,475 | 6,141,437 | 1,097,135 | 842,915 |
| **Total creditors at 31 March** | **8,111,184** | **6,738,594** | **1,143,332** | **975,146** |

The table above provides an analysis of the balances in Table 19.1 by contractor type.

## 20. Provisions for Liabilities and Charges

| | Nuclear Decommissioning £000 | Other Decommissioning And Restoration Costs £000 | Early Retirement Commitments £000 | Other £000 | Total £000 |
|---|---|---|---|---|---|
| At 1 April 2007 | 3,910,643 | 107,991 | 444,835 | 1,308,412 | 5,771,881 |
| Increase in Provision | 497,992 | 5,707 | 141,798 | 190,225 | 835,722 |
| Unwinding of discounting | 90,963 | 1,023 | 8,281 | (18,794) | 81,473 |
| Amounts released | (264,861) | (3,867) | (21,440) | (136,725) | (426,893) |
| Amounts capitalised | (21,501) | - | - | - | (21,501) |
| Utilised in year | (45,014) | (9,173) | (156,623) | (276,101) | (486,911) |
| **At 31 March 2008** | **4,168,222** | **101,681** | **416,851** | **1,067,017** | **5,753,771** |

Analysis of amount charged / (credited) to Operating Cost Statement

| | 2007-08 £000 | 2006-07 £000 |
|---|---|---|
| Charged/(credited) to: | | |
| Property management | 1,220 | (8,724) |
| Staff costs | 150,720 | 68,826 |
| Nuclear and Other Decommissioning provisions | 233,751 | (438,612) |
| War Pensions Benefits | - | 1,000 |
| Other costs | 23,138 | 97,938 |
| Net interest (receivable)/payable | 123,288 | 126,414 |
| **Total** | **532,117** | **(153,158)** |
| Made up of: | | |
| Increase | 835,722 | 564,343 |
| Release | (426,893) | (843,915) |
| | 408,829 | (279,572) |
| Unwinding of discount | 123,288 | 126,414 |
| Net increase in provisions | **532,117** | **(153,158)** |

## Nuclear Decommissioning

**20.1** Nuclear decommissioning provisions relate principally to: the cost of facility decommissioning, the treatment and storage of nuclear waste arising from operations at MoD sites and operation of Royal Navy submarines and to the Departmental share of planning and constructing a national repository for the eventual disposal of that waste. MoD is also responsible for the Atomic Weapons Establishment (AWE).

The liabilities include the costs associated with decommissioning and care and maintenance of redundant facilities (the conditioning, retrieval and storage of contaminated materials), research and development and the procurement of capital facilities to handle the various waste streams.

Calculation of the provision to cover the liabilities is based on schedules of information received by the MoD from major decommissioning contractors. These schedules are based on technical assessments of the processes and methods likely to be used to carry out the work. Estimates are based on the latest technical knowledge and commercial information available, taking into account current legislation, regulations and Government policy. The amount and timing of each obligation is sensitive to these factors and their likely effect on the calculation and amount of the liabilities is reviewed on an annual basis. For decommissioning operations with a finite end date costs have been calculated to that date; for operations of an ongoing nature (e.g. storage of materials) costs have been calculated up to financial year 2149-50.

The latest estimate of the undiscounted cost of dealing with the MoD's nuclear liabilities is £9,221,769,000 (2006-07: £8,384,950,000[4]).

The estimate of £4,168,222,000 (2006-07: £3,910,643,000) at 31 March 2008 represents the liabilities discounted at 2.2% to the balance sheet date and expressed in 2007-08 money values.

The estimated timescale over which the costs will need to be incurred is as follows:

|  | 31 March 2008 £000 |
| --- | --- |
| Up to 3 years | 285,134 |
| From 4 – 10 years | 1,044,294 |
| Beyond 10 years | 2,838,794 |
| **Total** | **4,168,222** |

In December 2007 the AWE Quinquennial Review Submission Report was presented to the Nuclear Installations Inspectorate (NII). The resulting estimates incorporate risk and uncertainty appropriate to each type of expenditure and form the basis of the 2007-08 AWE decommissioning costs.

## Other Decommissioning and Restoration

**20.2** Other decommissioning and restoration provisions relate primarily to contaminated sites where the Department has a constructive or a legal obligation to restore the sites for normal use. The estimated payments are discounted by the Treasury discount rate of 2.2% in real terms. There have been no new provisions created during 2007-08. Existing provisions have been used to offset expenditure on the removal of asbestos (£1,700,000), on the restoration of closed sites in Northern Ireland (£4,750,000), at the former DERA Ranges (£668,000) and for the removal of residual military equipment from the Pacific Island of Kiritimati. Following a review of the requirement, there has been a partial release of provision (£3,528,000) to the Operating Cost Statement, for the disposal of radioactive source material and dilapidations.

---

4 Following a review of nuclear provisions, the 2006-07 undiscounted cost has been restated from £8,385,008,000.

**Early Retirement Pensions**

**20.3** The Department meets the additional costs of benefits beyond the normal civil service pension scheme benefits in respect of employees who retire early by paying the required amounts annually to the pension schemes over the period between early departure and normal retirement date. The Department provides for this in full when the early retirement programme becomes binding by establishing a provision for the estimated payments discounted by the Treasury discount rate of 2.2% in real terms. During 2007-08, provisions were created for Locally Employed Civilian redundancies in Cyprus (£10,379,000), and for redundancies in Defence Equipment and Support (DE&S) TLB (£59,971,000). Increases of £71,449,000 were made to existing schemes. Early retirement/redundancy costs charged to provisions during the period amounted to £156,624,000.

**Other**

**20.4** Other provisions include costs arising from the disposal of fixed assets; redundancy and relocation costs associated with reorganisation and restructuring and amounts payable under guarantees, litigation and contractual arrangements. During 2007-08, provisions have been increased for legal claims (£144,372,000), an outstanding adjudication decision (£9,136,000) and Locally Employed Civilian pensions (£33,230,000). Following a review of the requirement, provisions have been released to the Operating Cost Statement in respect of an adjudication decision where an appeal is outstanding (£40,933,000), the disposal of Multiple Launch Rocket Systems (£57,273,000) and in respect of a potential loss arising from slippage in a procurement project which is no longer required (£9,835,000). Costs charged to provisions during the period amounted to £244,464,000 and included £102,808,000 for Army and RAF manpower reductions following decisions on organisational changes.

## 21. General Fund

The General Fund represents the total assets less liabilities of each of the entities within the accounting boundary, to the extent that the total is not represented by other reserves and financing items.

| | 2007-08 £000 | 2006-07 £000 |
|---|---:|---:|
| Balance at 1 April | 75,434,183 | 72,490,177 |
| Net Parliamentary Funding | | |
| – Drawn Down | 33,622,000 | 31,025,000 |
| – Deemed | 229,588 | 658,881 |
| Year end adjustment | | |
| – Supply (Creditor)/Debtor – current year | (346,673) | (229,588) |
| Net Transfer from Operating Activities | | |
| – Net Operating Costs | (36,223,006) | (33,948,669) |
| – CFERs paid and repayable to Consolidated Fund | (750,810) | (56,326) |
| Non-cash charges: | | |
| Cost of Capital (OCS) | 3,370,908 | 3,241,907 |
| Auditors' Remuneration (Note 10) | 3,600 | 3,600 |
| – Change in the Discount Rate – Pension Provision (Note 20) | 41,815 | (50,600) |
| Transfer from/(to) Revaluation Reserve (Note 22 ) | 1,266,589 | 2,321,586 |
| Transfer from/(to) Donated Asset Reserve (Note 22) | (394) | (21,785) |
| **Balance at 31 March** | **76,647,800** | **75,434,183** |

## 22. Reserves

| | Revaluation Reserve £000 | Donated Asset Reserve £000 | Investment Reserve £000 |
|---|---|---|---|
| At 1 April 2007 | 17,129,769 | 2,013,539 | 232,599 |
| Arising on revaluation during the year (net) | 4,589,279 | 385,591 | 7,181 |
| Additions during the year | - | 67,870 | - |
| Transfers | 2 | - | - |
| Transferred (to) / from Operating Cost Statement | - | 28,922 | - |
| Transferred (to) / from General Fund | (1,266,589) | 394 | - |
| **At 31 March 2008** | **20,452,461** | **2,496,316** | **239,780** |

## 23. Notes to the Cash Flow Statement

### 23.1    Reconciliation of operating cost to operating cash flows

| | Note | 2007-08 £000 | 2006-07 £000 |
|---|---|---|---|
| Net operating cost | OCS | 36,223,006 | 33,948,669 |
| Non-cash transactions: | | | |
| – Depreciation and amortisation charges | 10 | (6,173,005) | (5,644,119) |
| – Impairment in value of fixed assets | 10 | (74,346) | (175,705) |
| – Provisions to reduce value of stock to its net realisable value | 10 | (137,193) | (90,771) |
| – Stocks written off – net | 10 | (431,651) | (94,903) |
| – Auditors' remuneration | 10 | (3,600) | (3,600) |
| – Surplus / (deficit) arising on disposal of stock | 10 | 9,638 | (4,078) |
| – Surplus arising on disposal of tangible fixed assets | 10 | 682,647 | 123,135 |
| – Fixed Assets written off – net | 10 | (869,919) | (730,325) |
| – Capital project expenditure written off | 10 | (19,238) | (58,830) |
| – Bad debts written off | 10 | (29,607) | (26,557) |
| – Bad debts provision | 10 | 1,224 | (4,298) |
| – Movement in provisions for liabilities and charges (excluding capitalised provisions) | 20 | (408,829) | 279,573 |
| – Unwinding of discount on provisions for liabilities and charges | | (123,288) | (126,414) |
| – Cost of capital | 21 | (3,370,908) | (3,241,907) |
| | | (10,948,075) | (9,798,799) |
| Increase in stocks / WIP | | 501,231 | 169,875 |
| Increase in debtors | | 713,184 | 347,119 |
| (Increase) in creditors | | (1,540,776) | (206,751) |
| *Less movements in creditors relating to items not passing through the OCS* | | *640,212* | *(76,237)* |
| Use of provisions | | 100,342 | 287,357 |
| **Net cash outflow from operating activities** | | **25,689,124** | **24,671,233** |

### 23.2 Analysis of capital expenditure and financial investment

| | Note | 2007-08 £000 | 2006-07 £000 |
|---|---|---|---|
| Intangible fixed asset additions | 13 | **1,755,558** | 1,744,366 |
| Tangible fixed asset additions* | 14, 20 | **6,707,037** | 5,818,599 |
| Less movement on fixed asset accruals & creditors | | **(288,291)** | (301,213) |
| Proceeds on disposal of tangible fixed assets | | **(1,174,198)** | (489,808) |
| Loans made to Trading Funds | 15 | **-** | 4,400 |
| Repayment of loans made to the Trading Funds and QinetiQ | 15 | **(9,949)** | (8,479) |
| **Net cash outflow from investing activities** | | **6,990,157** | **6,767,865** |

*Tangible fixed asset additions at Note 14 are shown net of the movement in capitalised provision at Note 20 (Tangible fixed asset additions, from Note 23.2 above, £6,707,037,000 less movement on capitalised provision £21,501,000, from Note 20, is equal to £6,685,536,000 the total additions at Note 14).

### 23.3 Analysis of capital expenditure and financial investment by Request for Resources

| | Capital expenditure £000 | Loans etc £000 | A in A £000 | Net Total £000 |
|---|---|---|---|---|
| Request for Resources 1 | 7,338,426 | (9,949) | (1,174,198) | 6,154,279 |
| Request for Resources 2 | 835,878 | - | - | 835,878 |
| Request for Resources 3 | - | - | - | - |
| Net movements in debtors/creditors | 288,291 | - | - | 288,291 |
| **Total 2007-08** | **8,462,595** | **(9,949)** | **(1,174,198)** | **7,278,448** |
| Total 2006-07 | 7,562,965 | (4,079) | (489,808) | 7,069,078 |

### 23.4 Analysis of financing

| | Note | 2007-08 £000 | 2006-07 £000 |
|---|---|---|---|
| From the Consolidated Fund (Supply) – current year | 21, 18 | **33,622,000** | 31,025,000 |
| Repayment of loans from the National Loans Fund | | **(1,904)** | (1,797) |
| Capital elements of payments in respect of finance leases and on-balance sheet PFI contracts | | **(24,374)** | (9,020) |
| Repayment of other loans | | **(85,800)** | - |
| Net financing | | **33,509,922** | **31,014,183** |

### 23.5 Reconciliation of Net Cash Requirement to increase/(decrease) in cash

| | Note | 2007-08 £000 | 2006-07 £000 |
|---|---|---|---|
| Net cash requirement | | **(33,504,916)** | (31,454,292) |
| From the Consolidated Fund (Supply) – current year | 21, 18 | **33,622,000** | 31,025,000 |
| Amounts due to the Consolidated Fund received and not paid | 19 | **-** | 39,655 |
| Amounts due to the Consolidated Fund received in the prior year and paid over | | **(39,655)** | (102,983) |
| Movement on Collaborative balances | | **(37,253)** | (51,949) |
| Increase / (decrease) in cash | | **40,176** | **(544,569)** |

## 24. Notes to the Statement of Operating Costs by Departmental Aim and Objectives

The net costs of the Departmental Objectives are determined as follows:

### Objective 1: Achieving success in the tasks we undertake

| | 2007-08 | | | 2006-07 | | |
|---|---|---|---|---|---|---|
| | Gross £000 | Income £000 | Net £000 | Gross £000 | Income £000 | Net £000 |
| Operations | 2,218,138 | (22,101) | 2,196,037 | 1,463,977 | (20,604) | 1,443,373 |
| Other military tasks | 1,125,887 | (40,020) | 1,085,867 | 1,611,502 | (86,229) | 1,525,273 |
| Contributing to the community | 490,384 | (30,682) | 459,702 | 421,920 | (25,357) | 396,563 |
| Helping to build a safer world | 527,413 | (218,768) | 308,645 | 516,874 | (171,085) | 345,789 |
| Total | 4,361,822 | (311,571) | 4,050,251 | 4,014,273 | (303,275) | 3,710,998 |

Costs are identified as follows:

– *Operations* comprises the additional costs incurred deploying the Armed Forces in military operations, e.g. in Iraq and Afghanistan, over and above the costs of maintaining the units involved at their normal states of readiness.

– *Other military tasks* include ongoing military commitments, e.g. to security in Northern Ireland and Overseas Commands, and the costs of identifying and countering the threat of terrorist attack on the UK mainland, and of maintaining the integrity of UK waters and airspace.

– *Contributing to the community* includes ongoing support activities, e.g. search and rescue, administration of cadet forces. In addition, it includes the costs of assistance to other Government Departments and agencies, e.g. in counter drugs operations.

– *Helping to build a safer world* includes the costs of Defence diplomacy undertaken to build confidence and security with our allies. It also includes the Department's support of wider British interests.

### Objective 2: Being ready to respond to the tasks that might arise

The costs of delivering the military capability to meet this objective are analysed among force elements of the front line commands, including joint force units where these have been established, and a small number of centrally managed military support activities.

In addition to the direct operating costs of the front line units, they include the attributed costs of logistical and personnel support, identified by reference to the output costs of supplier Management Groupings.

In common with all objectives, these also contain a share of the costs of advising Ministers and accountability to Parliament, and apportioned overheads for head office functions and centrally provided services.

The total comprises the full costs, including support services, of force elements grouped under the following headings:

| | 2007-08 | | | 2006-07 | | |
|---|---|---|---|---|---|---|
| | Gross £000 | Income £000 | Net £000 | Gross £000 | Income £000 | Net £000 |
| **Royal Navy** | | | | | | |
| Aircraft carriers | 386,614 | (9,891) | 376,723 | 348,985 | (10,050) | 338,935 |
| Frigates and Destroyers | 1,527,946 | (36,940) | 1,491,006 | 1,677,001 | (58,421) | 1,618,580 |
| Smaller warships | 373,316 | (13,524) | 359,792 | 403,709 | (13,386) | 390,323 |
| Amphibious ships | 422,474 | (8,803) | 413,671 | 349,766 | (10,823) | 338,943 |
| Strategic sealift | 35,958 | (2,078) | 33,880 | 46,738 | (684) | 46,054 |
| Fleet support ships | 310,367 | (6,201) | 304,166 | 375,291 | (8,996) | 366,295 |
| Survey and other vessels | 158,721 | (5,484) | 153,237 | 97,893 | (3,759) | 94,134 |
| Naval aircraft | 1,153,225 | (30,447) | 1,122,778 | 1,117,280 | (34,106) | 1,083,174 |
| Submarines | 2,829,872 | (47,116) | 2,782,756 | 2,286,998 | (82,943) | 2,204,055 |
| Royal Marines | 568,272 | (19,835) | 548,437 | 577,469 | (20,530) | 556,939 |
| | 7,766,765 | (180,319) | 7,586,446 | 7,281,130 | (243,698) | 7,037,432 |
| **Army** | | | | | | |
| Field units | 9,964,310 | (292,933) | 9,671,377 | 9,134,183 | (311,830) | 8,822,353 |
| Other units | 1,724,888 | (135,022) | 1,589,866 | 1,993,020 | (109,495) | 1,883,525 |
| | 11,689,198 | (427,955) | 11,261,243 | 11,127,203 | (421,325) | 10,705,878 |
| **Royal Air Force** | | | | | | |
| Combat aircraft | 4,291,895 | (99,140) | 4,192,755 | 3,848,236 | (156,506) | 3,691,730 |
| Intelligence, Surveillance, Target Acquisition and Reconnaissance aircraft | 922,591 | (23,884) | 898,707 | 635,269 | (22,436) | 612,833 |
| Tankers, transport and communications aircraft | 1,074,904 | (49,560) | 1,025,344 | 1,262,576 | (51,779) | 1,210,797 |
| Future capability | 87,737 | (1,989) | 85,748 | 45,837 | (1,566) | 44,271 |
| Other aircraft and RAF units | 1,566,744 | (196,150) | 1,370,594 | 1,489,798 | (62,572) | 1,427,226 |
| | 7,943,871 | (370,723) | 7,573,148 | 7,281,716 | (294,859) | 6,986,857 |
| **Centre Grouping** | | | | | | |
| Joint and multinational operations | 784,515 | (23,849) | 760,666 | 448,581 | (23,744) | 424,837 |
| Centrally managed military support | 650,423 | (44,173) | 606,250 | 447,486 | (80,637) | 366,849 |
| Maintenance of war reserve stocks | 540,639 | (8,187) | 532,452 | 787,274 | (16,868) | 770,406 |
| | 1,975,577 | (76,209) | 1,899,368 | 1,683,341 | (121,249) | 1,562,092 |
| **Total Objective 2** | 29,375,411 | (1,055,206) | 28,320,205 | 27,373,390 | (1,081,131) | 26,292,259 |

Most groupings are self explanatory. The following, however, should be noted:

- *Smaller warships* includes mine hunting and offshore patrol vessels.

- *Amphibious ships* includes assault ships providing platforms for landing craft and helicopters, and Royal Fleet Auxiliary landing support ships.

- *Strategic sealift* is the Roll-On Roll-Off ferry facility supporting the Joint Rapid Reaction Force.

- *Fleet support ships* includes Royal Fleet Auxiliary ships providing tanker and replenishment support to warships.

- *Survey and other vessels* includes ocean and coastal survey and ice patrol ships.

- *Naval aircraft* include Sea King, Lynx and Merlin helicopters deployed in anti-submarine, airborne early warning, Royal Marine support, and reconnaissance and attack roles.

- *Submarines* includes the operating costs of submarines, nuclear weapons systems and logistical support of nuclear propulsion, including nuclear decommissioning.

- *Army – Field units* includes 1 (UK) Armoured Division, 3 (UK) Division, Joint Helicopter Command and Theatre troops.

- *Army – Other units* includes Regional Divisions and Land support and training.

- *Combat aircraft (formerly strike/attack and offensive support aircraft and Typhoon/Tornado F3 within defensive and surveillance aircraft))* includes Tornado GR4, Joint Force Harrier and Jaguar aircraft deployed in strike/attack and offensive support roles and Typhoon and Tornado F3 in air defence roles for the UK's standing commitments and contingent overseas operations. Typhoon will have a multi-role capability from mid 2008.

- *Intelligence, Surveillance, Target Acquisition and Reconnaissance (ISTAR) (formerly within defensive and surveillance aircraft and reconnaissance and maritime patrol aircraft)* includes Sentry AEW1, Sentinel and Nimrod aircraft deployed in UK contingent operations, NATO and UN peacekeeping commitments.

- *Tankers, transport and communications aircraft* includes C-17, Hercules, Tristar and VC10 aircraft providing air transport and air to air refuelling, and smaller transport aircraft (BAe 125/146 and Squirrel/Agusta 109 helicopters) used in a rapid communications role.

- *Future capability* includes the Joint Test and Evaluation Group and the development and use of geographic information.

- *Other aircraft and RAF units* includes ground forces (e.g. the RAF Regiment), miscellaneous aircraft not included elsewhere and the RAF Logistics Hub and Air Traffic Services.

- *Joint and multinational operations* includes Chief of Joint Operations HQ and the costs less receipts of UK participation in NATO.

- *Centrally managed military support* includes intelligence operational support and Special Forces.

- *Maintenance of war reserve stocks* includes the holding costs and charges of munitions and other stocks, above the levels required for planned consumption.

## Objective 3: Building for the future

This objective comprises the following elements:

| | 2007-08 | | | 2006-07 | | |
|---|---|---|---|---|---|---|
| | Gross £000 | Income £000 | Net £000 | Gross £000 | Income £000 | Net £000 |
| Research | 974,056 | (302) | 973,754 | 1,026,433 | (104) | 1,026,329 |
| Equipment programme | 1,893,357 | (28,691) | 1,864,666 | 1,925,892 | (44,882) | 1,881,010 |
| Total | 2,867,413 | (28,993) | 2,838,420 | 2,952,325 | (44,986) | 2,907,339 |

- *Research* comprises the costs, including capital charges, of the Science, Innovation, Technology TLB, and research expenditure incurred by other TLBs.

- *Equipment Programme* refers to the administration and programme costs incurred by DE&S TLB, associated with specifying requirements for and procurement of fighting equipment and other assets. The values of fixed asset additions are shown in Notes 13 and 14.

## Attribution to Objectives

Gross expenditure of £34,046,238,000 (90.5%) (2006-07 – 86.0%) and Operating Income of £1,047,357,000 (75%) (2006-07 – 74.1%) were allocated to tasks, force elements or activities directly supporting the Objectives. The rest was apportioned in one of two ways:

- by means of cost attributions to "customer" Management Groupings, using local output costing systems to identify the full local costs of services provided. Cost attributions from suppliers are analysed onward to final outputs on advice from the recipients. If specific advice is not given, attributed costs are assumed to follow the same pattern as locally incurred expenditure:

- as an element of central overhead, shared among objectives in proportion to all other attributions. The force elements etc. described above receive a share of the expenditure and income components of these overheads, on the basis of their net costs.

The central overheads comprised:

| | 2007-08 | | | 2006-07 | | |
|---|---|---|---|---|---|---|
| | Gross £000 | Income £000 | Net £000 | Gross £000 | Income £000 | Net £000 |
| Support for Ministers and Parliament | 11,840 | (9) | 11,831 | 15,062 | (19) | 15,043 |
| Departmental corporate services | 1,309,521 | (314,455) | 995,066 | 1,170,115 | (309,963) | 860,152 |
| Strategic Management | 252,440 | (6,151) | 246,289 | 240,183 | (1,822) | 238,361 |

- Support for Ministers and Parliament includes provision of advice to Ministers and the costs, wherever incurred in the Department, of dealing with Parliamentary business.

- Departmental corporate services comprises internal support functions, e.g. payment of bills, payroll administration and medical care for service personnel, and costs of Departmental restructuring.

- Strategic management includes policy making functions in strategic, personnel, scientific and medical matters.

## Capital employed

The deployment of the Department's capital in support of its objectives does not follow the pattern of operating costs. Net assets totalling £80,892,859,000 (81.1%) support the military capability required to meet Objective 2. The remainder comprises assets wholly attributable to tasks within Objective 1 (£3,237,559,000 – 3.2%), and intangible assets, Single Use Military Equipment (SUME) and other assets under construction, and assets related to equipment procurement within Objective 3 (£15,724,331,000 – 15.7%), and payment of War Pensions Benefits (-£18,393,000).

## 25. Capital Commitments

Capital commitments, for which no provision has been made in these financial statements, were as follows:

|  | 31 March 2008 £000 | 31 March 2007 £000 |
|---|---|---|
| Contracted but not provided for | 18,090,995 | 17,849,412 |

## 26. Financial Commitments

### 26.1    Commitments under operating leases:

Commitments under operating leases to pay rentals during the year following the year of these accounts are given in the table below, analysed according to the period in which the lease expires.

|  | Land and Buildings | | Other | |
|---|---|---|---|---|
|  | 31 March 2008 £000 | 31March 2007 £000 | 31 March 2008 £000 | 31 March 2007 £000 |
| The Department was committed to making the following payments during 2008-09 in respect of : |  |  |  |  |
| Operating leases expiring within one year | 14,455 | 8,984 | 38,045 | 84,439 |
| Operating leases expiring between two and five years | 18,017 | 11,298 | 118,991 | 104,359 |
| Operating leases expiring after five years | 166,158 | 156,482 | 7,072 | 11,700* |
|  | 198,630 | 176,764 | 164,108 | 200,498 |

*Re-stated. The prior year figure incorrectly included the whole life value of one contract; overstating the annual costs of leases expiring after five years by £676,873,000.

### 26.2    Obligations under finance leases:

Obligations under finance leases are as follows:

|  | 31 March 2008 £000 | 31 March 2007 £000 |
|---|---|---|
| Rentals due within 1 year | 43 | 2,595 |
| Rentals due after 1 year but within 5 years | - | 43 |
| Rentals due thereafter | - | - |
|  | 43 | 2,638 |

## 27. Private Finance Initiative (PFI) Commitments

### Charge to the Operating Cost Statement and future commitments

**27.1**    The total amount charged in the Operating Cost Statement in respect of off-balance sheet PFI transactions and the service element of on-balance sheet PFI transactions was £1,276,131,000 (2006-07: £1,147,660,000); and the payments to which the Department is committed during 2008-09, analysed by the period during which the commitment expires, are as follows:

| | 31 March 2008 £000 | 31 March 2007 £000 |
|---|---|---|
| Expiry within 1 year | 15,064 | 11,028 |
| Expiry within 2 to 5 years | 286,469 | 172,654 |
| Expiry within 6 to 10 years | 289,078 | 178,205 |
| Expiry within 11 to 15 years | 135,850 | 335,233 |
| Expiry within 16 to 20 years | 55,162 | 67,317 |
| Expiry within 21 to 25 years | 228,259 | 219,874 |
| Expiry within 26 to 30 years | 24,540 | 21,213 |
| Expiry within 31 to 35 years | 208,726 | 171,964 |

### Off Balance Sheet

**27.2**    The following information is provided for those schemes assessed as off Balance Sheet:

| Project Description | Capital Value* £000 | Prepayment 31 Mar 2008 £000 | Contract Start ** | Contract End |
|---|---|---|---|---|
| Training, Administration and Financial Management Information System: Provision of training administration and financial management information systems to the Army Recruiting and Training Division | 36,000 | - | Aug 1996 | Nov 2009 |
| Hazardous Stores Information System: Provision of an information management service for hazardous stores safety datasheets with 2,000 users | 1,000 | - | Oct 1997 | Oct 2008 |
| Defence Fixed Telecommunications System: Integration of 50 fixed telecommunications networks used by the Armed Forces and MoD, including the delivery of voice, data, LAN interconnect and other WAN services | 200,000 | - | Jul 1997 | Jul 2012 |
| Medium Support Helicopter Aircrew Training Facility: Provision of 6 flight simulator training facilities, covering three different types of helicopter, at RAF Benson | 114,000 | 6,440 | Oct 1997 | Oct 2037 |
| Hawk Synthetic Training Facility: Provision of replacement simulator training facilities at RAF Valley | 19,000 | 618 | Dec 1997 | Dec 2015 |
| Joint Services Command and Staff College (JSCSC): Design and delivery of a new tri-Service Command and Staff Training College infrastructure and supporting services, including single residential accommodation and married quarters. (Of the total amount, £58 million relates to on-balance sheet) | 87,196 | - | Jun 1998 | Aug 2028 |
| Attack Helicopter Training Service: Provision of full mission simulator, 3 field deployable simulators, ground crew, maintenance and armament training | 165,000 | - | Jul 1998 | Sep 2017 |
| Family Quarters Yeovilton: Provision of married quarters accommodation for 88 Service families at RNAS Yeovilton | 8,200 | - | Jul 1998 | Jul 2028 |
| RAF Lyneham Sewage Treatment: Refurbishment of existing sewage treatment facilities, serving a population of 7,000, to meet regulatory standards at RAF Lyneham | 3,809 | - | Aug 1998 | Aug 2023 |

| Project Description | Capital Value* £000 | Prepayment 31 Mar 2008 £000 | Contract Start ** | Contract End |
|---|---|---|---|---|
| Thames Water (formerly known as Tidworth Water and Sewage): Pathfinder project providing water, sewerage and surface water drainage, serving a population of 12,000 military and dependants at Tidworth | 5,000 | - | Feb 1998 | Aug 2018 |
| RAF Mail: Provision of informal messaging services for the RAF | 12,000 | - | Nov 1998 | Nov 2008 |
| Fire Fighting Training Units: Provision of fire fighting training for the Royal Navy | 22,500 | - | Apr 1999 | Jan 2021 |
| Light Aircraft Flying Training: Provision of flying training and support services for Air Experience Flying and University Air Squadron Flying Training | 20,000 | - | Apr 1999 | Mar 2009 |
| Tornado GR4 Synthetic Training Service: Provision of aircraft training service at RAF Marham and RAF Lossiemouth | 61,700 | 1,798 | Jun 1999 | Jun 2031 |
| Army Foundation College: Provision of teaching and training facilities for the further vocational education and military training of high-quality school leavers | 73,400 | - | Feb 2000 | Dec 2029 |
| RAF Cosford/RAF Shawbury Family Quarters: Provision of married quarters accommodation for 145 Service families at RAF Cosford and RAF Shawbury | 15,083 | - | Mar 1999 | Jun 2025 |
| Central Scotland Family Quarters: Provision of married quarters accommodation for 164 Service families in Central Scotland | 24,713 | 1,786 | Aug 1999 | Jan 2021 |
| Tri-Service Material Handling Equipment: Provision of Tri-Service materials handling capability | 35,000 | - | Jun 2000 | Jun 2010 |
| Commercial Satellite Communication Service (INMARSAT): Provision of world-wide commercial satellite communication system for Royal Navy Ships | 2,600 | - | Mar 2001 | Mar 2008 |
| E3D Sentry Aircrew Training Service: E3D Sentry simulators instructors and maintainers at RAF Waddington | 6,929 | 335 | Jul 2000 | Dec 2030 |
| Lynx MK 7 and 9 Aircrew Training Service: Provision for simulator training facility for Lynx MK 7 and 9 helicopter aircrew | 15,436 | 160 | Jul 2000 | Jul 2025 |
| Tri-Service White Fleet: Provision, management and maintenance of support vehicles in the UK | 40,000 | - | Jan 2001 | Jan 2011 |
| Family quarters at Wattisham: Provision of married quarters accommodation for 250 Service families | 34,200 | - | May 2001 | Mar 2028 |
| Family quarters at Bristol/Bath/Portsmouth: Provision of married quarters accommodation for 317 Service families | 78,010 | 4,092 | Nov 2001 | Sep 2028 |
| Defence Housing Information Systems: Provision of a management information system for Defence Housing | 11,600 | - | Oct 2001 | Sep 2010 |
| Marine Support to Range and Aircrew Training: Provision of management, manning, operation and maintenance of Air Support Craft and Range Safety Craft | 11,850 | - | Dec 2001 | Dec 2012 |
| Astute Class Training: Provision of a training environment for crewmen and maintainers to support Astute Class submarines for 30 years | 79,600 | - | Sep 2001 | Jan 2037 |
| Strategic Sealift (RoRo): Provision of strategic sealift services based on six RoRo ferries in support of Joint Rapid Reaction Force deployments | 175,000 | - | Jun 2002 | Dec 2024 |
| Material Handling Equipment: Provision of tri-service material handling equipment for Army, Navy and RAF storage depots | 7,821 | - | Aug 2002 | Jul 2010 |
| Aquatrine Project A: Provision of water and waste water services | 154,032 | 85,282 | Apr 2003 | Nov 2028 |
| Aquatrine Project B: Provision of water and waste water services | 86,440 | 29,604 | Sep 2004 | Mar 2030 |
| Aquatrine Project C: Provision of water and waste water services | 174,000 | 61,983 | Oct 2004 | Mar 2030 |
| Hayes Records and Storage: Pan-Government Records Management and Archive Services | 11,000 | - | Sep 2003 | Sep 2028 |
| Defence Sixth Form College: Development of a sixth form college to help meet the future recruitment requirements in the Armed Forces and MoD Civil Service | 20,000 | - | Jun 2003 | Aug 2033 |

| Project Description | Capital Value*<br>£000 | Prepayment<br>31 Mar 2008<br>£000 | Contract<br>Start ** | Contract<br>End |
|---|---|---|---|---|
| Colchester Garrison: Redevelopment, rebuilding and refurbishment to provide accommodation and associated services (messing, education, storage, workshops) | 539,000 | 145,813 | Feb 2004 | Feb 2039 |
| Skynet 5: Range of satellite services, including management of existing Skynet 4 satellites | 1,360,930 | - | Oct 2003 | Feb 2020 |
| C Vehicles: Provision of Earthmoving and Specialist plant, Engineer Construction Plant and Material Handling Equipment and support services | 703,000 | 36,302 | Jun 2005 | Jun 2021 |
| Portsmouth 2 Housing: Provision of 148 Family quarters in Portsmouth | 27,092 | 7,653 | Oct 2005 | Oct 2030 |
| Future Strategic Tanker Aircraft (FSTA): FSTA is an innovative PFI programme that will provide modern air-to-air refuelling and passenger air transport capabilities | 2,688,000 | - | Mar 2008 | Mar 2035 |

*The capital value is based on private sector partners' capital investment, where known, or otherwise the capital value of the public sector comparator.
**The date when the contracts were signed.

## On Balance Sheet

**27.3**    The following PFI projects are treated as on balance sheet. The service payment commitments for the year 2008-09 are included in the table shown at 27.1.

| Project Description | Capital Value*<br>£000 | Net Book Value<br>31 Mar 2008<br>£000 | Contract<br>Start ** | Contract<br>End |
|---|---|---|---|---|
| Defence Helicopter Flying School: Provision of helicopter flying training services | 93,027 | 20,871 | Apr 1997 | Mar 2012 |
| RAF Lossiemouth Family Quarters: Redevelopment and re-provision of 279 Service family quarters | 24,745 | 26,364 | Jun 1998 | Aug 2020 |
| Joint Services Command and Staff College: Command and Staff College for military and civilian personnel (also see JSCSC – Off Balance Sheet) | 58,188 | 71,429 | Jun 1998 | Aug 2028 |
| RAF Fylingdales: Provision of guaranteed power supply | 7,486 | 3,235 | Dec 1998 | Dec 2023 |
| Main Building Refurbishment: Redevelopment and management services for MoD Main Building | 347,914 | 233,739 | May 2000 | May 2030 |
| Naval Communications: Submarine fleet communications service | 58,491 | 40,513 | Jun 2000 | Dec 2030 |
| Defence Electronic Commerce Service: Strategic partnership to deliver e-business environment to share information between MoD and trading partners | 6,511 | 784 | Jul 2000 | Jul 2010 |
| Defence Animal Centre: Redevelopment of new office and residential accommodation, animal husbandry and training support | 10,047 | 11,970 | Aug 2000 | Nov 2026 |
| Heavy Equipment Transporters: Provision of vehicles to replace existing fleet and meet future requirements | 58,000 | 48,522 | Dec 2001 | Jul 2024 |
| Field Electrical Power Supplies: Provision of generator sets to support operational electrical requirements in the field | 73,410 | 65,717 | Jun 2002 | Jun 2022 |
| Devonport Armada Single Living Accommodation: Provision of Support Services and Fleet Accommodation Centre services at Devonport Naval Base | 44,513 | 34,167 | Jul 2004 | Mar 2029 |
| Project Allenby/Connaught: Rebuild, refurbishment, management and operation of facilities for Service accommodation at Aldershot, Tidworth, Bulford, Warminster, Larkhill and Perham Down | 1,117,332 | 117,991 | Mar 2006 | Apr 2041 |
| Northwood: Rebuild, refurbishment, management and operation of facilities for the Permanent Joint Headquarters | 161,521 | 25,076 | Jul 2006 | Oct 2031 |
| Provision of Marine Services: Provision of marine services at UK Dockyard Ports at Portsmouth, Devonport and Clyde and support to military exercises, training and deep water trials, worldwide. | 90,564 | - | Dec 2007 | Dec 2022 |

*The capital value is based on private sector partners' capital investment, where known, or otherwise the capital value of the public sector comparator.
**The date when the contracts were signed.

| Imputed finance lease obligations under on-balance sheet PFI contracts comprises: | 31 March 2008 £000 | 31 March 2007 £000 |
|---|---|---|
| Rentals due within 1 year | 22,401 | 18,391 |
| Rentals due after 1 year but within 5 years | 82,935 | 90,521 |
| Rentals due thereafter | 671,587 | 549,585 |
| | 776,923 | 658,497 |
| Less interest element | 60,857 | 64,460* |
| | 716,066 | 594,037 |

*Re-stated. The prior year analysis of interest understated the split between finance leases and PFI obligations.

## 28. Financial Instruments

**28.1**    FRS 13, Derivatives and Other Financial Instruments, requires disclosure of the role which financial instruments have had during the period in creating or changing the risks an entity faces in undertaking its activities. Because of the largely non-trading nature of its activities and the way in which government Departments are financed, the Department is not exposed to the degree of financial risk faced by business entities. Moreover, financial instruments play a much more limited role in creating or changing risk than would be typical of the listed companies to which FRS 13 mainly applies. Financial assets and liabilities are generated by day-to-day operational activities and are not held to change the risks facing the Department in undertaking its activities.

### Liquidity risk

**28.2**    The Department's revenue and capital resource requirements are voted annually by Parliament and are, therefore, not exposed to significant liquidity risks.

### Interest rate risk

**28.3**    A significant proportion of the Department's financial assets and liabilities carry nil or fixed rates of interest. The exposure to interest risk is, therefore, not significant.

### Foreign currency risk

**28.4**    The Department has in the past entered into forward purchase contracts with the Bank of England to cover its foreign exchange requirements. Details of the outstanding foreign currency contracts are as follows:

| Currency | Foreign currency US$/Euro 000 | Weighted average exchange rate (=£1) | 31 March 2008 Sterling £000 | 31 March 2007 Sterling £000 |
|---|---|---|---|---|
| | | | | **2007/ 2008 delivery** |
| US Dollar | 2,258,250 | 1.79 | | 1,263,836 |
| Euro | 1,957,000 | 1.43 | | 1,365,429 |
| | | | **2008/2009 delivery** | **2008/2009 delivery** |
| US Dollar | 2,073,000 | 1.81 | 1,145,771 | 1,145,771 |
| Euro | 2,126,000 | 1.42 | 1,498,720 | 1,498,720 |
| | | | **2009/2010 delivery** | **2009/2010 delivery** |
| US Dollar | 1,328,000 | 1.84 | 721,119 | 721,119 |
| Euro | 1,634,000 | 1.40 | 1,169,141 | 1,169,141 |
| | | | **2010/2011 delivery** | **2010/2011 delivery** |
| US Dollar | 919,000 | 1.88 | 487,944 | 487,944 |
| Euro | 1,087,000 | 1.39 | 784,205 | 784,205 |
| | | | **2011/2012 delivery** | **2011/2012 delivery** |
| US Dollar | 445,000 | 1.90 | 234,187 | 234,187 |
| Euro | 540,000 | 1.38 | 391,219 | 391,219 |
| Total | | | **6,432,306** | **9,061,571** |

**Fair values**

*Financial assets*

28.5    The Department's financial assets include investments in, and loans made to, MoD Trading Funds and QinetiQ Group plc. The net assets of these bodies (excluding MoD loans), the interest rates applicable to these loans and the market value of the shareholding in QinetiQ Group plc are shown in Note 15. Other financial assets' fair values approximate to their book values.

*Financial liabilities*

28.6    The Department's liabilities include loans from the National Loans Fund, obligations under finance leases and PFI contracts amounting in total to £823,397,000 (2006-07: £795,271,000). The fair values of these liabilities will be different from their book values but since these represent only 5.3% of the gross liabilities and provisions, the impact on the Department's net assets will not be material. The fair values of provisions for liabilities and charges are not materially different to their book values, which are stated after discounting at the Treasury rate of 2.2%. Other liabilities' fair values approximate to their book values.

## 29. Contingent Liabilities and Contingent Assets Disclosed under FRS 12

### Contingent Liabilities

29.1    Contingent liabilities estimated at some £1,698,012,000 (2006-07: £1,474,972,000) have been identified. The balance primarily comprises of site restoration liabilities of some £400,000,000 (2006-07: £400,000,000) relating to the British Army Training Units in Canada and indemnities, that are quantifiable, of £999,548,000 (2006-07: £886,800,000) granted to contractors and suppliers.

The Department has a number of sites where it may be necessary to carry out remediation work in respect of contamination. It is not cost effective or practicable to identify all levels of contamination at individual sites nor to assess the likely cost of any remediation work necessary. As any liability cannot, therefore, be quantified it is not appropriate to include a provision in accordance with FRS 12.

The Department signed a contract in May 2007 for Service Life Insurance which will enable Service personnel to access life insurance throughout their Service career. As at 31 March 2008 MoD's contribution to payments against qualifying policies amounted to £124,000. The amount for 2008-09 will show payments for policies falling due in 2008 but at this time the extent of the liability cannot be known. This unquantified liability has been reported to Parliament. A maximum theoretical liability of £4bn has also been reported to Parliament. Details of the scheme and key features can be found at www.servicelifeinsurance.co.uk

### Contingent Assets

29.2    A US salvage company, Odyssey Marine Exploration, has found what is believed to be the wreck of the British warship Sussex, which sank in the Western Mediterranean in 1694 carrying gold and silver coins estimated to be valued at the time at £1 million. If confirmed as the Sussex, the wreck and its contents are legally the property of Her Majesty's Government.

A licensing agreement was signed on 27 September 2002 between the Disposal Services Authority of the Ministry of Defence, on behalf of Her Majesty's Government, and Odyssey for further archaeological exploration of the wreck of the Sussex and recovery of artefacts et cetera. Full responsibility for the project, including the sale of the artefacts has been transferred to the Department. Proceeds from the sale of any artefacts will be surrendered to HM Treasury.

The Department will be responsible for the preservation of any part of the wreck brought up as part of the salvage effort.

# 30. Contingent Liabilities not Required to be Disclosed under FRS 12 but included for Parliamentary Reporting and Accountability

## Quantifiable (Unrestricted)

**30.1** The MoD has entered into the following quantifiable contingent liabilities by offering guarantees, indemnities or by giving letters of comfort. None of these is a contingent liability within the meaning of FRS12 since the likelihood of a transfer of economic benefit in settlement is too remote.

| UNRESTRICTED – Indemnities | 1 April 2007 £000 | Increase in year £000 | Liabilities crystallised in year £000 | Obligation expired in year £000 | 31 Mar 2008 £000 | Amount reported to Parliament by Departmental Minute £000 |
|---|---|---|---|---|---|---|
| Residual liability for the remediation of unidentified contamination in parts of the former Rosyth Naval Base which has been sold to Rosyth 2000 plc. | Up to 1,000 | | | | Up to 1,000 | 1,000 |
| Liabilities arising from insurance risk of exhibits on loan to the Army, Navy and RAF Museums. | 2,535 | 95 | | | 2,630 | |

## Quantifiable (Restricted)

**30.2** Details of restricted indemnities are not given because they are sensitive due to commercial confidentiality and/or national security.

## Unquantifiable (Unrestricted)

**30.3** The MoD has entered into the following unquantifiable contingent liabilities by offering guarantees, indemnities or by giving letters of comfort. None of these is a contingent liability within the meaning of FRS12 since the possibility of a transfer of economic benefit in settlement is too remote.

● Indemnity given in relation to the disposal of Gruinard Island in the event of claims arising from the outbreak of specific strains of anthrax on the Island.

● Indemnities to the Babcock Group in respect of nuclear risks under the Nuclear Installations Act 1965.

● Indemnities to the Babcock Group in respect of non-nuclear risks resulting from claims for damage to property or death and personal injury to a third party.

● Indemnity to Rolls-Royce Power for the non-insurance of the Rolls-Royce Core Factory and the Neptune Test Reactor facility for death and personal injury to a third party.

● Indemnity for residual commercial contracts claims liabilities arising from the disbanding of DERA as an MoD Trading Fund and the formation of QinetiQ on 1 July 2001.

● Indemnity for residual employee disease liability arising from the disbanding of DERA as an MoD Trading Fund and the formation of QinetiQ on 1 July 2001.

● Indemnity for public liability arising from the disbanding of DERA as an MoD Trading Fund and the formation of QinetiQ on 1 July 2001.

● Indemnity for environmental losses incurred by QinetiQ arising from certain defined materials at specific properties before the formation of QinetiQ on 1 July 2001.

## Unquantifiable (Restricted)

**30.4** Details of restricted liabilities are not given because they are sensitive due to commercial confidentiality and for national security.

These liabilities are unquantifiable due to the nature of the liability and the uncertainties surrounding them.

## 31. Losses and Special Payments

| CLOSED CASES: these comprise losses and special payments which have been formally signed off to date subsequent to a satisfactory completion of all the case work relating to the loss or special payment. Closed cases, therefore, include some cases which in the previous year were shown under Advance Notifications. | Arising in 2007-08 | Reported in 2006-07 as Advance Notifications |
|---|---|---|
| | £000 | £000 |
| Total (excluding gifts, special payments and War Pensions Benefits) under £250,000 each: 11,505 cases | 12,262 | |
| Total (excluding gifts, special payments and War Pensions Benefits) over £250,000 each: 26 cases (detailed below) | 143,188 | 179,088 |
| Totals | 155,450 | 179,088 |
| | | £000 |
| Total Value of Closed Cases – Arising in 2007-08 plus Cases Reported in 2006-07 as Advance Notifications | | 334,538 |
| Details of the 26 Closed Cases over £250,000 each are: | | |
| **Cash Losses** | | |
| Write-off of Control Account balances related to legacy military pay system issues. This represents 185 occurrences. (Central) | 301 | |
| **Bookkeeping Losses** Write-off of unsupported legacy asset balances formerly held in the Defence Procurement Agency and Defence Communication Services Agency prior to merger into DE&S, and following the migration of assets to the Single Balance Sheet Owner. The reported losses cover numerous items across a range of asset categories, principally in IT projects (£25,288K) and assets under construction (£21,156K). The items represent legacy balances that cannot be substantiated, and not a loss of assets. (DE&S) | 50,925 | |
| Write-off of unsupported balances following 2007-08 asset verification exercise. The loss consists of: £27.4M in respect of a duplicated asset (an Apache helicopter), £5.5M in respect of an asset sold in 2005 where the asset value incorrectly remained in the accounts and unverified assets of £3.8M. (DE&S) | 36,700 | |
| Write-off of unsupported assets under construction balances in British Forces Gibraltar. Capitalisation of various building projects was not possible due to errors in bookkeeping in a previous financial year. Consequently balances were unavailable to transfer to the Single Balance Sheet Owner. In consultation with the National Audit Office it was agreed that the expenditure should be written off. (CJO) | 17,772 | |
| A bookkeeping loss has arisen in respect of the write-off of an unsubstantiated debtor balance. The write-off has been accounted for during 2006-07. (DE&S) | | 12,893 |
| A bookkeeping loss has arisen in respect of the write-off of duplicated assets on the Fixed Asset Register following an asset verification exercise. (DE&S) | 10,349 | |
| Write-off of unsupported assets under construction following a verification exercise to clear unanalysed balances and legacy projects from Air Command's Fixed Asset Register (FAR). Following consultation with the National Audit Office, Air Command was advised that any balances which could not be substantiated would need to be written off prior to the year-end. The value written off relates to several projects which had been capitalised in error in a previous financial year and which were therefore, not transferred to the Single Balance Sheet Owner. (Air) | 8,099 | |
| A bookkeeping loss has arisen in respect of the write-off of a number of unsubstantiated Control Account Balances. The loss has been accounted for during 2006-07 and comprises erroneous balances on five Control Accounts that are believed to have been caused by system errors, spread over a period of four years. There has been no physical loss of cash. (DE&S) | | 7,180 |
| Write-off of Control Account balances due to an inability to reconcile balances for tax and National Insurance contributions paid to HM Revenue & Customs in 2000 with individuals' pay records. Impact is that transactions have been accounted for as overpayments resulting in write-off action. This represents 1,500 occurrences. (Central) | 3,627 | |
| Write-off of assets under construction unsupported balances where revenue expenditure was capitalised incorrectly. (Land) | 2,686 | |
| Write-off of unsupported assets under construction balances. In previous financial years, £2.6M of expenditure, mostly in Gibraltar, had been capitalised in error. (CJO) | 2,626 | |
| Write-off of unsupported legacy project balances during 2007-08. This is due largely to capitalisation of costs incurred after final delivery of the equipment. These balances are not transferred to the front line customer as asset deliveries once deliveries have been completed. A similar situation occurs, on a smaller scale, when Foreign Military Sales payments are made post closure of a project. (DE&S) | 2,220 | |
| Write-off of unsupported balances following the reconciliation of creditors prior to transfer of balances to the Purchase to Pay system. A number of creditor balances were understated. (Central) | 727 | |
| Write-off of refurbishment costs at HMS Collingwood Sport and Recreation Centre. The expenditure was capitalised in error during the preparation of the year-end accounts for financial year 2005-06. (FLEET) | 545 | |
| Write-off of asset balances following internal transfer without supporting evidence relating to the Princess Mary Hospital, Cyprus. (Central) | 514 | |

| CLOSED CASES: (continued) | Arising in 2007-08 £000 | Reported in 2006-07 as Advance Notifications £000 |
|---|---|---|
| **Losses of pay, allowances and superannuation benefits** | | |
| Write-off of Control Account balances related to legacy military pay system issues. This represents 82 occurrences. (Central) | | 1,479 |
| **Stores Losses** | | |
| The Cadet Hut, Kings School Winchester was destroyed by fire. (Land) | | 334 |
| **Claims waived or abandoned** | | |
| Following an annual review of the Service Level Agreement, a claim for Service Level Failure Charges against EDS waived. (Central) | | 3,715 |
| **Constructive Losses** | | |
| As a result of commitments under the Oslo Declaration on dumb cluster munitions, the Multiple Launch Rocket System containing the M26 bomblet was declared as out of service by the Secretary of State for Defence on 20 March 2007. The announcement also resulted in the withdrawal of the BL755 Air to Ground Unguided Cluster Bomb. Although plans were in place to dispose of the munitions, the revised out of service date has resulted in a write off of £112M (£101M for M26 and £11M for BL755). (DE&S) | | 112,000 |
| Reduction in the number of Integrated Biological Detection Systems following a strategic review of the United Kingdom's detection capability. In January 2006, the contractor (Lockheed Martin UK) reviewed the system and production performance achieved to date and, in agreement with the Integrated Project Team, extended the production schedule to include significant improvements to quality and performance control. However, during this period, the operational planning assumptions underpinning the biological detection Operational Analysis were reviewed and led to the reduction of the total number of systems required. (DE&S) | | 25,916 |
| The Nuclear, Biological and Chemical Battlefield System Application Project was cancelled by mutual agreement with the Contractor. Technical difficulties in pre-existing software introduced significant risks into the project which threatened its future success. (DE&S) | | 14,165 |
| Cancellation of a Radioactive Waste Processing Plant project following the decision to extend the life of the existing facility at Faslane. The project was beset by contractual, financial and timing problems and cancelled after external consultants had incurred expenditure on design activities. (DE&S) | 3,666 | |
| Additional Contractor costs arising from delays in installing Warship Electronic Chart Display and Information System (WECDIS) equipment. MoD was unable to provide the ships and installation guidance for the WECDIS project, and hence the Prime Contractor (Lockheed Martin UK) was unable to complete the work by the formal end date of the installation contract (31 December 2007). Under the terms of the contract the Prime Contractor is entitled to be paid on the basis that the Installation Teams were available to complete the work. (DE&S) | 1,510 | |
| Write-off relating to expenditure incurred by MoD in the preparation of infrastructure and instrumentation for a UK experiment incidental to a US explosive test to be conducted at the Nevada Test Site. The US test was subsequently cancelled. By way of compensation, the US Government has made available funds to the MoD to undertake tests at an alternative site in the US. (DE&S £466k and SIT £794k – 1 case) | 466 | 794 |
| A loss arising from the decision to close a 5 year old Sullage Treatment Plant as a result of a lack of a technical solution to suppress gas emissions, the need to replace corroded sullage vessels and a re-appraisal of the overall operational and financial effectiveness of the plant in light of changed circumstances. Construction costs of £1.3M have been offset by a recovery from the construction company who accepted liability of £0.6M in respect of the corroded sullage vessels. (DE&S) | | 612 |
| **Fruitless Payments** | | |
| Secondary contract and extra costs incurred for outstanding remedial work at the Composite Repair Facility at RNAS Culdrose, following a contractor liquidation. (FLEET) | 455 | |
| Totals | 143,188 | 179,088 |
| | | £000 |
| **Total of the 26 cases listed above** | | 322,276 |
| **International Courtesy Rules** Supplies and services provided on a reciprocal basis to Commonwealth and Foreign Navy vessels during visits to British Ports at Clyde, Portsmouth, Devonport and Gibraltar. (Central) | 2,587 | |
| **Special Payments** | | |
| Total under £250,000 each: 95 cases | 266 | |
| Total over £250,000 each: 2 cases (detailed below) | | 45,822 |
| Totals | 266 | 45,822 |

| CLOSED CASES: (continued) | Arising in 2007-08 | Reported in 2006-07 as Advance Notifications |
|---|---|---|
| | £000 | £000 |
| | | £000 |
| **Total Value of Special Payments – Arising in 2007-08 plus Cases Reported as Advance Notifications in 2006-07** | | 46,088 |
| Details of the 2 Special Payments over £250,000 each are: | | |
| Ex-gratia element of Northern Ireland Royal Irish Regiment redundancy payment relating to Normalisation arrangements in the Province. This represents payments made during 2007-08. Future payments are disclosed as an Advance Notification. (AG) | | 38,108 |
| Ex-gratia element of the Northern Ireland civilian redundancy payment relating to Normalisation arrangements in the Province. This represents payments made during 2007-08. Payments due to made in the period 2008 – 2010 are disclosed as an Advance Notification. (Land and DE) | | 7,714 |
| Total | | 45,822 |
| **Gifts** | | |
| Total under £250,000 each: 46 cases | **1,282** | |
| Total over £250,000 each: 3 cases (detailed below) | **4,311** | |
| Total | **5,593** | |
| Details of the 3 Cases over £250,000 each are: | | |
| Jaguar spares and a Challenger 2 Loader Trainer to the Government of Oman. Details of the transfer were notified to the House of Commons in a Departmental Minute dated 24 April 2007. (Central) | **1,174** | |
| 15 Up-armoured light protection vehicles (High Mobility Multi-Purpose Wheeled Vehicles) and a support package to the Government of Afghanistan. Details of the transfer were notified to the House of Commons in a Departmental Minute dated 10 July 2007. (Central) | **1,620** | |
| 25 Field Ambulances to the Government of Afghanistan. Details were notified to the House of Commons in a Departmental Minute dated 04 March 2008. | **1,517** | |
| Total | **4,311** | |
| **War Pensions Benefits (WPB):** | | |
| **Claims Abandoned-WPB** | | |
| Irrecoverable overpayments of war pensions relating to 2,622 cases amounting to £1,464,855 (2006-07: 2,623 cases amounting to £631,177) were written off. These represent overpayments of pensions which occur for a number of reasons outside of the MoD's control; this represented 0.14% of the total war pension payments budget of £1.027 billion. All overpayments are recorded as amounts outstanding and action is taken to recover these amounts. Where the overpayment was found to be irrecoverable, the decision was taken to waive the amount owed. | **1,465** | |
| Total | **1,465** | |
| **Special Payments-WPB** | | |
| Total number of payments made during the year was 533 (2006-07: 885) and amounted to £1,948,305 (2006-07: £5,215,885). These payments were for War Disability Pensions, and were made under the authority of Treasury Dispensing Instruments but outside the scope of the Service Pension order. These relate to the following payments: | | |
| (a)   Far Eastern Prisoners of War Ex-gratia payments | | |
| In the 2000 pre Budget speech, the Chancellor of the Exchequer announced that ex-gratia awards of £10,000 would be paid to surviving members of British groups held prisoner by the Japanese during the Second World War or their surviving spouses. Although the majority of cases have been paid in previous financial years, 39 claims were processed and paid in financial year 2007-08. The total payment amounted to £390,000. | | |
| Following a Judicial Review announced in November 2003, the scheme was expanded to allow payments to qualifying Gurkhas in Nepal. | **390** | |

| CLOSED CASES: (continued) | Arising in 2007-08 £000 | Reported in 2006-07 as Advance Notifications £000 |
|---|---|---|
| (b) Empire Air Training Scheme Pensions<br><br>These Payments relate to members of the Royal Australian Air Force who were trained under the Empire Air Training Scheme and were subsequently selected for service in the RAF. The British Government agreed in June 1942 that it would contribute towards pensions in respect of disablement or death due to the service with the RAF.<br><br>In 2007-08 the total number of cases was 274 (2006-07: 306 cases) and the cost amounted to £949,955 (2006-07: £1,110,189). | 950 | |
| (c) Noise Induced Sensorineural Hearing Loss<br><br>During financial year 2007-08 208 payments were made under the Dispensing Instruments totalling £540,471. (2006-07: 217 cases, £538,337). | 540 | |
| (d) Crown Agents Supplementation payments<br><br>Crown Agents Financial Services make payments to ex-members of the colonial forces who are resident in the UK and who have been awarded a disablement pension by the colonial government. The payment is a supplementation amount that increases the disablement pension to the rate equivalent to a UK war pension.<br><br>The Veterans Agency re-imburses Crown Agents Financial Services for these payments. During financial year 2007-08, the total number of cases was 12 (2006-07: 13 cases) and the amount payable was £67,879 (2006-07: £77,358). | 68 | |
| Total | 1,948 | |

| ADVANCE NOTIFICATIONS: these comprise losses and special payments, which arose during 2007-08 and prior years, but where the cases have not yet been formally signed off to date. A formal sign off cannot take place until all the work necessary to establish the validity of the loss or special payment, and the exact amount thereof, has been satisfactorily concluded. The amounts shown below are, therefore, only the best estimates, and are reflected in these accounts where appropriate. It is likely that, in many instances, the final value of these losses and special payments will differ from the estimates below when they are reported as closed in future years. Should the final value be less than £250,000, they will not be separately identified. | Arising in 2007-08 £000 | Reported in 2006-07 as Advance Notifications £000 |
|---|---|---|
| **Notified in prior years**<br>The value of 8 Chinook Mk3 helicopters has been written down by £205M under prudent accounting practices. The write down has arisen because, although the terms of the contract had been met, the helicopters do not currently meet the operational requirement and could not acquire Military Aircraft Release. The MoD intends to convert the Mk3 airframes to a modified Mk2 standard, with a revaluation of the 8 aircraft at the point of asset delivery. Whilst the value of the loss reported in the accounts is currently an estimate, the final write-off case, expected to be completed in 2008-09, will report the actual recalculated value of the loss. (DE&S) | | 205,000 |
| Slippage in the construction programme for two Landing Ship Dock (Auxiliary) caused delay in supplying design information and equipment to a contractor. This resulted in a claim on the MoD relating to the associated delay and dislocation costs. Following review, the potential loss has been reduced. (DE&S) | | 53,836 |
| A potential claim against a contractor on the Airborne Stand-Off Radar programme has been abandoned resulting in a loss, but other benefits have been secured in compensation. (DE&S) | | 28,000 |
| Cancellation of the Alternative Launcher Drive System programme has resulted in a potential write-off. (DE&S) | | 4,000 |
| A contractor is claiming extra costs resulting from the late delivery of unusable Global Positioning System chips in respect of the Storm Shadow missile programme, purchased via Foreign Military Sales. A related write-off of £1.8M for Variation of Price was recorded in the 2004-05 accounts. (DE&S) | | 4,000 |
| Write-off of unsupported balances following asset verification exercise. (DE) | | 2,983 |
| The payment of staff from public funds within a non-public organisation covering the period April 1999 to March 2007 – The British Möhnesee Sailing Club. (Land) | | 1,324 |
| The payment of staff from public funds within a non-public organisation covering the period April 1999 to March 2007 – The British Dümmersee Yacht Club. (Land) | | 1,313 |
| The estimated repair costs to the Type 45 Long Range Radar Antenna which was damaged during installation. (DE&S) | | 697 |
| In September 2006, four Sea King Gnome 1T engines were transported from Rolls-Royce East Kilbride to HMS Sultan using the Defence Storage and Distribution Agency. On arrival at HMS Sultan they were found to have been transported in the incorrect orientation, additionally one had suffered impact damage. All four engines had to be returned to the workshop for a full strip and overhaul at a total cost of £0.5M. (DE&S) | | 500 |

| ADVANCED NOTIFICATIONS: (continued) | Arising in 2007-08 £000 | Reported in 2006-07 as Advance Notifications £000 |
|---|---|---|
| A potential loss has been identified in respect of an overpayment made to a MoD contractor. Whilst repayment is being actively pursued, there is no assurance that the overpayment can be recovered owing to the statute of limitation restrictions. (Central) | | 372 |
| A food component was withdrawn from Operational Ration Packs following discovery in tests that deterioration of the product's packaging could over time compromise the safety of the contents. The Contractor accepted liability in principle for this defect and agreed to supply a replacement product utilising an alternative packaging arrangement, at no cost to MoD, subject to being able to develop a replacement product that could be warranted fully fit for purpose. This development work is continuing and, if successful, will substantially mitigate the overall loss to the MoD brought about by a combination of loss of use of the original product and the cost of its removal/ destruction. (DE&S) | | 315 |
| Mill Hill Garrison Pre-School Playgroup, a private enterprise, was allowed to trade from MoD property for the period April 1995 to March 2005 without due rent being raised. (Land) | | 267 |
| **Notified during the year** | | |
| **Cash Losses** | | |
| Ministry of Defence Police (MDP) Net Pay Deduction (NPD). Overpayments of salary were made to MDP officers between 1998 and 2008 due to a miscalculation of the rate of NPD for pension contributions. | 1,250 | |
| Minimum Drawing Rate (MDR) overpayments due to Joint Personnel Administration automation problems. (Central) | 700 | |
| **Bookkeeping losses and adjustments** | | |
| Write-off of unsupported balances following the reconciliation of legacy military pay control accounts prior to the transfer to the Joint Personnel Administration system. The loss is the estimated write-off following discussions with the contractor. (Central) | 3,580 | |
| Write-off following the reconciliation of the military Long Service Advance of Pay control account. This has arisen due to transfer from legacy pay systems to Joint Personnel Administration system where during reconciliation there was a difference between local records and the Joint Personnel Administration system. This represents the current estimate of write-off while the issue is under investigation. (Central) | 500 | |
| Write-off of unsupported control account balance from financial year 2003-04, following the internal transfer of responsibility for the management of computer training from Defence College of Management and Technology, Shrivenham to Defence Business Learning. (Central) | 331 | |
| **Losses of pay, allowances and superannuation benefits** | | |
| The introduction of an Infantry Financial Retention Incentive (FRI) in 2007-08 saw a number of infantry personnel receiving the FRI in error. (LAND) | 8,000 | |
| **Stores Losses** | | |
| Difference between Issue Transaction Summary and Unit holdings identified during an Equipment Capability Audit at 34 Field Hospital, HQ 2 Medical Brigade. Attributable to legacy equipment management and accounting issues from 2003 onwards. The loss represents a write-off of stock, which was disposed of in accordance with regulations, but not recorded in the accounts. (LAND) | 1,726 | |
| Loss of equipment at 34 Field Hospital, HQ 2 Medical Brigade identified during an Equipment Capability Audit in 2003. (LAND) | 339 | |
| **Constructive Losses** | | |
| Costs incurred by MoD as a result of the Department's failure to supply surplus Nimrod MR2 (Spey) engines to Rolls-Royce (RR) for refurbishment within the contractually agreed period. The Total Support Package for Nimrod is based on RR providing availability of engines and the MoD has contracted to release surplus engines within thirty days of an aircraft being withdrawn from service. A decision was taken to delay retirement of a number of Nimrod MR2 aircraft between July 2005 and May 2006, while the business case for the Nimrod MRA4 production contract was reviewed. Had the production contract for MRA4 been delayed or cancelled, the service life of the MR2 fleet would have had to be extended and their engines retained. The Rolls Royce claim is based on additional costs incurred in providing the contracted level of engine availability with a smaller pool of spare engines. (DE&S) | 953 | |

| ADVANCED NOTIFICATIONS: (continued) | Arising in 2007-08 £000 | Reported in 2006-07 as Advance Notifications £000 |
|---|---|---|
| **Fruitless Payments** | | |
| Cancellation of the Military Flying Management Information System (MFMIS) has resulted in nugatory expenditure. Technical difficulties and cost constraints, which introduced significant risk, had put in jeopardy the future success of the project. The decision was therefore taken to cancel the project. (DE&S) | 8,695 | |
| Write-off of the cost associated with the laying and removal of the slurry seal at RAF Brize Norton. Defence Estates and Royal Air Force Infrastructure Branch had instructed the contractor to use slurry seal as a surfacing material. However, the resurfacing began to fail after a few months as the slurry seal was not fit for purpose. The slurry seal treatment was abandoned and Marshall Asphalt laid instead. (DE) | 876 | |
| **Claims waived or abandoned** | | |
| Service Level Failure Charges against Electronic Data Services (EDS) waived by the Service Personnel and Veterans Agency during financial year 2007-08. The £9,323k represents the maximum sum which may be waived against service delivery failures under the Service Provision. The final assessments are still to be completed and in a few instances the maximum charge possible, or a proportion of it, may be invoked. A significant number of the charges were not invoked because service delivery failures were due to factors beyond EDS' control. (Central) | 9,323 | |
| A claim abandoned in respect of outstanding debts owed to MoD by Air Luxor, an airline which has ceased trading. (Air and CJO) | 733 | |
| Totals | 37,006 | 302,607 |

| | £000 |
|---|---|
| **Total Value of Advance Notifications – Arising in 2007-08 plus Reported and Arising in Prior Periods** | 339,613 |

| Special Payments – advance notifications requiring disclosure | Arising in 2007-08 £000 | Reported in 2006-07 £000 |
|---|---|---|
| **Notified in prior years** | | |
| Ex-gratia element of the Northern Ireland civilian redundancy payment relating to Normalisation arrangements in the Province. This represents payments due to be made in the period 2008 – 2010. Payments already made during 2007-08 are disclosed as a Closed Case. (Land and DE) | | 7,896 |
| Ex-gratia element of Northern Ireland Royal Irish Regiment redundancy payment relating to Normalisation arrangements in the Province. This represents payments due to be made. Payments already made during 2007-08 are disclosed as a Closed Case. (AG) | | 2,492 |
| **Notified during the year** | | |
| Armed Forces Memorial. The Armed Forces Memorial, located at the National Memorial Arboretum, Staffordshire, is dedicated to members of the UK Armed Forces killed on duty or as a result of terrorist action. In a Ministerial announcement to Parliament on 5 June 2008 the Department announced a Special Payment to cover an estimated £500k shortfall in the final construction cost. (Central) | 500 | |
| Totals | 500 | 10,388 |

| | £000 |
|---|---|
| **Total Value of Special Payments – Advanced Notifications Arising in 2007-08 plus Reported and Arising in Prior years** | 10,888 |

## Related Party Transactions

**32.1**    The Defence Science and Technology Laboratory, the UK Hydrographic Office, the Met Office, the Defence Aviation Repair Agency and ABRO operate as Executive Defence Agencies financed by Trading Fund.

The MoD has a 19.3% shareholding in QinetiQ Group plc and also holds a Special Share in the company; further details can be found at Note 15 – Investments. The MoD also appoints a Non-Executive Director to QinetiQ's Board; the appointment is currently held by Mr Colin Balmer.

The Navy Army Air Force Institutes (NAAFI), the Oil and Pipelines Agency and the Fleet Air Arm Museum, are Public Corporations.

The Trading Funds, QinetiQ Group plc, the Oil and Pipelines Agency, NAAFI and the Fleet Air Arm Museum are regarded as related parties outside the Departmental Boundary with which the Department has had material transactions. Transactions are carried out on terms which are contracted on an arms length basis, and are subject to internal and external audit. The values of transactions with some of these organisations are set out below and balances with the Trading Funds and NAAFI at year end, are in the following table:

| Organisation | Debtor Balances £000 | Creditor Balances £000 |
|---|---|---|
| Defence Science and Technology Laboratory | 5,438 | (86,602) |
| UK Hydrographic Office | 6,729 | (1,014) |
| Met Office | 7,294 | (9,814) |
| Defence Aviation Repair Agency | 4,506 | (5,546) |
| ABRO | 12,178 | (28,051) |
| NAAFI | 284 | - |

### Oil and Pipelines Agency (Public Corporation)

Agency Fees (excluding VAT): £1,800,000 (2006-07: £1,730,000)
Director General Joint Supply Chain and Director Defence Fuels Group are members of the Board of Directors.

### Fleet Air Arm Museum (Public Corporation)

Grant-in-Aid: £614,000 (2006-07: 593,000)
Assistant Chief of Staff (Carrier Strike Aviation), C-in-CFleet, Whale Island; Assistant Director Joint Manoeuvre, MoD, London; Director Operations, DG Helicopters, DE&S; Commanding Officer of the Naval Transition Team; Commanding Officer RNAS Culdrose and Commanding Officer RNAS Yeovilton are members of the Board of Trustees.

### Executive Non-Departmental Public Bodies (NDPBs)

**32.2** The following are Executive NDPBs of the MoD. They are designated NDPBs under the National Heritage Act 1983 and produce their own annual accounts, in accordance with the Charities (Accounts and Reports) Regulations 2005, on an accruals basis, and are regarded as related parties. During the period 1 April 2007 to 31 March 2008, each Executive NDPB had a material transaction with the Department, as listed below:

### National Army Museum

Grant-in-Aid: £5,489,000 (2006-07: £5,293,000)
The Department is not represented on the Board.

### Royal Air Force Museum

Grant-in-Aid: £7,019,000 (2006-07: £6,774,000)
The Department is not represented on the Board.

### Royal Marines Museum

Grant-in-Aid: £765,000 (2006-07: £741,000)
Director Royal Marines and Regimental Sergeant Major and the Corps Secretary, Royal Marines Corps are members of the Board of Trustees.

**Royal Naval Museum**

Grant-in-Aid: £873,000 (2006-07: £896,000)
Naval Base Commander Portsmouth and the Naval Secretary, CinCFleet, Whale Island were members of the Board of Trustees during the financial year.

**Royal Navy Submarine Museum**

Grant-in-Aid: £576,000 (2006-07: £562,000)
Rear Admiral Submarines is a member of the Board of Trustees.

**Other**

32.3     Sir Ian Andrews, Second Permanent Under Secretary of State, is a trustee of the Imperial War Museum. Mr Charles Miller Smith, until July 2007 a Non-Executive Director on the Defence Board, is the Chairman of Scottish Power. The Imperial War Museum and Scottish Power are therefore regarded as related parties of the Ministry of Defence and transactions between the organisations during the year were:

| | | £000 |
|---|---|---|
| Imperial War Museum | Various transactions-Payments | 62 |
| | Various transactions-Receipts | 3 |
| Scottish Power* | Various transactions-Payments | 12,972 |

*The prior year figure was incorrectly stated in the accounts. The value of transactions (payments) in 2006-07 was £12,131,000.

During the year various works of art and other items were transferred to and from the Imperial War Museum. No value was attributed to these items.

The Department also pays a number of grants to other bodies outside the Departmental Boundary. These include Grants-in-Aid to: the Council of Reserve Forces and Cadets Associations (CRFCA), prior to 2007-08 the CRFCA received grants which were accounted for as other expenditure at (Note 10 – Other Operating Costs), the Commonwealth War Graves Commission, the Royal Hospital Chelsea, the Marine Society & Sea Cadets, the Gurkha Welfare Scheme and Skill Force.

In addition, the MoD has had a number of transactions with other government departments and central government bodies. Most of the transactions have been with: the Foreign & Commonwealth Office, the Government Communications Headquarters, the Home Office, the Learning and Skills Council, the Department for Communities and Local Government, the Treasury Solicitor, the Cabinet Office, the Department for Work and Pensions, the Department for Environment Food and Rural Affairs, the National School of Government, HM Revenue and Customs and the Department for International Development.

**Joint Ventures**

32.4     There are no Joint Ventures within the Departmental accounting boundary. Some of the Trading Funds have set up Joint Ventures and the Department is involved in collaborative projects with various foreign countries for the development and production of Single Use Military Equipment.

## 33. Events After the Balance Sheet Date

**33.1** The Annual Report includes, under Future Developments, details of the formation of the Defence Support Group (DSG). As part of the process of setting up the new organisation the DARA Rotary Wing and Components businesses were sold to Vector Aerospace Ltd for £17M. The remaining elements of DARA merged with ABRO to form DSG. Completion of the sale and merger were effective from 1 April 2008 and will be reflected in the Department's 2008-09 Annual Report and Accounts.

**33.2** The financial statements included in the Annual Report and Accounts were authorised for issue on 17 July 2008.

## 34. Non-Operational Heritage Assets

**34.1** The Department owns a range of non-operational heritage assets from historically significant defence equipment, through archive information, to museum and art collections. In accordance with HM Treasury's Financial Reporting Manual (FReM), non-operational heritage assets are valued except where the cost of obtaining a valuation for the asset is not warranted in terms of the benefits it would deliver or where it is not possible to establish a sufficiently reliable valuation.

On the above basis, no non-operational heritage assets, except land, were valued at the year-end.

**34.2** The scope and diversity of the holdings of non-operational heritage assets which are not valued are illustrated by the examples detailed in the table below:

| Item | Location | Description |
|------|----------|-------------|
| HMS Victory | Portsmouth | HMS Victory is the world's oldest commissioned warship and is most famous for her role as Lord Nelson's Flagship at the Battle of Trafalgar. HMS Victory is open to the public, details are available at: www.hms-victory.com |
| Army Historic Aircraft Flight | Middle Wallop | Formed in 1977, the flight consists of seven aircraft and makes public appearances between May and September. Further information can be found at: http://www2.army.mod.uk/aac/display/ahaf_home/index.htm |
| Battle of Britain Memorial Flight | RAF Coningsby | The Memorial Flight operates 11 mainly World War II aircraft that appear at several hundred public events each year and can also be viewed at their hangar at RAF Coningsby. Further information is available at: www.bbmf.co.uk/index.html |
| Pickling Pond | HMNB Portsmouth | Pickling or mast ponds enabled long lengths of timber to be soaked before being used to build ships; well seasoned planks would not split or shrink in the water. |
| Enigma Machine | RAF Cosford | Cryptographic equipment captured during WW2 and used at Bletchley Park to assist in the breaking of German signal traffic. |
| Artefacts, records and artworks | Various locations | Over one hundred Regimental and Corps Museums and collections exist across the country. Ownership of the buildings and contents of the museums varies between the MoD, local authorities and regimental associations. The museums, which are open to the public, trace the history of the regiments and comprise displays of uniforms, weapons, medals and records. Further information is available at: http://www.army.mod.uk/events/museums/default.aspx |
| MoD Art Collection | Various locations | The MoD Art Collection comprises approximately 800 works of fine art and 250 antiques such as clocks and furniture. Many other miscellaneous items, such as photographs and manuscripts are contained in the archive. At the core of the collection are works commissioned by (and bequeathed to) the Admiralty during the 19th century, and those given to the Admiralty and to the War Office by the War Artists Commission at the end of the Second World War. Items from the MoD art collections are displayed in conference rooms and senior officers' accommodation throughout the Defence estate. The most important items are on permanent public display in the National Maritime Museum and on temporary loan to many other public museums and galleries. Further information is available at: www.mod.uk/DefenceInternet/AboutDefence/WhatWeDo/DefenceEstateandEnvironment/MODArtCollection |
| Records and artworks | London, Gosport, Stanmore | The Admiralty and Institute of Naval Medicine Libraries and the Air Historical Branch (RAF) comprise text and records of historical and research items. Although not open to the public, access is available on application. |

## 35. Entities within the Departmental Boundary

The entities within the boundary during 2007-08 were as follows:

**Executive Agencies**
Defence Analytical Services Agency
Defence Medical Education Training Agency
Defence Storage and Distribution Agency
Defence Vetting Agency
Ministry of Defence Police and Guarding Agency
People, Pay and Pensions Agency
Service Children's Education
Service Personnel and Veterans Agency

**Advisory Non-Departmental Public Bodies**
Advisory Committee on Conscientious Objectors
Advisory Group on Medical Countermeasures
Animal Welfare Advisory Committee
Armed Forces Pay Review Body
Central Advisory Committee on War Pensions
Defence Nuclear Safety Committee
Defence Scientific Advisory Council
National Employer Advisory Board
Nuclear Research Advisory Council
Review Board for Government Contracts
War Pensions Committees

Stakeholder Advisory Group – Op Telic Health Research Programme Review Board

Independent Monitoring Board – Independent Board of Visitors for Military Corrective Training Centre

## 36. Votes A Statement – Statement of Approved Maximum Armed Forces Numbers

36.1     Votes A provide the formal mechanism by which Parliament sets limits for and monitors the maximum numbers of personnel retained for service in the Armed Forces. They are presented to the House shortly before the start of each financial year (late February), and form part of the Parliamentary Supply process.

36.2     Votes A numbers represent uppermost limits for Service manpower; they neither predict actual strengths nor act as a control over numbers in the Services. Votes A includes a contingency margin to cover unforeseen circumstances. Manpower levels are monitored routinely, and if it is anticipated that the numbers could be breached, then a Supplementary Estimate may be required to increase the limit.

36.3     The tables included below compare, for each service, the numbers voted by the House of Commons with the maximum numbers maintained and the date at which this peak occurred. The aggregate maximum numbers maintained may not equal the sum of Officers plus Men and Women as these categories peak at different times of the year. The "Men and Women" categories represent the Services' Ratings and Other Ranks.

**36.4**   Maximum numbers of personnel to be maintained for service with the Armed Forces:

| | | Numbers voted by the House of Commons | Maximum Numbers Maintained | Peak Dates |
|---|---|---|---|---|
| **NAVAL SERVICE** | | | | |
| Royal Navy | Officers | 7,400 | 6,780 | April 2007 |
| | Men and Women | 26,670 | 24,590 | April 2007 |
| | Aggregate | 34,070 | 31,370 | April 2007 |
| Royal Marines | Officers | 930 | 820 | November 2007 |
| | Men and Women | 7,240 | 6,850 | March 2008 |
| | Aggregate | 8,170 | 7,650 | January 2008 |
| **ARMY SERVICE** | | | | |
| Army | Officers | 16,380 | 14,880 | June 2007 |
| | Men and Women | 104,900 | 94,440 | February 2008 |
| | Aggregate | 121,280 | 109,120 | February 2008 |
| | | | | |
| Gurkhas | Officers | 190 | 170 | October 2007 |
| | Men and Women | 4,315 | 3,980 | August 2007 |
| | Aggregate | 4,505 | 4,140 | August 2007 |
| | | | | |
| **AIR FORCE SERVICE** | | | | |
| Royal Air Force | Officers | 10,580 | 9,890 | April 2007 |
| | Men and Women | 37,780 | 35,480 | April 2007 |
| | Aggregate | 48,360 | 45,370 | April 2007 |

**36.5**   Maximum numbers of personnel to be maintained for service with the Reserve Forces:

| | | Numbers voted by the House of Commons | Maximum Numbers Maintained | Peak Dates |
|---|---|---|---|---|
| **NAVAL SERVICE** | | | | |
| Royal Fleet Reserve | Officers | 5,600 | 5,099 | April 2007 |
| (Navy) | Men and Women | 4,400 | 4,346 | March 2008 |
| | Aggregate | 10,000 | 9,035 | May 2007 |
| Royal Fleet Reserve | Officers | 420 | 363 | March 2008 |
| (Marines) | Men and Women | 1,350 | 1,278 | May 2007 |
| | Aggregate | 1,770 | 1,638 | May 2007 |
| Royal Naval Reserve | Officers | 1,160 | 886 | April 2007 |
| | Men and Women | 1,750 | 1,237 | April 2007 |
| | Aggregate | 2,910 | 2,123 | April 2007 |
| Royal Marines Reserve | Officers | 100 | 54 | April 2007 |
| | Men and Women | 920 | 769 | February 2008 |
| | Aggregate | 1,020 | 821 | February 2008 |
| Royal Naval Reserve List 7 | Officers | 900 | 724 | April 2007 |
| **ARMY SERVICE** | | | | |
| Army Reserve | Officers | 11,000 | 10,410 | March 2008 |
| | Men and Women | 26,000 | 24,290 | March 2008 |
| | Aggregate | 37,000 | 34,700 | March 2008 |
| Territorial Army | Officers | 7,500 | 4,610 | March 2008 |
| | Men and Women | 39,500 | 25,390 | March 2008 |
| | Aggregate | 47,000 | 30,000 | March 2008 |

| | | Numbers voted by the House of Commons | Maximum Numbers Maintained | Peak Dates |
|---|---|---|---|---|
| **AIR FORCE SERVICE** | | | | |
| Royal Air Force Reserve | Officers | 4,750 | 3,746 | August 2007 |
| | Men and Women | 15,250 | 7,940 | April 2007 |
| | Aggregate | 20,000 | 11,662 | April 2007 |
| Royal Auxiliary Air Force | Officers | 650 | 242 | February 2008 |
| | Men and Women | 2,400 | 1,230 | March 2008 |
| | Aggregate | 3,050 | 1,471 | February 2008 |

**36.6** Maximum numbers of personnel to be maintained for service as special members with the Reserve Forces:

| | | Numbers voted by the House of Commons | Maximum Numbers Maintained | Peak Dates |
|---|---|---|---|---|
| **NAVAL SERVICE** | | | | |
| Royal Naval Reserve | Officers | 720 | 108 | April 2007 |
| | Men and Women | 1,300 | 99 | October 2007 |
| | Aggregate | 2,020 | 204 | April 2007 |
| **ARMY SERVICE** | | | | |
| Territorial Army | Officers | 1,000 | - | - |
| | Men and Women | 5,000 | 85 | March 2008 |
| | Aggregate | 6,000 | 85 | March 2008 |
| **AIR FORCE SERVICE** | | | | |
| Royal Air Force Reserve | Officers | 150 | 58 | February 2008 |
| | Men and Women | 400 | 66 | January 2008 |
| | Aggregate | 550 | 123 | March 2008 |

The Armed Forces figure uses data from the Joint Personnel Administration system and is subject to validation; as a result, Army statistics from 1 April 2007, and Navy and RAF statistics from 1 May 2007 are provisional and subject to change

# Annexes

# Annex A

## Accountability to parliament

Ministers have accounted to Parliament during 2007-08 on all aspects of the Department's business. 4,497 Parliamentary Questions were tabled, Defence Ministers participated in 19 debates on defence issues in the House of Commons and six in the House of Lords and responded to 12 Adjournment Debates in Westminster Hall. Ministers made five oral statements to the House of Commons and four to the House of Lords. They also made 104 written statements to the House of Commons and the House of Lords. Details are published in Hansard.

## Evidence to House of Commons Defence Committee

Since 1 April 2007 the Ministry of Defence has also given evidence to the House of Commons Defence Committee on a number of occasions covering a wide range of issues, and the Government has responded to a number of the Committee's reports. All Committee publications, including published evidence given to the Committee, are available at: www.parliament.uk/parliamentary_committees/defence_committee.cfm

## Session 2006-07

Reports (Government Responses are listed in brackets after the report they relate to)

| | | |
|---|---|---|
| Twelfth Report HC 835 (HC 1026) | **Ministry of Defence Main Estimates 2007-08** | published 10 July 2007 |
| Thirteenth Report HC 408 (HC 1024) | **UK operations in Afghanistan** | published 18 July 2007 |
| Fourteenth Report HC 117 (CM 7620) | **Strategic Export Controls: 2007 Review** | published 7 August 2007 |
| Fifteenth Report HC 535 (HC 109) | **The Work of Defence Estates** | published 14 September 2007 |

## Session 2007-08

| | | |
|---|---|---|
| First Report HC 110 (HC 352) | **UK land operations in Iraq 2007** | published 3 December 2007 |
| Second Report HC 138 | **Costs of operations in Iraq and Afghanistan: Winter Supplementary Estimate 2007-08** | published 5 December 2007 |
| Third Report HC 107 (HC 375) | **UK/US Defence Trade Cooperation Treaty** | published 11 December 2007 |
| Fourth Report HC 181 | **The Iran hostages incident: the lessons learned** | published 14 December 2007 |

| | | |
|---|---|---|
| Fifth Report HC 61 | **Ministry of Defence Annual Report and Accounts 2006-07** | published 28 January 2008 |
| Sixth Report HC 274 | **The work of the Committee in 2007** | published 31 January 2008 |
| Seventh Report HC 327 | **Medical care for the Armed Forces** | published 18 February 2008 |
| Eighth Report HC 400 | **Operational costs in Afghanistan and Iraq: Spring Supplementary Estimate 2007-08** | published 10 March 2008 |
| Ninth Report HC 111 | **The future of NATO and European Defence** | published on 20 March 2008 |
| Tenth Report HC 295 | **Defence Equipment 2008** | Published on 27 March 2008 |

The Defence Committee also undertook a number of visits to military establishments both in the UK and overseas as part of its inquiries, as shown in the table below.

## Defence Committee visits to military establishments

| Date of Visit | Establishment | Related Inquiry |
|---|---|---|
| 17-20 Apr 07 | Afghanistan | UK operations in Afghanistan |
| 24 May 07 | Hounslow and Pirbright Barracks | Defence Estates |
| 14 Jun 07 | Headley Court | Medical Care for the Armed Forces |
| 21 Jun 07 | RCDM Birmingham | Medical Care for the Armed Forces |
| 7-12 Jul 07 | Iraq and Kuwait | UK operations in Iraq |
| 31 Jul 07 | FRES Trials of Truth at Bovington | FRES |
| 4 Oct 07 | RFA Argus (Portsmouth) | Medical Care for the Armed Forces |
| 10 Oct 07 | Army Medical Service Training Centre, Strensall | Medical Care for the Armed Forces |
| 11 Oct 07 | Redford Barracks | Medical Care for the Armed Forces |
| 2 Nov 07 | Frimley Park MDHU | Medical Care for the Armed Forces |
| 16 Nov 07 | Portsmouth MDHU | Medical Care for the Armed Forces |
| 23 Nov 07 | Northallerton MDHU | Medical Care for the Armed Forces |
| 23 Nov 07 | Derriford MDHU | Medical Care for the Armed Forces |

## Evidence to Select Committees of the House of Commons and House of Lords

Since 1 April 2007 the Ministry of Defence has also given written and oral evidence on various issues to the following Select Committees of the House of Commons and House of Lords: All Committee publications, including published evidence given to the Committee, are available at: http://www.parliament.uk/parliamentary_committees/parliamentary_committees11.cfm

### Session 2006-07

| Reports (Government Responses are listed in brackets after the report) | | |
|---|---|---|
| Joint Committee on Human Rights HL 128/HC 728 | **Monitoring the Government's Response to Court Judgements Finding breaches of Human Rights** | published 28 June 2007 |
| Science and Technology Committee HC 66-1 + HC 66-11 | **2007: A Space Policy** | Published on 17 July 2007 |
| HoC Science and Technology Committee HC 472-1 + HC 472-11 | **International Policies and Activities of the Research Councils** | published 31 July 2007 |
| Joint Committee on the Draft Climate Change Bill HL 170-1/HC 542-1 + HL 170-11/HC 542-II | **Draft Climate Change Bill** | published 3 August 2007 |
| HoL EU Committee HL 161 | **Current Developments in EU Defence Policy** | published 6 August 2007 |
| HoC Science and Technology Committee HC 470-1 | **Investigating the Oceans** | published 18 October 2007 |
| Environment Audit Committee HC 740 (HC 276) | **The Structure of Government and the challenge of Climate change** | published 29 October 2007 |

### Session 2007-08

| | | |
|---|---|---|
| HoL European Union Committee HL 62-1 | **The Treaty of Lisbon: an impact assessment** | published 13 March 2008 |

## Evidence to Public Accounts Committee and Reports

We have also given evidence to the Public Accounts Committee, as shown in the tables below.

### Session 2006-07

| Reports (Government Responses are listed in brackets after the report) | | |
|---|---|---|
| Thirteenth Report | Smarter Food Procurement in the Public Sector | HC 357 (Cm 6908) |
| Fourteenth Report | Delivering Digital Tactical Communications through the Bowman CIP Programme | HC 358 (Cm 7077) |
| Twenty First Report | Progress in Combat Identification | HC 486 (Cm 7151) |
| Thirty Fourth Report | Recruitment and Retention in the Armed Forces | HC 43 (Cm 7216) |
| Thirty Sixth Report | Reserve Forces | HC 729 (Cm 7216) |
| Forty Sixth Report | Major Projects Report 2006 | HC 295 (Cm 7275) |
| Sixty First Report | Managing the Defence Estate | HC 537 (Cm 7322) |

### Session 2007-08

| Reports (Government Responses are listed in brackets after the report) | | |
|---|---|---|
| **MoD Evidence** Major Projects Report 2007 | Oral Evidence given by Sir Bill Jeffrey KCB, Permanent Under Secretary, General Sir Kevin O'Donoghue KCBE, CBE and Lieutenant General Sir Andrew Figgures CBE, Deputy Chief of Defence Staff (Equipment Capability), Ministry of Defence | HC 433-i |
| Leaving the Services | Oral evidence given by Sir Bill Jeffrey, KCB Permanent Under Secretary, Mr Chris Baker, OBE, Director General Service Personnel Policy and Air Commodore Phil Miles, Director of Resettlement, Ministry of Defence | HC 351-i |
| The Privatisation of QinetiQ | Oral evidence given by Mr Bill Jeffrey, CB Permanent Under Secretary and Trevor Woolley, Finance Director, Ministry of Defence; Mr Peter Schofield, Director, Shareholder Executive; and Sir John Chisholm, Chairman QinetiQ. | HC 151-i |

## Public Accounts Committee Recommendations

Thirteenth Report (2006-07) Smarter
Food Procurement in the Public Sector

| PAC Recommendations | Response Reported in the Treasury Minute |
|---|---|
| **PAC conclusion (v): For many children and adults, publicly provided meals form a key element in their daily diet, but not all public bodies make the most of the opportunity to promote healthier eating. They and their contractors should assess regularly the dietary requirements of all their existing and potential customers, including the elderly and those from ethnic and religious minority communities, canvassing customer views as part of regular quality audits of catering services. Frontline organisations should work with contract caterers to introduce healthier food combined with educational events that encourage healthy eating, and introduce 'traffic light' systems to highlight the nutritional value of each menu option.** | The MoD accepts this conclusion. The MoD's nutritional policy is set by the Expert Panel on Armed Forces Feeding (EPAFF), whose overarching aim is to educate Service personnel about nutrition and healthy eating. Under the direction of EPAFF, a series of nutritional guides for commanders, caterers and individuals has been developed and issued. In addition, a nutritional DVD has also been made available to all Service units with a supporting presentation to reinforce the message being sent to recruit training units. The MoD also established a web-based service for personnel to seek nutritional advice from their consultant dieticians and nutritionists. |
| **PAC conclusion (vi): There are wide disparities in the prices paid by public bodies for the same food items, ranging from between 32 pence and £1.10 for a standard 800g loaf of wholemeal bread, and between 17 and 44 pence for a pint of milk. Following the example of the Ministry of Defence, Departments should conduct regular benchmarking surveys or draw upon publicly available or commercially generated pricing information, and secure explanations from frontline organisations where significant price variations exist. They should also encourage greater use of e procurement methods to stimulate increased competition and greater transparency of prices through, for example, e-auctions.** | The MoD accepts this conclusion. The use of e-auctions contributed to the savings achieved within food procurement as part of the Supply Chain Excellence Programme. The MoD continues to conduct regular benchmarking surveys and e-auctions. |

| PAC Recommendations | Response Reported in the Treasury Minute |
|---|---|
| **PAC conclusion (vii): A lack of commercial skills and knowledge about the specialist food and catering market undermines the ability of frontline procurers to strike good deals with the major national wholesale food or multi-national contract catering companies. The three Departments (the Department for Education and Skills, the Ministry of Defence and the NHS Purchasing and Supply Agency) and the Prison Service, working with the Office of Government Commerce, should use their collective purchasing power to negotiate with the major food and catering firms for a larger share of the £95 million earned annually by contract catering firms from their suppliers by way of volume discounts and rebates.** | The MoD does not accept that there is a lack of commercial skills/market knowledge within its organisation, which prevents it from placing competitive sourcing arrangements. The MoD has a dedicated commercial team and employs within the Defence Food Services Integrated Project Team, staff with specialist food and catering knowledge, who continue to refresh their knowledge of the market through training, development and research. The MoD has also invested in developing a Category Management Team that supports the activities of the commercial and catering staff and shares information with other Government Departments via the OGC's Food Procurement Group. |
| **PAC conclusion (xi): The Committee expects to see measurable progress within two years (by 2008-09) towards savings of some £20 million promised by the Ministry of Defence over the five year life of its new main food contract.** | The conclusion is accepted by the MoD, in so far as their contract will realise the quoted savings over the life of the contract. |
| **PAC conclusion (xii): The National Audit Office has demonstrated that it is possible for public bodies to increase the proportion of food purchased competitively from local or regional producers while complying with EU requirements. Following the lead of the Ministry of Defence in working with the UK meat industry, the three departments together with the Department of Environment, Food and Rural Affairs, should explore with UK food producers ways to increase the amount of UK produce purchased by the public sector. Public bodies should also be able to demonstrate that the animal welfare and food production practices of their suppliers adhere to the standards under which UK producers operate and satisfy themselves that enough independent spot checks and inspections are taking place.** | The conclusion is accepted, in part, by MoD as it reflects the present working practices within the Department, particularly in the context of the department's working relationship with the UK meat industry. The MoD does, however, need to ensure the year round availability of its 'Core List' commodities, which supply our worldwide operational commitments. This cannot be achieved, cost effectively, with a policy of local or regional buying alone. |
| **PAC conclusion (xiv): Public sector procurers should seek to increase the proportion of food purchased from 'Fair Trade' sources that offer the same standard at a competitive price. In some cases fair trade products will be more expensive but departments should work with the supply chain to improve competitiveness while still securing a fair price for producers.** | The conclusion is accepted by MoD. It is the intention of the MoD to test, through its Food Selection Panel, a wider range of fair trade products in the future for inclusion on the 'Core List'. |

Fourteenth Report (2006-07) Delivering Digital
Tactical Communications through the Bowman
CIP Programme

| PAC Recommendations | Response Reported in the Treasury Minute |
|---|---|
| **PAC conclusion (i): There is no individual within the Department with full responsibility for ensuring that the Bowman CIP project meets its objectives. In 2006, the Department belatedly appointed a senior officer to act as Senior Responsible Owner. But he lacks the authority and time to effectively discharge this onerous responsibility and is only supported by a small staff. In applying the Senior Responsible Owner concept, the Department should equip those appointed to such challenging positions with the funding, authority and trust to fully discharge their responsibilities in line with the guidance issued by the Office of Government Commerce.** | The Department notes the Committee's views and agrees that in its earlier stages the Bowman and CIP projects would have benefited from stronger high-level governance arrangements. The Department believes that the governance arrangements, which were developed in the light of the OGC guidance in 2003 and as the programme evolved provide a robust framework for delivering the Bowman CIP programme. The senior officer now responsible for the delivery of networks such as Bowman CIP that underpin Network Enabled Capability (NEC) has the authority, position within the Department and support to ensure that obstacles to delivery are addressed and overcome while maintaining coherence with other projects supporting the wider NEC capability.

It is the Department's policy that large and complex projects or groups of projects will have a senior responsible owner appointed on behalf of and accountable to the Defence Management Board. In addition, under the Department's Defence Acquisition Change Programme, the Directors of Equipment Capability will fulfil the senior responsible owner role for each of their projects that are not covered by specific SRO appointments. Although the senior responsible owner may not have full financial or command/line management authority over all those delivering the projects, he or she will be empowered, have a good knowledge of the requirement, be competent to resolve conflicting priorities and be able to exert influence outside traditional management or command chains. This is consistent with the OGC guidance. |

| PAC Recommendations | Response Reported in the Treasury Minute |
|---|---|
| **PAC conclusion (ii): The Department took nine months to approve the revised deal struck with General Dynamics UK in October 2005. Time is money for the Department and its contractors, and delaying delivery of a much-needed capability could also cost lives. The Department intends to action the relevant recommendations from its Enabling Acquisition Change review to improve its in-house approvals processes. The Department should also engage the Treasury and other relevant government departments in developing a leaner, more responsive approval process so that decisions can be made in a more-timely manner.** | The Department agrees that responsiveness is an important attribute of the investment approvals process, alongside the need to ensure that proposals are soundly based and provide good value for money.<br><br>Implementation of the recommendations of the Enabling Acquisition Change report is being taken forward through the Defence Acquisition Change Programme.<br>A number of changes to the approvals process have already been made. These include:<br><br>• the involvement of the Defence Management Board in the most significant investment decisions;<br><br>• the addition of the Defence Commercial Director to membership of the Department's Investment Approvals Board; and<br><br>• the delegation of the approval of the lower value lower risk equipment and support projects to the new Defence Equipment and Support organisation.<br><br>Other changes that will be introduced shortly include:<br><br>• a more streamlined scrutiny process which aims to ensure that project teams have, at an early stage, a clearer picture of the information required at the main decision points and simplifies the production of business cases;<br><br>• for larger projects, the inclusion of support costs in Main Gate equipment approvals;<br><br>• independent cost estimates; and<br><br>• the requirement to carry out commercial due diligence before contract signature.<br><br>The Department is engaged with HM Treasury to develop a more responsive procurement approvals process. Although engagement with other Government Departments does take place in the context of the approvals process, this does not impact on approval timelines. |

| PAC Recommendations | Response Reported in the Treasury Minute |
|---|---|
| **PAC conclusion (iii): The Bowman CIP project timescale was clearly unrealistic, and the inherent complexity and technological challenges were under-estimated. The Department should re-design its scrutiny processes and better align these and its assurance processes so that they are fit to deal with the challenges of modern defence acquisitions and to take into account the culture of over-optimism endemic in much defence procurement.** | The Department accepts the general thrust of the Committee's views. The Department recognises that the timescales set for the Bowman and CIP projects were challenging and was aware of the potential technical and complexity challenges, but on balance believed that the risks were worth taking in order to achieve coherence between the two projects and the earliest possible delivery of this important new capability. The deployment on operations of a militarily useful Bowman CIP from April 2005 was an important step forward. The Department recognises, as a general issue, the need for greater realism in the planning of defence capability and agility in the acquisition system.<br><br>Changes being introduced through the Defence Acquisition Change Programme, including the streamlining of process, better cost estimating and greater use of incremental acquisition are aimed at improving the acquisition system to provide better delivery of capability to the front line, and improved value for money for the taxpayer. |
| **PAC conclusion (iv): The vehicle conversion challenge posed by the unexpected variation in the land vehicle fleet could have been predicted if the fleet had been properly surveyed before contracts were placed. The problem was compounded by the absence of good data on vehicle configurations, and the practice, particularly in the army, of modifying vehicles without managing and tracking the modifications. Until the Department obtains adequate standing information on vehicle condition and configuration, it should re-emphasise to Users the importance of maintaining standard configurations wherever possible and should survey representative samples of vehicles before commencing modification work.** | The Department accepts that there is an issue with capturing and tracking information about modifications to vehicles. The UK armed forces' vehicle fleet consists of many types, which in some cases are themselves sub-divided into many variants according to role and parent unit. This fleet is, in some cases, up to 40 years old and over time and for good reasons has been subject to extensive modifications to meet the evolving operational or safety environment.<br><br>Given the general knowledge the Department had about the age and condition of the vehicle fleet, it was recognised that configuration control was an issue at the outset of Bowman conversion. A platform presentation programme was put in place that brought some commonality to the fleets but could not allow for platform-to-platform variations. The Department accepts in retrospect that more detailed survey and preparation work would have enabled the true scale of the variations present in the vehicle fleets to be better understood and the conversion programme to have proceeded more smoothly.<br><br>As a result in part of experience with the Bowman CIP conversion programme the Department is working hard to address vehicle configuration control issues and believes significant improvements will flow as more capable electronic engineering and configuration management systems enter service. Until then, the better use of existing data alongside revised processes within the Army will deliver worthwhile improvements. |

| PAC Recommendations | Response Reported in the Treasury Minute |
|---|---|
| **PAC conclusion (v): Complex new systems such as Bowman CIP are more expensive to support and will require more on-going training than their simpler predecessors. To encourage more serious consideration of Through Life Management issues and better inform future investment decisions, the Department should validate the quality of the key data underpinning decisions on the delivery of through life management capability including measures of financial maturity, and clarity about the capability needed.** | The Department agrees that clarity on requirements and the quality of data are key factors in the successful delivery of through life capability management. The Defence Acquisition Change Programme is addressing these issues. For example, the Department's capability planning process has been reformed to support through life capability management and now follows a multi-stage process to establish capability requirements, identifying risk and pressures relating to such areas as the industrial capacity, funding and maintaining the effectiveness of current capability.<br><br>Implementation of this process is expected to mature towards the end of 2007. Much of the data that underpins this work is generated by the newly formed Defence Equipment and Support (DE&S) organisation through its equipment Through Life Management Plans (TLMPs). The DE&S has initiated a programme of work to simplify and improve the design of TLMPs and complete a 100 per cent refresh of the data they contain by the end of the current financial year. |
| **PAC conclusion (vi): Bowman CIP was accepted in service in March 2004 with 27 major provisos that reflect the limited operational capability of the initial system. The Department should only accept that General Dynamics UK has cleared the provisos on the basis of robust trials-based evidence and should not pay any outstanding amounts until it is satisfied that the Armed Services are getting the capability they asked for.** | The Department agrees with the Committee on the importance of robust testing and trialing as a basis for accepting equipment into service. Acceptance of the next increment of Bowman CIP (Bowman CIP 5) will be based on the evidence gathered through extensive trialing activity in 2006 and 2007. These trials will graduate from highly demanding technical field trials to operational field trialing in the hands of the user. This trialing methodology will ensure that the capability delivered by General Dynamics UK is fully verified and validated before it is deployed on operations.<br><br>Included in this process is the clearance of outstanding provisos against full systems acceptance. In order to ensure the delivery of the required capability a number of significant outstanding payments to General Dynamics UK remain and will be held pending the delivery of the contracted requirement. |

| PAC Recommendations | Response Reported in the Treasury Minute |
|---|---|
| **PAC conclusion (vii): The Department has removed several important capabilities from the existing Bowman CIP programme. The Department has developed plans which it is confident will now deliver the most vital aspects of capability without further delay. The capabilities being delayed, such as the ability to communicate with allies, remain important, not least to reduce the risk of further friendly fire deaths. The Department is confident that, to date, no lives have been lost due to this deferral. It should, within the next year, develop a realistic forward plan to ensure the Armed Forces do not have to forego these capabilities for longer than is absolutely necessary.** | The Department remains confident that the revised Bowman CIP programme approved in 2006 will deliver the coherent and stable austere Bowman CIP capability necessary to provide the basis for Network Enabled Capability in the land environment. The Department notes that this level of capability, Bowman CIP 5, will improve on the ability of the current version to communicate with allies by secure voice by also providing an ability to transfer standard formatted messages or e-mail with allies, as explained in the supplementary memorandum of evidence submitted in response to Question 155. Bowman CIP will therefore increasingly contribute to our Combat Identification capability and the minimisation of the risk of fratricide.<br><br>The Department continues to believe that the deferral of technically risky capability from the current Bowman CIP programme was prudent. The Department confirms that it is working to define plans for future capability releases beyond Bowman CIP 5 and expects to consider these plans as part of its routine planning process. Among the factors that will shape these plans are the ability of the front line to absorb further large-scale changes and the constraints imposed by operational tempo.<br><br>The Department envisages a periodic capability release programme providing both capability enhancements and maintenance that will be informed by the current validation work on the delivery of deferred capability. |

| PAC Recommendations | Response Reported in the Treasury Minute |
|---|---|
| **PAC conclusion (i): The Department has failed to develop viable Combat Identification solutions to counter the risks of friendly fire incidents, despite their devastating effects, and despite the recommendations made by the Committee of Public Accounts in both 1992 and 2002. Some improvements have been made, for example for air and naval operations, but the Department needs to address the outstanding areas without further delay.** | The Department fully recognises the importance of Combat Identification in enabling the Armed Forces to conduct military engagements quickly and decisively with the minimum overall casualties and to minimise the risk of fratricide in combat. The Department notes for example the historically very low overall level of combat casualties in war fighting operations in Iraq in 1991 and 2003 as an important measure of military effectiveness to which Combat Identification contributes. However, the Department accepts that there is more that can be done to improve the Combat Identification capability of the Armed Forces. To this end, a Senior Responsible Owner for Combat Identification was appointed in 2004 to lead the Department's Combat Identification programme in a step change improvement in the Department's capability. The Department also identified priority areas for improving Combat Identification capability, broadly the challenging ground to ground and air to ground environments and when fighting alongside coalition partners. |
| | The Department has a well defined policy on Combat Identification and continues to invest heavily in a range of equipment systems that contribute to Combat Identification capability, to play a leading role in co-ordinating Allied efforts on interoperable technical and procedural solutions and to pursue improvements across all elements of military capability, including organisation, concepts and doctrine, information and training as well as equipment. The Department's view is that, given the nature of warfare, the complete elimination of the risk of fratricide is not a realistic aim. |
| | The Department's Combat ID programme is addressing current operations and establishing enduring capability for the long term. Improved capability, such as the Bowman secure tactical radio communications system, has been deployed on operations, as well as equipment to meet specific operational requirements such as blue force tracking systems, improved targeting pods for ground attack aircraft and ground-to-air radios which enable UK ground patrols to talk directly to Coalition aircraft. Improved equipment for forward air controllers is also being delivered and improved tactics; techniques and procedures for air-to- ground operations have been introduced. It is also planned to introduce into theatre later this year a significantly enhanced reconnaissance and surveillance capability using the Reaper (formerly known as Predator B) and Hermes 450 Unmanned Aerial Vehicle (UAV) systems. |

| PAC Recommendations | Response Reported in the Treasury Minute |
|---|---|
| | For the longer term, the introduction over the next few years of new capabilities such as the ASTOR airborne radar surveillance system will improve enduring capability. To guide longer-term activity, a full-scale audit of Combat Identification capability to identify current capability and shortfalls is being conducted, building on earlier work. This, together with more use of operational analysis and human factors research will help to address balance of investment issues and inform decisions to be made on investment in new or enhanced capability. The Department continues to work closely with the United States and NATO partners on achieving interoperability within Combat Identification. For example, the Department is actively involved in Exercise BOLD QUEST, a multinational technology demonstration in the United States in September 2007 that will help to inform UK decisions on investment in interoperable air-to-ground capability and will explore a more networked approach to Combat Identification.<br><br>The Department is also reviewing the implementation of its Combat Identification programme to ensure that it conforms to the Office of Government Commerce best practice model for change programmes. |
| **PAC conclusion (ii): Over half of the equipment programmes for Combat Identification have been delayed, deferred or re-scoped during the last four years. A Battlefield Target Identification System will not be available until early in the next decade. Equipments such as Blue Force Tracker and Bowman communications system may improve situational awareness in the meantime, but the inevitable time lag in analysing and collating information from these systems will restrict their potential for positive target identification. The Department therefore needs to develop a timetabled plan for introducing a credible target identification system.** | Improvements in situational awareness through developments such as Bowman will undoubtedly contribute significantly to Combat Identification; but the Department accepts that introducing such capability to provide reliable positive identification in near real time in the complex ground and air-to-ground environments within the foreseeable future is not realistic, given the challenges involved. Target identification systems are likely to remain a pillar of Combat Identification capability. The Department accordingly continues to work on improving target identification systems with a focus on the priority areas of the ground and air-to-ground environments. Technical solutions have been slow to mature and while the Battlefield Target Identification System concept was initially seen as promising, it has been clear for some time that such a target identification system would not on its own effectively address the risk of fratricide across the priority areas.<br><br>The Department has therefore identified, in close co-operation with allies, a range of potential target identification technologies (including the Battlefield Target Identification System) that could provide interoperable solutions across the priority areas. Coherent programmes for credible target identification systems based on interoperable technologies will be considered as part of the Department's routine planning process and, subject to normal scrutiny and prioritisation, timetabled plans will be developed. |

| PAC Recommendations | Response Reported in the Treasury Minute |
|---|---|
| **PAC conclusion (iii): Progress in procuring the Battlefield Target Identification System has been held up for six years awaiting allies' decisions. The Committee recommended in 2002 that the Department develop methods of co-operation with allies on Combat Identification, but preliminary decisions are yet to be made. The Department needs to reach agreement with allies on procuring a system, or introduce, as an interim, a more limited national programme, focusing on the key risk areas such as ground-to-ground combat.** | The Department accepts that – partly as a result of the technical complexity of the problem – it has taken longer than we would have wished to reach a common position with allies on the technology to be used for the Battlefield Target Identification System. Following active engagement by the Department, the principal allies have now reached consensus on a technical solution. The United States for example now has funding for a programme that is compatible and aligned with the UK's continuing Battlefield Target Identification System programme. The Department currently expects the UK programme to proceed to Initial Gate in early 2008 with a primary focus on the ground environment. Other allies are moving towards acquiring similar capability. Given that the risks associated with the international solution are being overcome, the Department therefore does not intend to proceed with a limited national solution, which would provide no benefit in coalition operations.

As indicated in the previous response, the Department continues to work actively with the United States and other allies to reach agreement on technical and procedural solutions for other aspects of the priority areas with current efforts focused mainly on air-to-ground combat. This reflects the increasing emphasis on air-to-ground combat in contemporary coalition operations and that air-to-ground fratricides have historically resulted in greater loss of life. |
| **PAC conclusion (iv): The Department's Senior Responsible Owner on Combat Identification has no budgetary or line management responsibility. The Department should identify what impact the Senior Responsible Owner has been able to make since the role was established in 2002, and determine whether giving greater management authority would increase the effectiveness of the role.** | It is the Department's policy that large and complex projects or groups of projects have a Senior Responsible Owner appointed on behalf of and accountable to the Defence Management Board. Although the Senior Responsible Owner may not have full financial or command/line management authority over all those delivering the capability, he or she will be empowered, have a good knowledge of the requirement, be competent to resolve conflicting priorities and be able to exert influence outside traditional management or command chains. This is consistent with Office of Government Commerce guidance. |

| PAC Recommendations | Response Reported in the Treasury Minute |
|---|---|
| | Since the Combat Identification appointment was made in 2004, the Senior Responsible Owner has made a number of important interventions. In particular, he has represented Combat Identification as a discrete and important enabling capability within the Department's planning process, ensuring that proper consideration is given to its priority. He has represented the UK internationally and particularly with the United States as the key ally on Combat Identification. For example, he attended a senior US Army and Marine Corps meeting during a crucial discussion of the way ahead. The Senior Responsible Owner was the focus for UK hosting of the important multinational exercise URGENT QUEST in 2005, which paved the way for decisions on Battlefield Target Identification System technology and is playing a similar role for UK participation in the multinational US-hosted exercise BOLD QUEST in September 2007, which will look at air-to- ground Combat Identification issues. The Senior Responsible Owner is leading the review of the implementation of the Combat Identification programme.

The Department believes that the current arrangements for the Combat Identification Senior Responsible Owner role are working well but will keep the position under review as the programme progresses. |
| **PAC conclusion (v): During Operation TELIC the Department produced 60,000 Aide Memoire cards to raise awareness of Combat Identification, but failed to distribute them to front line troops. The Department regretted this failure, which it attributed to more general difficulties with supplies in Iraq. Cards are now given to personnel before deployment. The Department should determine how successful they have been in raising awareness among the troops concerned.** | The content of the original Combat Identification aide memoire cards has now been subsumed into the generic All Arms Tactical Aide Memoire to which theatre specific tactical aides memoir are addenda. It is generally very difficult to assess the operational benefit of a specific element of training in a rigorous way, but no incidents of fratricide involving UK forces similar to those that occurred during Operation TELIC in March 2003 are known to have occurred since that time. However, the Department agrees that the scope for assessing the general effectiveness of tactics, techniques and procedures for Combat Identification should be investigated. This will be pursued by the Senior Responsible Owner for Combat Identification. |

| PAC Recommendations | Response Reported in the Treasury Minute |
|---|---|
| **PAC conclusion (vi): As the Committee recommended in 2002, the Department has developed a database on the fratricide incidents, but does not collate data on fratricide rates of our allies or on non-combatant casualties. The Department should update the database regularly and expand it to include data on allied fratricide rates and non-combatant casualties. The Committee also recommended in 2002 that the information gathered in the database be analysed and disseminated appropriately within the United Kingdom and to allies. The Department should share the database with our allies to promote greater joint interest in finding effective solutions.** | The Department agrees that collating; analysing and sharing information about casualties resulting from fratricide incidents is an important research activity that underpins work on improving Combat Identification capability. The Department maintains research data on fratricide incidents and has participated in international collaborative research on the subject with key allies to promote greater collective understanding of the issues. For reasons explained to the Committee (supplementary memorandum submitted by the Ministry of Defence 27 July 2006), the Department's research data does not include non-combatant casualties. |
| **PAC conclusion (vii): It took between eight and 28 months to conclude the Boards of Inquiry investigations into the four friendly fire incidents during Operation TELIC, and in one case it was a further 27 months before the findings were made publicly available. There will inevitably be variations in the time taken to complete investigations due to differing levels of complexity and the possibility of criminal prosecutions. But once complete, the Department should make every effort to publish the findings of Boards of Inquiry within one month of the investigation being concluded.** | The Department accepts that every effort should be made to publish as soon as possible the findings of Boards of Inquiry dealing with high profile cases. Following a recent review of policy, Departmental guidance has been issued on the proactive publication of information about the reports of Boards of Inquiry in cases where there is likely to be significant public interest, such as operational and training fatalities or serious injuries and major equipment loss or damage.

This guidance responds to the requirements of the Freedom of Information Act 2000 and requires the convening order, terms of reference, findings, recommendations and Convening Authority/Reviewing Authority comments of such Boards of Inquiry to be published as a defined class of information in the MoD Publication Scheme under the Act. The Department therefore expects that Board of Inquiry reports that fall into this category will normally be made available to the general public via the MoD website within two months of completion of the report to allow time to brief the next of kin on its contents and to prepare the report for publication. |

| PAC Recommendations | Response Reported in the Treasury Minute |
|---|---|
| **PAC conclusion (viii): It took the Department over six months to inform the Committee that it could not provide information on allied fratricide rates and non-combatant casualties requested at the hearing. The Department should in future provide promised information no later than four weeks after the hearing. Where more time is required, the Department should agree an appropriate timetable for delivery within a week of the hearing.** | The Department accepts the need for timely responses to requests for information made during Committee hearings. In line with Treasury guidance, the Department will aim to send such follow up information to the PAC Committee normally within a fortnight of the hearing. If it is likely to take longer, perhaps because further research is required, the aim is to provide information by a month after the hearing. If additional information needs to be sent later or if it has proved impossible to gather, the Department will inform the PAC Committee as soon as possible. |

Thirty Fourth Report (2006-07) Recruitment and Retention in the Armed Forces

| PAC Recommendations | Response Reported in the Treasury Minute |
|---|---|
| **PAC conclusion (i): There are shortfalls of personnel in all three Services. In April 2007 the shortfall was 5,850 and the Armed Forces as a whole were of 3.2 per cent under strength.** | The Department accepts the conclusion of the Committee. The current shortfall is higher than we would wish. In part, this is a result of current restructuring work where strengths are falling before corresponding decreases in manning requirements. The Department recognises the importance of taking the necessary steps to address the shortfall, and has action in place.<br><br>All three Services are carrying out a range of activities to increase recruitment. The Royal Navy (RN) is examining more flexible approaches to the employment of its manpower and developing an Integrated Recruitment and Retention Strategy to foster higher levels of retention. In future Naval recruitment staff will work more closely with regional commanders to raise awareness of the Royal Navy and its career opportunities. The Army recruiting organisation has initiated the One Army Recruiting (OAR) change programme, which will provide a more efficient and effective recruiting process across both the Regular and Territorial Army. The Royal Air Force is already seeing some success from the recent marketing campaign, which has resulted in an increase in both officer and airmen recruits. |

| PAC Recommendations | Response Reported in the Treasury Minute |
|---|---|
| **PAC conclusion (ii): The increasing frequency of deployments on overseas operations and time away from home are factors causing people to leave the Armed Forces.** | The Department partly accepts the Committee's conclusion. There are many reasons why people leave the Services each year and these are dependent on age, rank and personal circumstances. It is true that one of the reasons given in the NAO survey for leaving was 'time away from home' (around 35 per cent of those surveyed cited this as a reason) and frequency of deployments (again approximately 35 per cent). However this needs to be balanced against one of the main satisfaction factors of job security. Over the last 10 years voluntary outflow rates taken across the Services have fluctuated only marginally year on year. However, the Department continues to monitor the situation carefully.

The Department's recruitment and retention levels compare favourably with the public and private sector and other parts of the public sector. The Chartered Institute of Personnel Development Report on Recruitment and Retention Turnover 2006 gave turnover for the Production Industry at 8.2 per cent compared with the MoD's 5.2 per cent. It suggests that the Armed Forces are good at keeping their people, which is particularly important as we have limited opportunity to recruit laterally, unlike other employers. Through the Continuous Attitude Surveys (CAS), the Department monitors Service personnel's views on a raft of retention issues.

The buoyancy of the job market will inevitably exert a degree of 'pull' on people's decision to leave the Services and individuals with particular skills, such as qualified pilots and communications engineers, will always be in demand. However, the Professional Aviator and other financial retention initiatives (FRIs) for RAF aircrew are good examples of targeted retention policies.

A number of measures are also being implemented to manage better the time between deployments, such as the Royal Navy's Rebalancing Lives initiative, which was introduced in 2002. The Army is seeking, where appropriate, to contractorise Regular Army Assistance to Training (RAAT) tasks, to reduce support to training tasks and minimise equipment maintenance without having a detrimental effect on Army outputs. Meanwhile the RAF has increased the Military Provost Guard Service to reduce the guarding task for RAF regular personnel, increase the employment of short term contract manpower to cover pressure points, reduce the number of un-established commitments and place new focus on conditions of service and work life balance. |

| PAC Recommendations | Response Reported in the Treasury Minute |
| --- | --- |
| **PAC conclusion (iii): There are indicators of overstretch in specific areas, such as severe shortfalls in personnel in some specialist trades, such as nurses, linguists and Leading Hands, and the routine breaking of harmony guidelines.** | The Department accepts that there are shortfalls in some specialist trades and that they are stretched. A Manning Pinch Point Steering Group meets quarterly to review manning figures and to initiate action to alleviate pressure on pinch point trades. Measures implemented range from reviewing current establishments, mobilising Reserves, seeking assistance from the other two Services, rank ranging appointments and extending engagements to considering a financial retention incentive.<br><br>Before a Financial Retention Incentive can be considered, a thorough manning review is required. This examines all the issues surrounding the population, their causes and potential financial and non-financial solutions. FRIs will be recommended by AFPRB as part of a comprehensive financial and non-financial package upon which the MoD is required to provide annual progress updates. |
| **PAC conclusion (iv): Financial incentives have met with some success in retaining people in the short term, but several key factors for people leaving, such as workload, inability to plan ahead outside work and the impact on family life, have not been addressed sufficiently.** | The Department accepts the conclusions of the Committee, and welcomes their conclusion. However, it should be acknowledged that while our Forces are heavily committed there is going to be pressure on certain areas. The Department has expanded its research programme through the development of Valuing and Investing in Service Personnel (VISP) and the Armed Forces Continuous Attitude Survey (AFCAS) in order to understand better the reasons for people leaving and to apply appropriate measures to encourage them to stay. A wide range of measures is in place to improve retention including: career management, improvement to conditions of service and work/life balance, extensions to normal engagement lengths, commitment bonuses and targeted Financial Retention Incentives. |
| **PAC conclusion (v): The Department lacks information on the costs of its recruitment and retention measures and has performed limited investment appraisal on its range of financial incentives.** | The Department accepts the conclusions of the Committee. The Department, in conjunction with the 3 Services, has revised the policy guidance for all future FRI submissions. In future, each case will contain details of key performance indicators, comprehensive details of the issue and details of the post project evaluation to be completed. In addition, these will include cost benefit analyses to quantify the benefits achieved in each case. The new Joint Personnel Administration system will provide a better source of management information. |

| PAC Recommendations | Response Reported in the Treasury Minute |
|---|---|
| **PAC conclusion (vi): The Department does not have a long-term strategy to ensure a steady supply of highly qualified specialist personnel especially where there are shortages.** | The Department does not accept the conclusion of the PAC. The Service Personnel Plan, which was introduced in 2006, provides a structure for the prioritisation and delivery of Service personnel policy over the next 15 years. It reflects the challenges and opportunities that the operational environment, demographic changes and the changing expectations of personnel and their families present to the MoD. Under the auspices of the Service Personnel Plan, work is underway to ensure the effective delivery of financial and non-financial conditions of service to achieve the recruitment, retention and motivation of sufficient, capable individuals to meet manning requirements. In addition work is underway to develop a retention positive and coherent Armed Forces Terms and Conditions package, which initially will focus on proposals for more flexible working arrangements. |
| **PAC conclusion (vii): Short term cuts in recruitment have had long term impacts on manning levels which are almost impossible to recover from and appear to have more money to mitigate in the long run.** | The Department partly accepts the conclusions of the Committee. The Department recognises the need to learn from lessons from the past, including the decision to slow Royal Navy recruiting in the mid-1990s in response to 'Options for Change'. The RAF has applied these lessons to its recent reductions, using careful management of normal outflow and redundancy to meet the reduced target while still maintaining a steady flow of new recruits. Around £3 million of additional marketing funding was expended to raise the profile of RAF careers and remind potential recruits that despite the RAF reducing in size, many rewarding career opportunities remain.

Despite the restructuring process, recruiting was good in 2006-07 with the Service intake up by 1,210 (6.7 per cent) on their achievement in the previous year. Over recruiting in certain areas is used where possible, but rescheduling training and using temporary facilities limits the extent to which this can balance out shortfalls. |

| PAC Recommendations | Response Reported in the Treasury Minute |
|---|---|
| **PAC conclusion (viii): The Department sets annual targets for recruitment but they do not take account of the need to fill in some of the gaps resulting from previous recruiting shortfalls.** | The Department does not accept the conclusion of the Committee. The Department routinely adjusts its annual recruitment targets to take account of the previous year's performance and other forecasts. Annex 34.1 illustrates this point.<br><br>A number of initiatives have been introduced to deal with earlier shortfalls. The Royal Navy, for example, have developed a scheme to speed up promotion for General Service Ratings who joined in the mid-90s. Other measures being considered include, lateral recruitment, Recruiting Bounty Scheme Golden Hellos for new recruits and Transfer Bonuses for Service personnel from other trades. The In-service Training Total (ITT) targets are calculated annually to allow for past performance and are balanced against our training schools capacity in any one-year. |
| **PAC conclusion (ix): Nine out of ten of the Army's top ten officers were educated at independent schools, whilst three quarters of Army scholarships in 2006-07 went to students from independent schools.** | The Department accepts the conclusions of the Committee. However, a more balanced insight can be gained from a breakdown of officers from this year's intake of the Advanced Command and Staff Course. See Annex 34.2.<br><br>This course is designed to provide selected officers with a broad understanding of the full range of operational and management issues across Defence as preparation for potential promotion to the senior ranks. It is a highly competitive course and only the top 10 per cent of OF3 & 4s (Major or Lt Col equivalents) of each Service are selected; it is designed to capture the very best in each service who have the potential to achieve the highest ranks. The majority of entrants (around 56 per cent) to the Royal Military Academy Sandhurst are now from the State Sector. |

| PAC Recommendations | Response Reported in the Treasury Minute |
|---|---|
| **PAC conclusion (i): All of the Volunteer Reserve Forces face significant shortfalls in manpower from some 16 per cent in the Territorial Army to some 36 per cent in the Royal Auxiliary Air Force.** | The Department accepts the Committee's conclusion. Since these figures were published, the manning position has improved considerably. Major efforts, by all three Services, supported by appropriate resources, are underway to address the manning shortfalls and many of the Committee's recommendations, such as improving the training and support available for Reservists, have been successfully implemented. |
| | The Royal Navy Reserves (RNR) is now on course to meet its projected manning levels, the Royal Marine Reserves (RMR) position has now started to improve and is now increasing in strength, and Royal Auxiliary Air Force (RAuxAF) recruiting has improved since the position last year. For the Territorial Army (TA), who made up a large majority of the Reserve Forces, 2006 was the best manning year since 1999, and the Department continues to closely monitor TA manning levels. A new programme to incentivise ex-Regulars to join the Volunteer Reserves was announced in August 2007. |
| **PAC conclusion (ii): People have been joining the Territorial Army despite failing basic fitness tests.** | The Department accepts the Committee's conclusion. While most recruits who join the TA meet our basic fitness requirements, if individuals do not, and their potential is recognised, they are given a training programme and encouraged to try again when they have improved their level of fitness. Many join the Reserves because of the opportunities offered there to develop their fitness but, conversely, research indicates that fitness is a barrier to others. There can be a perception that people believe they are "not fit enough" to join the Reserves. The Department believes that rather than losing potential recruits, it must strike the right balance between fitness on entry and potential. |
| | In line with the conclusions of the Report, to look creatively as ways to increase the options available for those wising to join. The Armyfit website, which offers free tailored on-line fitness programmes, was launched in February 2007, and has received nearly a million unique visitors. Of these, over 4,000 have gone on to complete an online application form to join the Army – Regular or TA. |
| | However, great care is taken to ensure that all Reservists who are mobilised for service on operations meet a prescribed level of fitness commensurate with their role in theatre, and the Department takes precautions to ensure Reservists and Regulars alike are fit to operate in demanding environments such as those of Afghanistan and Iraq. Where individuals fail their pre-deployment tests, they are given time to undertake further training to improve their fitness levels to ensure they are prepared properly to deploy. Individuals may be stopped from deploying where they are unable to meet the required fitness standards in the time available. |

| PAC Recommendations | Response Reported in the Treasury Minute |
|---|---|
| **PAC conclusion (iii): The Department does not know if, on operations, Reservists are more likely than Regulars to experience fitness problems which require evacuation back to the United Kingdom.** | The Department accepts the conclusion of the Committee. Since the report's publication, the situation has improved considerably. The RMR achieve the same levels of fitness as their Regular comrades before deploying on Operations. TA personnel are required to take and pass Military Annual Training Test Level 2, and on deployment are required to meet Level 1 – the same standard as Regulars.<br><br>The Department does necessarily deploy some members of the TA on operations, who cannot do this, having been accepted 'at risk' by the receiving formation. This can only occur where the individual Reservist has been judged and assessed by a Training Review Board, which includes representation from the Receiving Unit. This Board mitigates the risk, and ensures that the Commander of the receiving Unit is aware of it. No one, who fails this Board, is deployed. In most instances, this occurs when the individual has essential skill sets, such as a surgeon whose role is judged to be less physically demanding than that of a frontline soldier and the Department is therefore able to accept a lower level of fitness in order to ensure their vital skills are available. |
| **PAC conclusion (iv): On routine training and on pre-deployment training, Reservists are not being given the opportunity to train alongside Regulars, nor with the equipment they will use on operations.** | The Department agrees with the Committee's conclusion. Since the report was developed, the Department has introduced a number of steps to implement the NAO's recommendation encouraging greater synergy between regulars and reservists deploying on operations. The majority of those deploying on operations are now given the opportunity to train alongside their Regular colleagues. Every effort is made to ensure that mobilised Reservists get the same opportunities as Regulars, but by the nature of some specialisations and the mobilisation process itself, there may still be times when some individuals are unable to train with the Unit that they will serve with.<br><br>Where practicable, integrated training takes place alongside Regulars. For example, 40 Commando RM recently deployed on Operation HERRICK (Afghanistan) with nearly 80 Reservists, mostly RMR, who are being mobilised for 12 months in order that they are fully trained and integrated into the Unit. They were mobilised in April, and having completed their training, deployed to Afghanistan in October.<br><br>Reservists are issued exactly the same personal equipment as the Regulars on mobilisation. |

| PAC Recommendations | Response Reported in the Treasury Minute |
|---|---|
| **PAC conclusion (v): The Royal Naval Reservists rarely go to sea, as the Reserve is increasingly confined to force protection duties.** | The Department accepts the conclusion of the Committee. Following the NAO report's publication, the RNR have implemented the Reserves Integration Project, which addresses the terms and conditions of service needed to provide a flexible career path between the Regulars and the Reserves. Fundamental to this is the alignment of branches and skill sets.

The Royal Navy is working to ensure that all RNR Recruits will go to sea within 18 months of joining, and RNR's provide extensive support to Exercises at sea, such as the recent NOBLE MARINER, when many specialist billets in the Embarked Maritime Headquarters were filled by RNR.

On Operations, apart from individual deployments, the General Service Seaman (Reserve) branch has an enduring commitment to Force Protection for the Gulf Royal Fleet Auxiliaries for the next two years. This requires around 30 Reservists to be deployed at any time. |
| **PAC conclusion (vi): A number of Reservists have valuable civilian skills, which are not systematically utilised at present.** | The Department accepts the conclusion of the Committee. In line with its recommendation, the Department is developing a method of capturing the civilian skills of Reservist based on the Office for National Statistics' Standard Occupational Classification, and it is the Departments ambition to incorporate this facility onto Joint Personnel Administration (JPA is the new Tri-Service defence personnel administration system). Separately, the RNR already operates a civilian skills database.

Where operationally necessary, a Commander may make full use of a Reservist's civilian qualifications and skills (and as the Committee heard this was the case in the early stages of Operation TELIC in Iraq). It must, however, be understood that many Reservists join up to undertake duties and skills that would normally not be available to them in their civilian life. Current policy, taken from "Future Use of the UK's Reserves", published by DRFC on 7 February 2005, is that *"We will not mobilise a Reservist to take advantage of his or her civilian skills if he or she joined to serve in a different role, except with the express agreement of the Reservist and his or her employer."* The policy ensures that unless there is a clear operational necessity for a particular skill or trade, a Reservist will not be mobilised solely on the basis of their civilian skills.

This recognition is vital if the Department is to maintain relationships with both the Reservist and their employer. The Department is aware of the vital support given by employers to the functioning of the Reserves, and it would be unwise to jeopardise this by laying itself open to accusations of getting skilled personnel 'on the cheap' by appearing to take trained staff from an employer. |

| PAC Recommendations | Response Reported in the Treasury Minute |
|---|---|
| **PAC conclusion (vii): Reservist personnel have not been receiving prioritised medical treatment for either physical injury sustained on operations or for mental health problems, which develop post-mobilisation.** | The Department partially accepts the conclusions of the Committee. While mobilised, all Reservists are entitled to the same access to medical treatment as Regulars; that includes access for physical injury and / or illness and mental illness. At the time of their demobilisation, Reservists have the opportunity to declare medical problems and undergo medical examination.

The Reserves Mobilisation and Training Centre at Chilwell, where most reservists are demobilised, has access to rapid MRI scans through the Tri-Service Regional Rehabilitation Unit at RAF Cranwell to obtain definitive diagnosis for musculo-skeletal problems. Access is provided within 10 days of request. Medical Officers at Chilwell then have rehabilitation services on site to treat musculo-skeletal conditions and have accelerated access to the Ministry of Defence Hospital Unit Host Trusts in the same way as regular soldiers for all specialties. However, many Reservists choose to return home for referral. Under these circumstances, they will be treated along NHS timelines based on clinical need. Where medical issues are identified prior to demobilisation, the period of mobilisation can be extended to continue to treat the soldier until he is well enough to return to civilian life. Once demobilised reservists medical support is provided by the NHS.

For Reservists with mental health problems, it is long established that once they are demobilised, medical care becomes the responsibility of their own local NHS primary care trust and the majority of Veterans' physical and mental health needs are met by these provisions. However, the MoD recognises that it has an expertise to offer in certain specific circumstances, and in November 2006, it launched a new initiative – the Reserves Mental Health Programme (RMHP). The RMHP is open to any current or former member of the UK Volunteer and Regular Reserves, who has been demobilised since 1 January 2003 following an overseas operational deployment as a reservist, and who believes that the deployment may have adversely affected their mental health; take-up for this programme has been low thus far. |

| PAC Recommendations | Response Reported in the Treasury Minute |
|---|---|
| **PAC conclusion (viii): The welfare support most used by Reservists and their families is provided by their Reserve unit, but not all units have dedicated welfare resources.** | The Department accepts the Committee's conclusion. Since the Report was published, much has been done to improve the support available for the families of mobilised Reservists along the lines recommended by the Committee, and the Departments aspiration is that support available to Reservists and their families, when a Reservist is mobilised, be no different to that offered to Regular personnel.<br><br>As examples of the improvements made, Reserve Units can now mobilise personnel specifically for welfare duties when personnel from that Unit are mobilised – depending on the circumstances of the Unit involved. Once around 20-30 Personnel are mobilised, the Unit will be automatically authorised to mobilise others to support them, and their families at home. Also, the Single Point of Contact scheme is being extended to cover the families of mobilised Reserves, as well as Regulars, on Operations. |
| **PAC conclusion (ix): The Department has made some major decisions about the future of the Reserve Forces, yet does not know what they cost.** | The Department accepts the conclusion of the Committee and has fully adopted its recommendations. Work is well advanced on a project aimed at improving the cost information the Department has available on the Reserves by initiating a detailed study of the costs and outputs of Volunteer Reserves. A report is due by the end of 2007 – the Department hopes this will aid future balance of investment decisions relating to the Reserves. |
| **PAC conclusion (x): The Department monitors and collects information on areas of diversity such as race and gender, but not on the socio-economic or educational background of its Reserve personnel whether on recruitment or promotion.** | The Department accepts the conclusion of the Committee. The intention is to record such information in future, but this will require substantial amendment to the Joint Personnel Administration system, and will therefore take some time to implement. |

Forty Sixth Report (2006-07) Ministry of
Defence: Major Projects Report 2006

| PAC Recommendations | Response Reported in the Treasury Minute |
|---|---|
| **PAC conclusion (1): The Department's Review of 20 of its largest projects cut their forecast costs by £781 million, but £448 million of this expenditure did not result in a saving to the Department as a whole as it was transferred to other budgets. The Department will have to forgo other – so far unspecified – activities, which might otherwise have been financed from those budgets. As an integral part of any further reviews, the Department should quantify the opportunity cost to the recipient's budget of having to absorb such transfers of expenditure, and the impact on their continued ability to plan and deliver the capabilities originally expected from those budgets.** | The Department accepts this conclusion. The principle applied to the transfers was to ensure that costs were allocated in such a way that the performance of individual project teams in controlling direct project costs could be effectively measured, for example maintaining defence-critical industrial capability, in accordance with the Defence Industrial Strategy. This generally cannot be controlled at an individual project level. Other costs, not directly related to delivery of the project, were transferred to other lines where it made sense to manage them and where any necessary trade-offs could be made to live within our means. In making these decisions the Department took full account of the potential impact on the receiving area and will continue to do so. Where such instances arise in the future the Department will take steps to ensure any opportunity cost is quantified. |

| PAC Recommendations | Response Reported in the Treasury Minute |
|---|---|
| **PAC conclusion (2): The Department has made investment decisions based upon inaccurate forecasts. Such decisions should be contingent on the outcome of an expert independent assessor's examination of the technical, financial and commercial maturity of the major projects and the likelihood they will deliver military benefits anticipated, similar to the examination conducted on the Future (Aircraft) Carrier.** | The Department broadly accepts this recommendation. As part of the Defence Acquisition Change Programme a number of measures are being put in place to ensure the technical, financial and commercial maturity of major projects. These include requiring all major projects to provide evidence that cost estimates have been created or verified by suitably expert organisations independent of the project and that independent technical advice has been obtained from an agreed expert source. "Independent" in this context need not mean external to the Department; this will be dependent on the nature and scope of the project.

In addition, the Department has established a due diligence unit to examine the commercial maturity of major projects before contract award. Projects with an "adverse" rating will not be permitted to proceed to contract and will be referred back to the Department's internal approving authorities.

The Department agrees with this conclusion. The Defence Industrial Strategy has provided a catalyst for the assessment of the industrial capability necessary to support submarine design and build activities. The establishment of the Astute Key Supplier Forum (KSF) is evidence of the resultant good working practices being developed between Department and Industry. These are already bringing benefit to the Astute programme through innovative design solutions and improved collaboration. Importantly these benefits will flow through to the Successor programme.

The KSF is very much an active, joint engagement strategy, regularly reviewed and constantly alive to suggestions regarding more efficient ways of working. In addition, within our wider key supplier management and supply network processes, the Department is monitoring the supply chain for existing and potential weaknesses, to assess to project and cost implications, and develop mitigating strategies. This improved, constructive and open dialogue is building a common understanding of risks and opportunities, enabling a better understanding of the cost of industrial sustainment across the submarine design and build enterprise. The Department plans to do the same for others areas of capability. |

| PAC Recommendations | Response Reported in the Treasury Minute |
|---|---|
| **PAC conclusion (3): The cost increases and delays on the Astute Class submarine project in part stem from failure to preserve the submarine supply chain. The Defence Industrial Strategy, introduced in December 2005, provides a framework against which to make judgements on the sustainment of critical industrial capabilities. The Department should routinely quantify the cost implications and operational benefits of sustaining critical defence capabilities for individual projects. The Department will also need to apply the learning from the Astute project in planning for a successor to the nuclear deterrent.** | The Department agrees with this conclusion. The Defence Industrial Strategy has provided a catalyst for the assessment of the industrial capability necessary to support submarine design and build activities. The establishment of the Astute Key Supplier Forum (KSF) is evidence of the resultant good working practices being developed between Department and Industry. These are already bringing benefit to the Astute programme through innovative design solutions and improved collaboration. Importantly these benefits will flow through to the Successor programme.

The KSF is very much an active, joint engagement strategy, regularly reviewed and constantly alive to suggestions regarding more efficient ways of working. In addition, within our wider key supplier management and supply network processes, the Department is monitoring the supply chain for existing and potential weaknesses, to assess to project and cost implications, and develop mitigating strategies. This improved, constructive and open dialogue is building a common understanding of risks and opportunities, enabling a better understanding of the cost of industrial sustainment across the submarine design and build enterprise. The Department plans to do the same for others areas of capability. |

| PAC Recommendations | Response Reported in the Treasury Minute |
|---|---|
| **PAC conclusion (4): The Government has announced plans to embark on a major project to build a successor to the nuclear deterrent, which is estimated to cost in the region of £19 billion and take up to 18 years. Many of the cost overruns on older projects have been due to over-ambition in the original design and a failure to properly understand and budget for costs. The Department will need to apply the learning from Astute to this new project, including how to realistically plan and use Computer-Aided Design, keeping to the required timescale in the design and build cycle; and using new methods of construction pioneered in the United States of America.** | The Department agrees, but provides the following clarification. The White Paper *The Future of the UK's Nuclear Deterrent* gave initial procurement cost estimates in the range of £11-14 Billion (at 2006-07 prices), and a timeline of 17 years to design, manufacture and commission a new class of submarines. The programme has just entered the concept phase during which cost estimates will be refined and detailed programme plans will be developed. Clearly these plans will need to draw heavily on lessons learned from the Astute programme. In particular, the programme will work to a construct that is similar, but not identical, to the arrangements in place for the successful Vanguard programme.

The role of Design Authority will revert back to the MoD to provide both a better balance between risk and major investment decisions, and to use the technologies developed through the Astute programme where possible to reduce the risks associated with introduction of the new class. Finally, work with the United States of America will continue, as outlined in an exchange of letters between Mr Blair and President Bush in December 2006, including building on progress made through Astute to further refine submarine design and build processes.

The Department accepts this recommendation. Since formation of Defence, Equipment and Support (DE&S) organisation on 2 April 2007, a range of additional HR flexibilities have been delegated by the Department to enable this. These include the ability to promote, in a limited number of cases, Team or senior Project Leaders, in situ. This delegation, based on both individual merit and achievement, provides continuity and stability at critical stages within a project. Minimum tour lengths are now agreed for DE&S staff on appointment to projects in order to better manage personnel succession planning, staff retention and provide greater stability in project management.

DE&S seeks to undertake active career management intervention. This provides for the managed advancement of key staff and conversely, where performance is not judged acceptable, individuals are provided with opportunities that better match their skill sets. Poor performance is not tolerated. |

| PAC Recommendations | Response Reported in the Treasury Minute |
|---|---|
| | DE&S is piloting a Reward and Recognition strategy to further enhance and link improvements in business performance with the effectiveness, and hence efficiency, of Business Units, Teams and the individual.

DE&S seeks to share learning and best practice with a range of other Government Departments. As an example, DE&S is represented at a senior level at the HR Director's Forum (South West). |
| **PAC conclusion (5): Key staff are neither held to account for a project's failure, nor rewarded for its success. The Department will now promote staff in post to retain vital skills, and continuity at key stages of projects, or move staff on in the case of failure. The Department should document its approach and how it will measure success, so as to evaluate the expected benefits against the outcomes; and it should share its learning with other government departments.** | The Department accepts this recommendation. Since formation of Defence, Equipment and Support (DE&S) organisation on 2 April 2007, a range of additional HR flexibilities have been delegated by the Department to enable this. These include the ability to promote, in a limited number of cases, Team or senior Project Leaders, in situ. This delegation, based on both individual merit and achievement, provides continuity and stability at critical stages within a project. Minimum tour lengths are now agreed for DE&S staff on appointment to projects in order to better manage personnel succession planning, staff retention and provide greater stability in project management.

DE&S seeks to undertake active career management intervention. This provides for the managed advancement of key staff and conversely, where performance is not judged acceptable, individuals are provided with opportunities that better match their skill sets. Poor performance is not tolerated.

DE&S is piloting a Reward and Recognition strategy to further enhance and link improvements in business performance with the effectiveness, and hence efficiency, of Business Units, Teams and the individual.

DE&S seeks to share learning and best practice with a range of other Government Departments. As an example, DE&S is represented at a senior level at the HR Director's Forum (South West). |

- Media and communications;

He has delegated the following responsibilities to his subordinate Ministers, who chair a number of other top-level committees and boards on specific issues as required:

- the Minister of State for the Armed Forces is responsible for Defence policy and planning; operations; the Armed Forces (Regular and Reserves); regional issues and the devolved administrations; the Defence Estates Committee; and Defence equipment and support business in the Commons;

- the Minister of State for Defence Equipment and Support is responsible for Defence Equipment and Support; Commercial policy throughout the Department; the defence equipment programme through life; defence logistics support; Defence Industrial Strategy; defence science and technology; defence exports; International aspects of defence equipment and support; and Defence issues in the House of Lords;

- the Under Secretary of State for Defence and Minister for Veterans is responsible for service personnel issues; veterans affairs; Defence Estates; civilian personnel policy and casework; MoD Police; health and safety; Hydrographic Office and Meteorological Office; Non-Departmental Public Bodies; low flying; visits by Peers and MPs; and the Armed Forces Parliamentary Scheme.

These delegations change from time to time as the Secretary of State directs.

## The Defence Ministerial Committee

Since April 2008 the Defence Ministerial Committee has brought together Ministers and the Department's most senior officials to ensure that Ministers collectively are regularly engaged in the business of the Department. It is chaired by the Secretary of State and comprises the other Defence Ministers, the Permanent Under Secretary, the Chief of Defence Staff, the three Single Service Chiefs of Staff, the Second Permanent Under Secretary, the Vice Chief of the Defence Staff, the Chief Scientific Adviser and the Finance Director. The Chief of Defence Materiel and Defence Board Non-Executive Directors may be invited to attend on occasion. The Secretary

of State takes and is responsible for the decisions of the Committee. It meets about eight times per year.

## The Ministry of Defence

Beneath Ministers lies the top management of the MoD. The Secretary of State has two principal advisers: the Chief of the Defence Staff and the Permanent Secretary. They share responsibility for much of the Department's business, reflecting the input that both military and civilian personnel make to political, financial, administrative and operational matters. The CDS is the professional head of the Armed Forces and the principal military adviser to the Secretary of State and the Government. The PUS has primary responsibility for policy, finance and administration in the Department. He is the MoD's Principal Accounting Officer and is personally accountable to Parliament for the stewardship of the resources within the Ministry of Defence's control. PUS and CDS each have a deputy: the Second Permanent Under Secretary and the Vice Chief of the Defence Staff, who jointly oversee the MoD Head Office.

The Head Office is responsible for leading the Defence contribution to the development of the Government's foreign and security policy and wider objectives, and for translating those objectives into departmental policy and the Defence capability needed to deliver it. As well as being the United Kingdom's Strategic Military Headquarters, the Head Office has four main roles:

- advising government on Defence;

- making policy and setting departmental strategy;

- planning and resource allocation; and

- management of Defence.

## The Defence Management Board

For the majority of 2007-08 the Defence Management Board (DMB) acted as the senior non-ministerial committee of the Ministry of Defence and was responsible for directing a number of key processes, in particular the bi-annual re-costing of the Defence programme and the Departmental planning process. The DMB was chaired by the Permanent Secretary and comprised the other Service and official members of the Defence Council and several non-executive directors appointed by PUS. It advised PUS on implementation of his responsibilities to Ministers for the full range of Defence business, other than the conduct of operations, and as Departmental Accounting Officer. It was responsible for the delivery of the Defence Aim, set by the Secretary of State for Defence and reflected in the Department's Public Service Agreement with the centre of Government:

*To deliver security for the people of the United Kingdom and the Overseas Territories by defending them, including against terrorism; and to act as a force for good by strengthening international peace and stability.*

The DMB delivered the Defence Aim, making the most cost-effective use of the resources that the Government provides, through pursuing three high-level Departmental objectives set out in our Public Service Agreement (PSA):

● Achieve success in the military tasks we undertake, at home and abroad;

● Be ready to respond to tasks that might arise;

● Build for the future.

It monitored Departmental performance against our PSA and other performance targets, using the Defence Balanced Scorecard, and formally reviewed performance and associated top-level risks at least quarterly. In delivering the Defence Aim, the DMB's core tasks were:

● Role of Defence - helping to define and articulate our strategic direction, and provide a clear vision and set of values for Defence;

● Targets and Objectives - establishing the key priorities and Defence capabilities necessary to deliver the strategy;

● Resource Allocation - ensuring that Defence priorities and tasks are appropriately resourced;

● Performance Management - managing corporate performance and resources in-year to deliver the required results.

The DMB placed emphasis on investment in key management issues such as providing:

● better and earlier guidance to the Department on key strategic issues;

● closer alignment of strategic objectives and resource allocation;

● greater rigour in addressing the resource challenge, and greater clarity about how it is to be addressed; and

● sharper focus on performance, through rigorous definition of performance standards and targets against a small number of key strategic objectives.

It generally met once or twice a month. Twice a year it had an 'away day' at which it reviewed the way it was working, considered strategic issues in greater depth and in a less formal context than its regular meetings, and provided top-down direction for any follow on work.

From 1 January 2008 under the Head Office streamlining programme the Defence Management Board was replaced by the Defence Board, placing a greater emphasis on the Board's strategic oversight and direction of defence. The Defence Board is the Department's senior non-Ministerial decision-taking body. Its principal function is to make the high level decisions necessary to ensure that Defence delivers its final outputs. It also provides strategic direction to the Department and manages performance. The Board has collective responsibility for the management of all aspects of the Department and the Armed Forces in the best interests of Defence, and for planning and performance with the exception of planning for, and conduct of, military operations. Its remit includes defence policy and strategy, major investment decisions, resource planning and prioritisation, setting and managing Departmental performance against objectives, and assurance.

The Board, chaired by PUS, meets formally on a monthly basis, though it may meet more frequently if required. PUS and CDS have executive responsibility to take decisions, with all Board members accepting corporate ownership of those decisions. Board members supporting PUS and CDS are 2nd PUS, VCDS, the three single Service Chiefs of Staff, the Chief of Defence Materiel, the Chief Scientific Adviser, the Finance Director, and Non-Executive Directors. PUS, as Chairman, in close consultation with CDS, takes and is responsible for the decisions of the Board, advised by its members and determines the Board's agenda.

In providing direction and initiating action on strategic issues the Board will:

- advise on the Department's strategic direction and communicate it;

- provide a clear vision and set of values for Defence;

- direct policy and strategy;

- manage strategic risk;

- establish the key priorities and defence capabilities necessary to deliver the strategy, and take action to ensure long term delivery;

- ensure that Defence priorities and tasks are appropriately resourced;

- provide direction, prioritisation and co-ordination of major change programmes.

In managing the performance of the Department, the Board will:

- set the Department's performance regime;

- regularly review the Department's performance and in-year management, taking the outputs of the Departmental performance and financial management mechanisms;

- hold individual Top Level Budget Holders to account;

- review assurance matters brought to its attention by the Chair of the Defence Audit Committee (DAC) and advise PUS as Accounting Officer on the annual statement of Internal Control;

- Agree Public Service Agreement and/or Departmental Strategic Objectives reports and the Department's Annual Report for the Secretary of State's consideration.

The DMB was, and the Defence Board is, supported by a dedicated secretariat located within the Finance Director's organisation until March 2008, and from April 2008 as a combined Defence Boards Secretariat working directly to PUS and CDS. The secretariat's role is to:

- manage the future programme of business for the Board and, from April 2008, the Defence Ministerial Committee and Chiefs of Staff Committee;

- provide advice on the preparation of papers, presentations and other material commissioned for the Board and, from April 2008, the Defence Ministerial Committee and Chiefs of Staff Committee;

- arrange meetings and awaydays, prepare agendas and circulate papers for in-and out-of-committee consideration;

- brief the chairman on the handling of business;

- support other Board members as required;

- record and circulate the decisions taken by the Board and, from April 2008, the Defence Ministerial Committee and Chiefs of Staff Committee, and track progress on them to conclusion.

The minutes of meetings are the responsibility of the Secretariat, acting under the Chairman's authority. They are the formal record of the proceedings, reflecting the key points of discussion and decisions. Summaries of the Defence Management and Defence Boards' decisions, together with the Agendas of their meetings and lists of the papers they have considered are published on the Ministry of Defence Website in support of the Department's implementation of the Freedom of Information Act.

Beneath the DMB there were throughout 2007-08 a wide range of boards and committees within the Head Office, responsible for day-to-day oversight of specific elements of the Department's business on behalf of the Board. These included:

- the Defence Audit Committee, responsible for ensuring corporate governance requirements are met, advising on the adequacy of internal controls and effective risk management;

- the Investment Approvals Board, responsible for the approval of major investment projects and oversight of the approvals process through which approval is sought;

- the Defence Estates Committee, responsible for development and implementation of policy for the Defence estate;

- the Efficiency Delivery Board, responsible for the Department's Efficiency Programme and ensuring its effective governance;

- the Defence Environment and Safety Board, responsible for policy on and oversight of environmental matters and health and safety; and

- the Policy and Programmes Steering Group, responsible for advice to the DMB on major balance of investment issues, the capability implications of significant changes in resources or policy, and production of coherent capability and policy options for consideration in the planning process.

A simplified supporting board and committee structure was introduced from April 2008 under the Head Office Streamlining programme to strengthen personal authority and accountability at senior levels within the Head Office. The Defence Audit Committee, the Investment Approvals Board and the Defence Environment and Safety Board continue to discharge the corporate functions set out above on behalf of the Defence Board. Other supporting boards and committees ceased directly to support and derive their authority from the Defence Board. Some continue to meet to advise the empowered Head Office 3-stars and Process Owners who are personally accountable to the Board. In addition, the new Defence Operating Board was established.

The Defence Operating Board is the means by which the decisions of the Defence Board and Chiefs of Staff Committee are made to happen and seen through. 2nd PUS and VCDS as the joint Chief Operating Officers have the authority to use the Defence Operating Board as the means of running Defence business. Business is conducted in groups configured for the purpose, including to resolve high level differences between TLBs, Head Office 3-stars

and/or Process Owners on cross-cutting issues, to settle high level Defence estate matters, and to ensure that Senior Responsible Owners are challenged and supported in delivering their change programmes. The Defence Operating Board is supported in its work by the Defence Boards Secretariat

The Code of Good Practice recommends that Boards engage in succession planning and talent development. The DMB's and Defence Board's ability to do this for their own members was and is heavily constrained. In particular, the five Chiefs of Staff (CDS, VCDS and the Chiefs of the Naval, General and Air Staffs) are members of the Defence Council, the Defence Ministerial Committee and the Defence Board in respect of their military appointments. The DMB had and the Defence Board has no role in the selection and appointment of its military members, who are appointed to their posts on the basis of their specialist military skills and experience, in accordance with procedures governed by Queen's Regulations. The Defence Board does maintain responsibility for and oversight of skills planning and talent development for the Defence civil service as a whole but most civilian Board members are Permanent Secretary appointments overseen by the Civil Service Commission and the Cabinet Office.

## Independent non-executive DMB and Defence Board members

The DMB had, and subsequently the Defence Board has, at least two external non-executive members appointed by PUS, who bring independent scrutiny, wider perspective and greater objectivity to Board discussions. Non-executives are independent in character and judgement, and are required to certify before taking up appointment that they have no relevant potential conflicts of interest. Non-executives are appointed in accordance with Cabinet Office best practice guidance for making external appointments. They are provided with written terms of reference including the specification of their roles, line of accountability and terms of appointment, which includes how their performance will be appraised. They are also provided with induction material to ensure they obtain the necessary background to perform their roles effectively. PUS holds personal meetings with the non-executives singly or collectively as he sees fit.

## Corporate Planning

The policy baseline from which Departmental planning is conducted is set out in Defence Strategic Guidance, which is reviewed every two years. It sets out the Board's strategic priorities for activity and planning throughout the Department and the Armed Forces. It includes:

- **The Defence Aim and Vision**, which set out the Government's highest-level objectives for defence, and how they will be achieved;

- **The Strategic Context**, which outlines the global strategic environment, including an assessment of threats and their implications;

- **The Defence Planning Assumptions**, which contain detailed guidance for planning future military capability, setting out what the Armed Forces should be capable of doing in terms of "What, Where, When, With Whom and for How Long";

- **The Defence Relations Strategy**, which provides high-level guidance for regional engagement strategies; and

- **Future Capability Development**, which gives strategic direction on the evolution of capabilities effectively to deliver defence policy.

Overall the guidance sets the broad policy and strategic context, establishes the key planning parameters and assumptions, and gives direction on areas of priority for resource allocation and for the development of future capabilities. Substantial elements of the guidance are classified, but the Defence Planning Assumptions provide the basis of the Department's periodic policy White Papers.

The Planning Round takes its cue from Defence Policy. It focuses on defining the required military capability and other outputs and allocating resources to Top Level Budget organisations in line with those outputs. The process is essentially one of prioritisation: enhancements require savings elsewhere in the programme. It examines our planned resource consumption on an accruals basis, constructed around the Treasury Control Framework, and the resources provided by HM Treasury in the Spending Review are prioritised and allocated to

budget holders. The overall programme is then reviewed by the Defence Board for agreement by the Secretary of State. The control totals for the Top Level Budget organisations are published alongside the Defence Plan containing the Department's top level performance targets.

## Performance Management

The Board uses the Defence Balanced Scorecard to manage performance against the objectives set out in the Defence Plan. The Board reviews performance against the Scorecard objectives every quarter alongside details of the emerging financial position for the year. By tracking progress against the objectives in the Defence Plan, the Scorecard focuses the Board's attention on what is important to delivering outputs and achieving results, and on areas where the Department might be falling behind, so that the Board can take action as necessary. The Defence Balanced Scorecard is underpinned by scorecards at TLB level and more generally across the Department. Under the Head Office Streamlining Programme the Department has created a new Strategy Director post, and is reviewing the arrangements for corporate planning and performance management.

## Risk Management

Effective management of risk is crucial to the delivery of the Defence Aim. The Board considers risk on two levels: strategic risks (top down), which are set by the context within which Defence operates; and risk to the achievement of the objectives set out in the Defence Plan (bottom up). Strategic risks are categorised into realms, as set by the Board from time to time. For each realm a Board member leads work in the area, supported by a second Board member in the role of 'inquisitor'. The leader is responsible to the Board for the assessment and management of the risks within their realm, and to raise issues to the Board as the need arises. The inquisitor's role is to challenge to leader and encourage debate in the Board. The current realms cover operational or other failure; making the defence case; departmental decision making; attracting and keeping talent; maximising technological opportunities whilst minimising vulnerabilities; and perception of the Armed Forces at home and abroad. In June 2008 the Board added a further realm, for information risk. Specific risks to the achievement of the Defence

Plan are presented to the Defence Board in the Quarterly Performance Report, alongside the Defence Balanced Scorecard. The Board then considers whether any of these 'bottom-up' risks are sufficiently serious to merit specific action by the Board or inclusion in the strategic risk register.

## Performance Reporting

Specific performance information collected for the Defence Balanced Scorecard is used to prepare both the Defence Board's performance reviews and external reports of progress against Public Service Agreement targets and Departmental Strategic Objectives. A full account to Parliament of Departmental Performance, covering performance against all of the MoD's objectives and priorities, internal and external, is published in the Ministry of Defence Annual Report and Accounts.

## Defence Industrial Strategy and Defence Acquisition Change Programme

The Acquisition Policy Board, chaired by the Minister for Defence Equipment and Support, is the Department's senior board for addressing strategic acquisition issues and defence industrial policy, with a key responsibility for oversight of the implementation of the Defence Industrial Strategy. The Board provides direction, assesses progress and strengthens cross-cutting initiatives. The Defence Acquisition Change Programme (DACP) was set up in 2006 as a single coherent acquisition reform programme to deliver the structural, process, culture and behavioural change to implement the recommendations from the Enabling Acquisition Change report and facilitate good through life capability management as identified in the Defence Industrial Strategy. PUS is the Senior Responsible Owner for the DACP accountable to the Defence Management Board/Defence Board for its delivery, and chairs a top level Sponsoring Group. Day-to-day management is oversee a Programme Director with overall implementation responsibility, supported by a Programme Management Office, who chairs the Programme Board.

## Defence Change Portfolio

The Defence Change Portfolio was launched in 2002. 2nd PUS is the Senior Responsible Owner. It links the major business change initiatives across Defence through strong central guidance and direction, to produce a single, coherent and prioritised modernisation programme. It ensures key initiatives have robust governance and plans, driving through improvements in departmental business processes for improved efficiency and effectiveness, so as to maximise investment in front-line operational capability. Each initiative is sponsored by one of the Department's Ministers and supported by rigorous governance structures including a Senior Responsible Owner personally accountable to the Defence Management Board/Defence Board for maximising the delivery of benefits. During 2007-08 the Defence Change Portfolio was overseen by the Change Delivery Group, co-chaired by the 2nd PUS and VCDS. This directed and managed the Defence Change Portfolio overall and provided challenge and support to individual major change initiatives. From April 2008 this function was subsumed within the Defence Operating Board.

## Internal controls

The Board places great importance on corporate governance and the management of risk. Within the Head Office a number of senior-level process owners and stewardship holders are responsible for setting and monitoring pan-departmental processes and standards. They are ultimately accountable for the efficient and effective operation of these systems to the Permanent Secretary through the Defence Board. They define the standards and requirements for key activities (such as security, health and safety, personnel management and financial management) which take place across the various business units, to ensure that they operate consistently and effectively across Defence. Details are set out in the Department's annual Statement on Internal Control, and the operation of these arrangements is scrutinised annually by the Defence Audit Committee under its review of the Statement on Internal Control. The control and assurance arrangements operated by the Head Office are currently being reviewed under the Head Office Streamlining programme.

The Defence Audit Committee (DAC), chaired by an independent member of the Board, is at the heart of the assurance process. It uses a risk-based approach to review the condition of the Department's internal control systems and advise the Permanent Secretary on his annual Statement on Internal Control in the Departmental Resource Accounts. The terms of reference for the DAC can be found at www.mod.uk. DAC meetings are attended by the Director of Defence Internal Audit and senior National Audit Office representatives. Since 2004-05 we have published an annual report on the work of the audit committee on the Department's website alongside the Annual Report and Accounts.

The system of internal control covers a number of dimensions (such as efficient organisation and budgetary structures, sound business processes, and robust internal audit) but is, in particular based on a continuous process designed to identify and prioritise the risks to achievement of Departmental policies, aims and objectives, to evaluate the likelihood of these risks being realised - and the impact this would have - and to manage them efficiently, effectively and economically. The Department has a clear Corporate Governance policy, which is periodically reviewed and updated as necessary. This sets out managers' responsibility to anticipate risks, exploit opportunities and implement control and mitigation activities as a means of optimising performance and delivering continuous improvement. It also facilitates the Department's ability to:

● protect its people;

● harness its resources to manage more effectively the risk to the achievement of objectives;

● avoid disasters or catastrophes by managing those physical and other risks that have the potential to damage its assets, people or members of the public, or effect the environment; and,

● assess and manage risks associated with working with other nations and public and private organisations.

As Departmental Accounting Officer, PUS is personally accountable for the economic, efficient and effective use of Defence resources. He is also responsible for the prudent administration of the Department and the regularity and propriety of Defence expenditure. In recognition of these responsibilities, PUS is supported by the Director of Defence Internal Audit (DIA) who is responsible for evaluating the adequacy and effectiveness of the Department's risk management, control and governance processes, and providing the Permanent Under Secretary with an annual opinion. Following discussion with senior management and stakeholders, DIA produces an annual audit programme for approval by the DAC.

## Management Structure

Most Defence activity takes place outside the Head Office and is managed through Top Level Budget Holders and Trading Funds not included in the TLB structure. PUS grants each TLB holder extensive delegated powers over personnel, infrastructure and budget. The Royal Navy and Royal Air Force have single TLBs. The Army had separate TLBs for its Operational and Personnel commands throughout 2007-08, which were consolidated into a single TLB on 1 April 2008. On 1 April 2008 the single Service Chiefs of Staff became TLB Holder for their Service TLB. The other TLBs are Defence rather than single Service organisations. These are:

● Chief of Joint Operations/Permanent Joint Headquarters, responsible for the planning and execution of joint (tri-Service) operations, and for the management of Permanent Joint Operating Bases in Cyprus, Gibraltar, the Falkland Islands and Diego Garcia;

● Defence Equipment and Support, which procures equipment and provides logistics support to the armed forces;

● Defence Estates, which delivers estate maintenance, works and services, and manages service housing;

● The Science, Innovation and Technology TLB, which is responsible for delivering expert advice and developing scientific and technological solutions to satisfy Defence needs and problems; and,

- The Central TLB, including the MoD Head Office and providing corporate services to other TLBs.

During 2007-08 each TLB Holder had a 'contract' with the Head Office, known as a Service Delivery Agreement, which specified the outputs he was required to deliver, the resources he was given to deliver these outputs, and the authority delegated to TLB holders by PUS. From 1 April 2008 TLB Holders' output setting and resource allocation were subsumed within the Defence Plan, with their delegated authorities from PUS set out separately. Within the TLB structure are a number of specialist agencies spanning a range of Defence support activity including personnel administration, security vetting, and policing. The Secretary of State owns and is ultimately accountable for the performance of Defence Agencies and Trading Funds.

TLB Holders are required to account annually for their management of their organisations to PUS in the context of the Department's Statement on Internal Control. They are advised on this by a TLB Audit Committee, generally chaired by a non-executive member of the TLB management board, performing the same function for the TLB Holder as the DAC provides for PUS. TLB Audit Committee meetings are attended by representatives of both Defence Internal Audit and the National Audit Office.

## Non-Departmental Public Bodies

The Department sponsors five executive and eleven advisory Non-Departmental Public Bodies (NDPBs), two Public Corporations, one Stakeholder Advisory Group and an Independent Monitoring Board. A brief description of the Executive NDPBs is below. Details of their funding from the Defence Budget and total gross expenditure can be found in the Departmental Resource Accounts. More detailed information on these and the other bodies sponsored by the department can be found at the MoD website at www.mod.uk.

## Executive NDPBs

The Department's Executive NDPBs are Service museums with charitable status, each of which retain close links with the Armed Forces (the Royal Naval Museum, the Royal Navy Submarine Museum, the Royal Marines Museum, the National Army Museum and the RAF Museum). A sixth museum, the Fleet Air Arm museum is formally classified as a Public Corporation. The arrangements between the Department and these bodies on the conditions governing payment and expenditure of the Grants in Aid made by the MoD are set out formally in a Financial Memorandum.

# Annex C

## PSA Target 2: Detailed Assessment Against Performance Indicators

### A. Afghanistan: Partly met.

By end 2007-08: Accountable and democratic structures for Afghanistan's governing institutions and Armed Forces, representing Afghanistan's ethnic diversity, and operating with respect for human rights.

Good progress was made overall in 2007-08, building on activities in the previous two years. The UK government focussed on building effective state institutions and better governance, through funding of over £100M. Progress on these in the south has been limited by ongoing insurgency and limited Government of Afghanistan capacity. The Afghan National Army (ANA) led a successful operation to clear the Taliban for Musa Qala, allowing the Afghan government to begin to provide stabilisation and governance. British Forces continued to train and provide specialist advice to the ANA, which is making good progress; 50,000 of a total projected strength of 80,000 are now deployed. Efforts to address the under-performance of the Afghan National Police continue and the UK contributes to the European Police Mission. UK government-funded activities aimed at further strengthening the rule of law, including counter-narcotics, and building public confidence have focussed on mentoring and training.

### B. Balkans: Partly met.

By end 2007-08: Western Balkan states at peace within and between themselves and continuing on the path to closer integration with the EU and NATO.

The countries of the Balkans remain at peace, though inter-ethnic tensions persist. Kosovo declared independence on 17 February 2008. While the overall situation is stable, there have been violent incidents in the (Serb-majority) north. Serbia's improved cooperation with the Tribunal for the Former Yugoslavia had led to the initialling of its EU Stabilisation and Association Agreement (SAA), though recent attacks against Embassies in Belgrade and statements condoning violence are concerning. Macedonia made renewed reform progress while Montenegro concluded its EU SAA. Bosnia inched towards police reform, allowing movement. The UK government has continued to support the Western Balkans' Euro-Atlantic integration, and has been particularly active on resolving Kosovo's final status. UK government programmes focus on government capacity and accountability; on security and justice sector reform; on refugee and internally displaced person returns; and on assisting minority communities and inclusive economic growth.

### C. Democratic Republic of Congo (DRC): Partly met.

By end 2007-08: Reduced cross border interference in Eastern DRC, a stable government in Kinshasa overseeing accountable security services and a reduction in militia operating outside such democratic government control. (This target will focus on DRC but will necessarily take account of wider Great Lakes dynamics)

With support from the UK government, the DRC government is making credible efforts to resolve conflict politically. DRC and Rwanda are cooperating to dismantle the Democratic Forces for the Liberation of Rwanda militia. However, fighting has occurred in eastern DRC between the Armed Forces, rebel soldiers and other illegal militias, resulting in extensive civilian displacement. The UK government is contributing substantially to work to stabilise the Kivus and a successful disarmament, demobilisation, repatriation, reinstallation and reinsertion programme has largely pacified Ituri district. The UK government has called for action on impunity and justice for victims of abuses by the armed forces.

## D. Iraq: Partly met.

By end 2007-08: A stable, united and law abiding state, within its present borders, cooperating with the international community, no longer posing a threat to its neighbours or to international security, abiding by all its international obligations and providing effective, representative and inclusive government for all its people.

Overall, security improved in Iraq in 2007-08. The US 'surge', combined with the tribal awakening and the growing capabilities and confidence of the Iraqi Security Forces, saw real gains. These were reflected in the transfer of security responsibility in six provinces, including Maysan and Basra. All four provinces in the south-east have now transferred. Serious challenges remain in Basra, but the authorities have shown they are able to maintain security and initiate key reforms. Although there were setbacks in 2007, including the withdrawal of Sunni parties from government, there has been some political progress in late 2007 and early 2008. The council of Representatives has passed legislation on amnesty for detainees, provincial powers and de-ba'athification. The Executive Council, a small group of senior politicians representing the key political groups, provides a forum for reaching agreement on key decisions. Iraq's relations with neighbouring states are improving from a low base, with regular meetings of the Neighbours Group. Both the EU and the UN have shown signs over the last year of engaging more positively with Iraq.

## E. Middle East Peace Process (MAPP): Not met.

By end 2007-08: Maximising the opportunity of Israeli withdrawal from Gaza and parts of the West Bank, significant progress towards a negotiated settlement resulting in the emergence of an independent, democratic, and viable Palestinian state with a reformed security sector, living side by side in peace and security with Israel.

Under the guidance of the United States, following the Annapolis meeting, the two sides have started bilateral talks. But challenges on the ground threaten to disrupt the political process.

Israel continued military operations in Hamas-controlled Gaza and incursions into area A in the West Bank. Rocket and mortar attacks from Gaza continue and the first suicide bombing for a year took place on 4 February 2007. The UK has tried to ensure that the international community's approach is balanced and positive, maintaining a focus on improving the Palestinian economy and supporting the Palestinian Authority (PA). The UK continues to encourage the political process, supporting leadership by the US. In June 2007 the UK government resumed direct support to the PA, providing £31M bilaterally to the Palestinians in 2007-08 and contributing to the Palestinian treasury through a European Union mechanism. Project work with Israeli and Palestinian civil society continues to focus on peace promotion through encouraging policy change. The UK government is also providing funding for: an NGO-managed project which has moved the route of the separation barrier closer to the green line; a project which aims to tackle planning problems for Palestinian villages in Israeli-controlled areas; and a project looking at systematic failures in due process in the Israeli military courts. The UK government continues to encourage sustainable security sector reform in the West Bank through providing technical expertise to the US Security Coordinator's team. This includes the deployment of a British Support Team based in Ramallah that can liaise directly with the PA.

## F. Nepal: Partly met.

By end 2007-08: A stable Nepal with a durable ceasefire in place with the Maoists, democratic institutions restored with respect for human rights and significant progress towards a constitutional settlement.

Nepal has continued to make progress towards the restoration of democracy though elections to a Constituent Assembly have twice been postponed. Following a recent agreement between the government and groups representing the Madhes, elections are set to take place in April 2008. Working with the government, political parties, the UN and international partners, the UK has helped to co-ordinate efforts to move the peace process forward towards a lasting peace including through a significant development assistance programme. Through the UN, we were able to secure an extension to the United Nations Mission in Nepal's mandate to July 2008.

## G. Nigeria: Partly met.

By end 2007-08: Local and central government effectively managing and resolving conflict and a reduction in the number of people affected by conflict.

Politically-motivated crime levels have not increased, though political tensions continue over the outcome of the April 2007 presidential election. Anti-corruption and the Delta remain UK government priorities in Nigeria. Recent successes include anti-money laundering investigations and engagement with communities in the Delta on governance and stakeholder participation. Also successful have been projects to foster inter-religious understanding in the north. However, the Delta continues to be unstable with bouts of urban violence in Port Harcourt, though the Joint Task Force recently intervened to stop an outbreak of gang violence. Inter-communal fighting between Christian and Muslim communities in the north is becoming more regular.

## H. Sierra Leone: Met.

By end 2007-08: Ongoing stable and democratic government overseeing accountable security services and a reduction in regional militia.

Sierra Leone has a democratically elected, stable government following elections in August/September 2007. The elections were judged free and fair, although 7% of polling stations were disqualified due to greater than 100% voter turnout. The security services performed well and the elections were largely peaceful despite some evidence of the use of former combatants to intimidate opposing parties. The UK government's intense political lobbying and substantial assistance helped to ensure the professionalism and accountability of the security services and the effective performance of the National Electoral Commission. It also made effective voter education and a nation-wide local electoral observer network possible. The UK government continues to provide a large amount of technical assistance to help increase the sustainability of the security sector.

## I. Sudan: North/South: Partly met. Darfur: Not met.

By end 2007-08: A fully implemented comprehensive peace agreement between the Government of Sudan and the SPLM, progress towards a stable and democratic government, a reduction in militia operating outside democratic control, and a reduction in the number of deaths through violent conflict.

*Sudan:* Progress against the Comprehensive Peace Agreement (CPA) is on course for national elections by July 2009. Most regular army units have redeployed in line with CPA; some irregular groups have not. Progress on Joint Integrated Units of northern and southern Sudanese forces remains slow but the UK is leading work to improve their operational effectiveness. The National Congress Party and the Sudanese People's Liberation Movement have not agreed an administration in the disputed area of Abyei, nor demarcation of the north-south border. Commissions in the north and south have adopted a national strategy for disarmament, demobilisation and reintegration but they have not agreed how to co-operate in the transitional areas or when to start demobilisation. A draft white paper sets out a framework for transformation of the Sudanese People's Liberation Army. Community security is limited in the south and more effort is needed on reconciliation processes.

*Darfur:* The PSA indicator for Sudan was drawn up before the conflict in Darfur, but we have nevertheless made a separate assessment. Progress to resolve the conflict is still limited: a UN-AU peacekeeping force (UNAMID) has been agreed but will not deploy fully until the end of 2008. The UK led efforts to establish the Darfur Community Peace and Stability Fund designed to promote peace at the local level. Violence, largely banditry, is endemic and constraining humanitarian relief efforts. Malnutrition is worsening in internally displaced persons' camps. Fighting between regular forces and irregular militia has flared up in West Darfur in the first quarter of 2008 and across the border in Chad since the end of November 2007. The political process is still stalled because of divisions between groups in Darfur.

## J. UN Peacekeeping: Partly met.

By end 2007-08: All potential UN peacekeeping missions should follow the principles of integrated and comprehensive planning set out in the Brahimi Report of 2000, incorporating these from the onset of the planning process and carrying them forward into mission deployment with appropriate training of personnel and systematic processes for learning lessons and applying best practice.

The UK government has worked to maintain momentum on implementation of the Integrated Mission Planning Process (IMPP) through lobbying in New York, the Special Committee on Peacekeeping Operations (C34), and by providing financial support to the Department of Peacekeeping Operations (DPKO). The application of the IMPP has not been systematic. DPKO used IMPP to guide efforts during the initial planning phase for the United Nations-African Union Mission in Darfur, and set up an Integrated Operating Team to ensure IMPP principles were applied. However, the mission did not fully apply IMPP, citing a lack of user-friendly manuals as a key obstacle. UK government officials continue to use the C34 to push for proper utilisation of IMPP.

## K. UN Peacekeeping: Met.

By end 2007-08: A 5% increase in the number of states contributing effective peacekeepers to regional and international Peace Support Operations (PSOs) under a UN mandate, with adjustment where necessary for changes in the demand for peacekeepers.

Field-based peacekeeping personnel deployed to UN-led missions have seen a 5% increase during 2007-08. 119 different countries now contribute troops. The UK government, with other donors, provided a range of training to build capacity of existing and potential troop contributing countries and senior mission leaders, which contributed to the overall increase in the number of effective peacekeepers in UN-mandated peace support operations.

## L. African Peacekeeping: Partly met.

By end 2007-08: Increased capacity in the African Union (AU) and sub-regional security organisations to manage peacekeeping missions.

UK support has been instrumental in assisting the African Standby Force (ASF) to develop. Training, logistics and rapid deployment are moving forward. However, progress on the ASF remains limited by weak capacity at the African Union and in African regions. Progress on five regional brigades remains uneven. There is new momentum in the Eastern Africa Standby Brigade, with the UK as lead partner, and the Southern African Development Community launched its brigade in August 2007. Much UK effort focuses on the Economic Community of West African States, which remains the most advanced region. The UK government continues to make a major contribution to increasing the number of trained African peacekeeping personnel (over 11,000 trained since 2004) including through UK training teams in Africa.

# Annex D

## Performance Management

Since 2000, the strategic management of the MoD has been underpinned and facilitated by the Defence Balanced Scorecard. At the highest conceptual level, the Defence Balanced Scorecard is a framework that helps the Defence Board translate strategy into operational objectives that drive both behaviour and performance. This is articulated in the Departmental Plan that sets out the Department's top level strategic objectives, including its Public Service Agreement (PSA) targets and Departmental Strategic Objectives (DSOs). The Defence Balanced Scorecard tells the Board how well the Department is doing in terms of the objectives that underpin the Plan and thus provides insight into its ability to achieve the Defence Vision.

The first Balanced Scorecards were devised for private sector bodies. As a public sector organisation, with outputs not expressed in financial terms, the Department has adapted the model to reflect better the nature of defence. Accordingly, the four perspectives of the Defence Balanced Scorecard (Purpose, Resources, Enabling Processes and Future) summarise the breadth of defence activity and cover the MoD's main areas of business. This Balanced Scorecard for 2007-08 is illustrated below.

## Purpose

### Are we fit for today's challenges and ready for tomorrow's tasks?

**Current Operations:** Succeed in operations and Military Tasks today

**Readiness:** Be ready for the tasks of tomorrow

**Policy:** Work with allies, other governments and multilateral institutions to provide a security framework that matches new threats and instabilities

**Defence in the Wider Community:** Work with other Government Departments to contribute to the Government's wider agenda, including on sustainable development

## Resources

### Are we using our resources to best effect?

**People:** Manage our people to provide sufficient, capable and motivated Service and civilian personnel

**Finance & Efficiency:** Maximise our outputs within allocated financial resources

**Estate:** Maintain and develop estate infrastructure of the right capability and quality

## Enabling Processes

### Are we a high performing organisation?

**Equipment & Support:** Equip, support and sustain our Armed Forces

**Safety, Security, Business Continuity:** Enable safe, secure and resilient operational capability

**Reputation:** Enhance our reputation amongst our own people and externally

## Future

### Are we building for future success?

**Future Capabilities:** Develop the capabilities required to meet the tasks of tomorrow

**Change:** Develop flexible and efficient organisations, processes and behaviour to support the Armed Forces

**Future Personnel:** Deliver the personnel plans to meet the needs of current and future tasks

There are a number of strategic objectives in each perspective – and 13 in total. Performance against each objective is assessed to an agreed timescale (either quarterly, six-monthly, or annually) reflecting the nature and volatility of the underlying data. Against each objective, targets setting out required levels of performance are agreed with those in the Department who are responsible for achieving the objectives – for delivery. Detailed Performance Indicators and metrics are also agreed. The Performance Indicators are a mixture of lag indicators (which inform the Board about actual achievements) and lead indicators (which are used to encourage different behaviours). Assessments may be quantitative or qualitative, and will either be provided by objective sources or subjected to lower level scrutiny and audit – by Front Line Commands or the Resources and Plans Directorates, for example. Agreeing the objectives, targets, performance indicators and metrics is an annual exercise, conducted prior to the publication of the Departmental Plan.

The Defence Board receives a performance report four times a year. When an objective is being assessed, the report will include an assessment of actual performance from the previous report, the current quarter, and a forecast of performance at the end of the next three to four financial years. Analysis of the issues highlighted by the performance assessments is included in the report, together with an assessment of the key risks that could jeopardise the achievement of objectives. In addition to the Defence Board's Strategic Risk process, a 'bottom up' risk picture is presented associating individual risks with particular objectives from the Departmental Plan. This is drawn from the Risk Register consolidated from those maintained by TLBs and Process Owners. The information, and assessments, that the Defence Board receive are used to inform board discussion and decision – they may, for example, support decisions to adjust strategic direction and priorities, or the reallocation of resources. And as the Department's performance against PSA targets and DSOs is reported and assessed in the Defence Balanced Scorecard, these assessments underpin the Department's performance reports to Parliament, No 10, HM Treasury and the Cabinet Office.

The Department's approach, and the data systems underpinning it, are formally reviewed about every two to three years,, in 2002 by the Department's internal auditors, and in 2003-04 and 2006-07 by the National Audit Office for the 2002 and 2004 Spending Review PSA data systems respectively. The December 2006 *Third Validation Compendium Report* on the quality of data systems underpinning the 2004 Spending Review PSAs was generally positive about the Department's data systems, none of which were assessed as 'not fit for purpose'. And it found no weaknesses in the quality of disclosure in the Department's public performance reports. In addition, in June 2005 the NAO published a report on the Department's arrangements for assessing and reporting military readiness following an extensive review which concluded that the Department had a good and continuously improving system for reporting readiness; and in October 2005 the NAO published a report on Joint Targets, including the Joint Target for Conflict Prevention shared by MoD, FCO and DfID.

More specifically:

● on **Operations** (SR04 PSA target 1) the Department provides a periodic and formal overall assessment through its Public Service Agreement and Annual Performance Reports. These assessments are underpinned by an appropriate and robust system for judging performance on operations and military tasks against the objectives established by Ministers. Further details are set out in the Department's supplementary memorandum to the House of Commons Defence Committee, published in its report on the MoD Annual Report and Accounts 2005-06 (HC 57 dated 28 November 2006). In the *Third Validation Compendium Report* the NAO concluded that the data system is "fit for the purpose of measuring and reporting performance" against this target;

● on **Conflict Prevention** (SR04 PSA target 2, joint with FCO and DfID) the NAO concluded in the *Third Validation Compendium Report* that the data system addressed the majority of risks to data quality, but needed strengthening to ensure that remaining risks were adequately concerned. In particular, the processes for assessing performance needed to be documented more clearly. The report noted that procedures had been put in place to address this. The results were reflected in the relevant Departmental Spring Performance Reports;

- on **Readiness** (SR04 PSA target 3) the NAO found in its 2005 report on *Assessing and Reporting Military Readiness* that the Department has a good system for defining, measuring and reporting the readiness of the Armed Forces which compares well with those used by other countries. It noted that the readiness reporting system is continuously evolving to incorporate further improvements. In the *Third Validation Compendium Report* it concluded that while broadly fit for purpose the PSA readiness reporting system should be further strengthened, primarily to establish a system to report performance against the ability to deploy, sustain and recover the Armed Forces. This work was concluded in time to inform the Annual Report and Accounts for 2006-07. Work to further refine the Department's readiness reporting system in light of the implications of the continuing high level of operations is set out in the Essay on pages 56 to 57 of the Annual Report

- on **European Security** (SR04 PSA target 4, joint with FCO) the NAO concluded in the *Third Validation Compendium Report* that, as with conflict prevention, the compilation and assessment process needed to be documented more thoroughly to ensure consistency of judgement over time. Further work was taken forward to address this point;

- on **Manning Balance** (SR04 PSA target 5) the NAO concluded in the *Third Validation Compendium Report* that the data system was fit for the purpose of measuring and reporting performance. Some of the underpinning data streams have been temporarily affected by the introduction of the Joint Personnel Administration system. This is reflected as necessary in the footnotes to the relevant tables in this report; and

- on **Equipment Procurement** (SR04 PSA target 6), the NAO's annual Major Projects Report covers cost, time and performance data for a sample of large projects. The NAO

concluded in the *Third Validation Compendium Report* that the data system was fit for the purpose of measuring and reporting performance.

Additionally, the financial data underpinning assessment of the 2004 efficiency target ultimately derives from the Departmental Resource Accounts, which are audited by the NAO. Defence Internal Audit validates logistics efficiency data every year, in 2006-07 reviewed the efficiencies achieved by the People Programme, and is currently conducting a wider validation exercise on conclusion of the SR04 efficiency programme, as indicated in the Annual Report. Defence Internal Audit's reports are visible to the NAO. The NAO itself conducted a wider review of the Government's efficiency programme in 2006-07 *(The Efficiency Programme: A Second Review of Progress)*. This included reporting on a number of the programmes within the defence efficiency programme, and specifically cited as an example of good practice the comprehensive auditing framework established to assess efficiencies arising from the Defence Logistics transformation Programme (which comprises some 40% of the Department's efficiency programme by value).

The Department's approach to strategic management and performance continues to attract interest from wider audiences, including other Government Departments, local authorities, and other nations' Ministries or Departments of Defence. In addition, MoD performance managers are regularly invited to address and take part in international strategic and performance management symposia. This interaction provides the opportunity to share ideas and pick up examples of good practice from others that can help improve the strategic management of the Department.

# Annex E

## Defence Agency Performance

### Defence Agency Performance

| Name | Overall performance Number and % of targets achieved[1] | | | Year on year performance – number and % of targets met which were directly comparable with the previous year | | Performance relative to target against comparable Key Targets in 06/07 (better/same/worse) |
|---|---|---|---|---|---|---|
| | 07/08 | 06/07 | 05/06 | 07/08 | 06/07 | |
| Defence Analytical Services Agency[1] | 8/14 57% | 10/12 83% | 8/10 80% | 7/11 64% | 8/9 89% | 1/7/3 |
| Defence Medical Education and Training Agency[2] | 6/7 86% | 4/6 67% | 3/6 50% | 5/5 100% | 4/6 67% | 3/1/1 |
| Defence Storage and Distribution Agency | 3/5[3] 60% | 6/6 100% | 6/6 100% | 3/5 60% | 6/6 100% | 1/1/3 |
| Defence Vetting Agency | 6/9 66% | 8/9 89% | 11/16 69% | 5/8 63% | 7/8 88% | 2/2/4 |
| MoD Police and Guarding Agency | 4/8 50% | 4/10 40% | 3/8 38% | 3/7 43% | 1/3 33% | 1/1/5 |
| People, Pay and Pensions Agency | 14/21 66% | 8/9 89% | 8/8 100% | 3/3 100% | 5/6 83% | 1/0/2 |
| Service Children's Education | 21/34 62% | 25/30 83% | 27/34 79% | 18/29 62% | 25/30 83% | 10/1/18 |
| Service Personnel and Veterans Agency | 8/12 67% | 16/17 94%[4] | 16/17 94%[4] | 3/4 75% | n/a | 2/1/1 |

Footnotes:
[1] Where there are multiple elements to a target, these have been counted separately.
[2] Agency status removed 1 April 08
[3] Performance against sixth key target still to be confirmed
[4] combined total for Armed Forces Personnel and Administration Agency and Veterans Agency which merged to form the SPVA on 1 April 07.

## Organisational changes

On 1 April 2008 agency status was removed from the Defence Analytical Services Agency and the Defence Medical Education and Training Agency.

## Defence Analytical Services Agency

DASA delivered against the majority of its Key Targets despite being faced with particular challenges in 2007-08. The main problem has been a consistently high level of vacancies throughout the year that contributed to the agency failing to meet its Service Level Agreement delivery targets and has consequently led to a reduction in Customer Satisfaction index. Recruitment and retention of specialist statistician and economist staff remains an issue and was hampered to a degree by uncertainty over MoD Head Office Streamlining plans and the need to move a team from RAF Innsworth to RAF High Wycombe as part of an RAF Relocation programme. This gave rise to loss of staff, dislocation and a certain reduction in output. Another key issue has been the quality of data available from the main departmental Management Information systems, particularly Joint Personnel Administration system, which continues to present problems.

## Defence Medical Education and Training Agency

DMETA continued to train and prepare secondary care personnel to meet the Commanders' in Chief requirements to support deployed operations and exercises. Adjustments were made to manage both the increased operational tempo and the numbers of casualties being repatriated to the UK. This has required expansion of clinical and supporting activities in Selly Oak Hospital, Birmingham, accomplished by reorganisation and enhancement of the Royal Centre for Defence Medicine and the Defence Medical Rehabilitation Centre at Headley Court.

Despite uncertainty over the application process for medical training within the NHS, DMETA successfully secured training places for all medical officers selected for entry into specialist training. All Nurse and Allied Health Professionals' training has now relocated to the Defence School of Secondary Health Care in Birmingham, where uniformed graduates achieve consistently higher numbers of

distinctions than their civilian peers. The Agency met all its key targets and sub-targets, other than one relating to harmony/separated service, which was narrowly missed.

## Defence Storage and Distribution Agency

DSDA has delivered almost all of its Future Defence Supply Chain initiative (FDSCi) headcount and service commitments two years ahead of schedule, as well as delivering additional headcount reductions. By June 2008, the final site closure will be complete and the business should be operating with approximately 2,337 posts less than it did three years ago. The operating costs of the business will reduce by a further £22M in the current financial year and savings are ahead of the Future Defence Supply Chain Initiative targets. Since October 2007 DSDA has been delivering over 90% of routine demands to the Unit or point of embarkation within seven calendar days compared with 49 days in December 2005. The Agency failed to meet two sub-targets relating to customer requirements as a result of the introduction of more demanding targets and consolidation of the DSDA estate, whilst performance against its efficiency target has yet to be confirmed.

## Defence Vetting Agency

The Agency met six out of nine of its Key Targets and sub-targets, failing the Key Target relating to routine clearances, which had three sub-elements. Even there, performance improved over the course of the year and the target was met in the last six months. The Agency is developing its IT system and customer access by way of a vetting transformation programme to help deliver the government's vision of a national security vetting service. The customer base and exposure to a wide variety of personnel security requirements continued to widen from the Defence area into a large portfolio of other government departments, organisations and national settings. This has resulted in approximately another 4% of national security vetting work being awarded from other departments which will be processed from 1 April 08, with a further 3-4% of new work likely to be awarded in 2008-2009.

## Ministry of Defence Police and Guarding Agency

The Agency continues to deliver an effective policing and guarding service to the Defence Estate in support of the Defence Mission and wider MoD objectives. The Agency performed well against a very challenging set of key targets that were agreed in a very difficult financial climate, meeting four out of eight targets and sub-targets. Customer satisfaction with the Ministry of Defence Police increased to 95%. Although satisfaction with the Ministry of Defence Guard Service and achievement of customer tasking were slightly down, the levels achieved should be viewed in the context of the financial constraints that were in place throughout the year. The Agency also missed its Key Target relating to the Crime Detection Rate, which can be attributed to the way that crime is investigated and detected although satisfaction with the Military Guard Service was slightly down, as was the achievement of customer tasking. The Agency also missed its Key Target relating to the Crime Detection Rate, which can be attributed to the way that crime is investigated and detected and the impact of the Home Office Accounting Rules. Considerable progress to address the shortfall between the Agency's budget allocation and the cost of delivering policing and guarding outputs has been made over the past twelve months through a partnership approach between the Agency and its customers and stakeholders.

## People, Pay and Pensions Agency

During its second full year of operation the PPPA completed the roll out of remaining HR services, including external recruitment and case advisory services. A full range of services are now in place and working. The Agency has performed close or to its agreed Service Level Agreement standards this year despite the higher than expected volumes of work and the launch of some of the new services. A number of the targets were broken down this year into their constituent elements, which has made it difficult to compare performance with the previous year. The agency met 14 out of 21 of its targets and sub-targets, very narrowly missing sub-targets relating to the timeliness of expenses payments, the accuracy of pension awards and satisfaction with pay/pensions/expenses. The performance of the civilian pay system was maintained despite the

necessary work and changes required to support the final transition and full operation of the new system which was completed by July 2007. The service is now operating with some 95,000 employees across eight different payrolls. The concept of Lean was introduced across parts of the Agency, successfully identifying ways in which processes could be simplified and improved.

## Service Children's Education

The Agency met 21 out of 34 of its Key Targets and sub-targets, with particularly high achievement at Key Stages 1 and 3, where it was notionally ranked third and first out of the 150 English Local Authorities. Although the progress made over the past few years at Key Stage 2 was not continued this year, with the five key sub-targets narrowly missed, the results remain around the (England) National average. Changes to the OfSTED inspection process led to the previous Key Target 5 being dropped for 2006-07, with a revised Key Target 4 being adopted for 2007-08 onwards. A total of 12 SCE schools were subject to the new short-notice inspection with all schools being ranked at least Satisfactory and nine of the twelve being assessed as Good or Outstanding. GCSE results again outstripped the National average as did performance at "A"-Level. The final key target confirmed that parental satisfaction remains exceptionally high at 94% of respondents.

## Service Personnel and Veterans Agency

The formation of the Agency has enabled a more integrated and through life approach to delivering services to Service Personnel, Veterans and their dependants. The Agency's challenging targets included the full roll out of Joint Personnel Administration (JPA) and a rationalisation and change programme following merger. The Agency achieved a high standard of delivery across a wide range of services, meeting eight of its twelve Key Targets and sub-targets. It very narrowly missed the accuracy element of the Key Target for delivery of Service Pay by 0.01%, and also missed Key Targets relating to time for clearing claims under the War Pensions Scheme and Armed Forces Compensation Scheme, response times to written complaints and efficiency savings.

Following the successful implementation of JPA, individual Servicemen and women now receive much of their administrative support directly via self service computer terminals and an SPVA Enquiry Service backed up by specialist back office teams. As a result of merger there has been a particular attention to integrating the separate pensions and compensation components of the business and this has identified a number of synergies and revised processing which will be both more efficient and deliver an improved service to customers.

# Trading Funds

## Defence Trading Fund Performance

| Name | Overall Performance Number and % of targets achieved | | | Year on Year Performance – number and % of targets met which were directly comparable with the previous year | | Relative performance against comparable targets in 06/07 (better/same/ worse) |
|---|---|---|---|---|---|---|
| | 07/08 | 06/07 | 05/06 | 07/08 | 06/07 | |
| ABRO | 4/5 80% | 4/5 80% | 4/5 80% | 1/2 50% | 4/5 80% | 1/0/1 |
| DARA | 4/4 100% | 4/4 100% | 3/4 75% | 3/3 100% | 3/3 100% | 2/1/0 |
| Defence Science and Technology Laboratory (DSTL) | 6/5/8 81% | 5/6 83% | 8/10 80% | 3/4 75% | 4/5 80% | 0/4/0 |
| Met Office | 4/4 100% | 4/4 100% | 5/5 100% | 2/2 100% | 2/2 100% | 2/0/0 |
| UK Hydrographic Office (UKHO) | 4/4 100% | 3/6 50% | 3/6 50% | 3/3 100% | 3/5 60% | 3/1/0 |

### ABRO

The service that ABRO provides to the Armed Forces continued to meet Customer demands for repair and maintenance across the full range of land based equipments both from its own workshops and an increasing number of in-barracks support locations. Ministers announced on 22 May 2007 the intention to create a new defence support organisation by merging ABRO, retained business units from the Defence Aviation Repair Agency (DARA) and certain other defence support facilities. Following a period of Trades Union consultation, Ministers confirmed this in statements to Parliament on 25 July 2008. Following the appropriate legislative process, this new organisation, the Defence Support Group (DSG), began formal trading on 1 April 2008. Its remit is to focus solely on the delivery of the Defence Industrial and Technology Strategies by being a flexible, responsive, operationally excellent organisation that provides a cost competitive in-house maintenance, repair, overhaul and upgrade capability in support of the Armed Forces, while operating in partnership with industry.

While the sterling performance put in by ABRO's employees in meeting customers' requirements should be commended, a major disappointment from a business perspective was the fact that the costs incurred in delivering this output were so great that ABRO posted an operating loss during the financial year. This poor result has adversely affected the Return on Capital Employed Key Target, which is one measure against which ABRO's success is calculated. Subsequent investigations have revealed a significant control weakness in the business reporting and management information systems, which did not provide adequate warning that the risk of cost overruns were becoming more likely. Plans are already in place and action is underway to strengthen business and risk-reporting systems, which will help ensure this failure to achieve our business goals is not repeated in the future.

Despite the disappointment in failing to achieve all the Key Targets against which the business is measured in its final year of trading as ABRO, there were laudible successes which should be acknowledged. Employees delivered critical equipment to the Armed Forces operating in Theatre and supported operations by deploying to Afghanistan, Kuwait and Iraq. Their performance during the year was notable and praised by their service colleagues who are acknowledging the equipment ABRO provided was helping save lives in extreme combat conditions.

## DARA

The Defence Aviation Repair Agency (DARA) provided deep level maintenance, repair and overhaul (MRO) services for VC10 aircraft, systems and components. The MoD defence-related work accounted for the majority of DARA's revenue, either directly to the MoD or as a sub-contractor to defence Original Equipment Manufacturers (OEMs).

Ministers announced on 22 May 2007 the intention to create a new defence support organisation by merging DARA's retained business units with ABRO and certain other defence support facilities. Following a period of

trades union consultation, Ministers confirmed the merger in statements to Parliament on 25 July 2008. Following the appropriate legislative process, this new organisation, the Defence Support Group (DSG), began formal trading on 1 April 2008. Its remit is to focus solely on the delivery of the Defence Industrial and Technology Strategies by being a flexible, responsive, operationally excellent organisation that provides a cost competitive in-house maintenance, repair, overhaul and upgrade capability in support of the Armed Forces, while operating in partnership with industry.

As well as working on the successful merger programme, many DARA employees were also closely involved in the sale of DARA's Rotary and Components businesses to Vector Aerospace International Ltd, which was successfully concluded on 31 March 2008. Throughout the reporting period, employees produced an impressive performance to achieve all the key targets set by Ministers and deliver solid, profitable and tangible results in DARA's final year of trading. With no major quality concerns, an increase on planned profit, reducing costs, better than anticipated efficiency targets and an improved Return on Capital Employed (RoCE) against plan resulted in a notable trading performance that will allow DARA to fully exploit its strengths in the new DSG organisation.

## Defence Science and Technology Laboratory

Dstl's core role is to provide independent, objective, high quality, scientific, analytical, technological and engineering advice and services to the MoD and UK Armed Forces. It carries out only work which it would be inappropriate to undertake in the private sector. Its mission is to create the winning edge for the UK Armed Forces and Government through the best use of science and technology, by delivering timely advice and solutions to the Government's most important defence and national security related problems in the most efficient and effective manner.

Dstl has continued to perform robustly this year. Turnover rose from £366.8M (in 2006-07) to £378.9M. Group turnover amounted to £379.9M. Excluding Ploughshare, Dstl's profit for the financial year fell from £22.8M in 2006-07 to £18.9M and Return on Capital Employed (ROCE) fell from 7.9% to 5.5% over the same period, this was mainly due to costs being incurred on non-capital infrastructure investments relating to the i lab transition programme and a new Financial/HR system. Manpower change rates continued to be held below the target for the sixth consecutive year, indicating a reduction in real terms of the cost to customers.

This year we have achieved or exceeded all our financial targets in terms of cash flow management and continuing affordability of our internal investment. We have established our customer-focussed Programmes Area to strengthen the coherence of our services and products, and embedded account management within Dstl and have improved management of our customer processes. We have established a Sales and Order Book to enable us to assess our future business prospects and priorities more accurately. Levels of customer satisfaction remain high at 73.5% for our overall service provision and feedback demonstrates that we are having an impact on our customers' most important issues, from support through to policy thinking and from military capability development through to major acquisition programmes, to direct support to defence and security-related operations in theatre.

Dstl inherited a range of scientific and technical capabilities. We have established the planning framework that will enable us to identify and develop the capabilities we will require for the future. A key element of this has been to agree, with our Owner, an initial set of core capabilities that Dstl will sustain to underpin MoD and other government department requirements. Dstl's wholly owned technology management company, Ploughshare Innovations Ltd (PIL), established in 2005 as a specialist technology transfer organisation has successfully managed the sales of Acolyte Biomedica Ltd to 3M Healthcare, and the assets of a second company have also been sold. PIL has also formed four new spin-out companies and has tripled the annual income received from licence fees and royalties.

Looking to the future, Dstl is continuing to develop its partnerships in line with the Defence Industrial Strategy and the Defence Technology Strategy. This includes the new Defence Equipment and Support organisation, other customers, industry and science and technology providers. We do this while continuing to invest in Dstl's future capabilities. The strategic integrated laboratory improvement programme 'i lab' remains a key enabler to this, with the most significant issues over the next two years being (a) to rationalise the Dstl estate to three core sites in order to maximise synergy and coherence of delivery to customers, and to reduce unnecessary duplication in laboratories, facilities and support functions, and (b) to ensure Dstl has in place an integrated corporate business environment by the end of 2008-09. These themes are reflected in Dstl's new Key Targets.

## Met Office

2007-08 was another successful year for the Met Office, meeting all of its Key Performance Targets for the third year running. We provided excellent forecasts of a number of very high profile weather events, notably the major flooding of summer 2007, the storm surges of November 2007 and the severe gales of March 2008. Following the flooding events of last summer, the Met Office has informed many lessons learned reviews and enquiries, including those by Sir Michael Pitt, the Environment Food and Rural Affairs Committee of the UK Parliament and the Scottish Parliament's Rural Affairs and Environment Committee. Contributions by the Met Office included factual accounts of the weather which led to the disruption; how it worked with other organisations to ensure they were well informed with accurate and up to date information: and improvements which have been identified both internally and externally. While the Met Office's contribution was mostly very good, it recognises that further improvements can be made to the benefit of the public and emergency response community. In this context, the Met Office made enhancements to the national Severe Weather Warning Service during the year including the introduction of a new tier of alert, the Advisory, which supplements the Met Office's Early and Flash warnings.

In response to customer requirements, the Met Office conducted a review into the provision of services to Defence which has resulted in the development of a new service delivery concept. Following consultation with the Trade Union, a new network structure has been designed which will enable the more efficient and effective delivery of Met services in the future. The Met

Office has also continued to provide support to the Armed Forces through the Mobile Met Unit, with members deployed in a number of locations, including Iraq and Afghanistan.

The Intergovernmental Panel of Climate Change (IPCC) was jointly awarded the Nobel Peace Prize in recognition of "their efforts to build up and disseminate greater knowledge about man-made climate change, and to lay the foundations for the measures that are needed to counteract such change". Met Office scientists were part of the IPCC delegation at the award ceremony, which reflects their prominence throughout the 20 year history of the IPCC – 21 Met Office staff have acted as lead authors or editors, and 34 more as contributing authors – and underlines the Met Office's key role in climate science on a global scale. The importance of the Met Office's work on climate research and prediction to the UK Government was reflected in the introduction of the Met Office Integrated Climate Programme. This five-year, £91M programme, brings together all its climate change work for the MoD and Defra. The main focus of the Programme is to improve the understanding of regional effects, the risks of dangerous climate change, the impacts for various mitigation paths and to quantify and reduce uncertainty.

Turnover in 2007-08 was £176.6M compared to £171.0M in 2006-07. Commercial revenue increased slightly compared to 2006-07 at £27.0M (2006-07 £26.9M), thus reversing the recent trend of falling revenue. Operating profit increased from £7.9M in 2006-07 to £12.7M in 2007-08. This was as a result of the Met Office maintaining its trading year position and the non recurrence of the exceptional charges encountered in 2006-07. Business profitability, a measure of profitability on revenue from services provided on a commercial basis rose from £3.9M in 2006-07 to £4.4M in 2007-08. Return on Capital Employed (ROCE) increased from 4.0% in 2006-07 to 6.1%, and remains above the 3.5% target.

The Met Office has been reviewing key elements of its strategy and has identified some areas of business where improvement is needed to deliver future success and profitability. In some instances, this will lead to strategic amendments to the current Met Office Corporate Plan, while in others further work is being carried out which will be incorporated into the next Corporate Plan due by the end of 2008.

## UK Hydrographic Office

The UKHO has four Top Level objectives:

- Operational Support to defence
- Support to the UK's "Safety of Life at Sea" treaty obligations
- Developing profitable business streams
- Organisational Excellence

UKHO's vision is "to remain the world leader in the supply of marine navigational information and services" and has recently developed the following new digital vision to help protect the organisation into its digital future: "UKHO will be the market leader in sales of carriage compliant navigational products and provide value added services". The products and services supplied to the defence customer (primarily the Royal Navy) are crucial to the conduct of operations globally. The UKHO also plays a central role in support of the Maritime and Coastguard Agency, in discharging the UK's Treaty obligations under the UN Safety of Life at Sea convention. In addition the UKHO has established a significant commercial business, supplying navigational charts, publications and other services to mariners throughout the world.

Financially the UKHO has enjoyed a successful year. Turnover increased by 11.7% to £94.3M. The growth in UKHO sales continued to be mostly generated from commercial customers, a rise of £9.0M to £78.2M. Sales to the MoD were up £0.2M to £11.8M. MoD sales as a percentage of total UKHO turnover represented 13.1% of the annual turnover. The cost base increased by 11.3%, much of this growth was fuelled by continuing investment in trainee compliers to meet planned future retirements. This gave a profit on ordinary activities of £7.9M; And a net profit of £0.6M after provision for an exceptional charge of £7.9M for redundancy costs linked to an announced future rationalisation programme (see below). A dividend of £7.9M has been provided this year: made up of £4.9M dividend of £7.9M has been provided this year: made up of £4.9M and a special dividend of £3M bringing the total to £54.9M since the Trading Fund was formed in 1996.

It has been a very successful year in terms of performance against the key targets being fully achieved. Teething problems experienced during the introduction of new technology last year have been overcome and are consistently achieving Key Target 1 for safety. Key Target 2 – Delivery of Defence Programme has been consistently achieved and the new Customer Supplier Agreement with the MoD was signed by 2nd PUS and UKHO Chief Executive in March 2008.

Following the launch of the Admiralty Vector Chart Service in April 2008, challenges for the UKHO now include the establishment of a strong position in the digital market through the development of various "value-added" products, services and supporting infrastructure and the implementation of the Production Systems Programme fully into operation.

A status review, conducted in 2007 to establish the optimum structure and ownership arrangements, concluded that the UKHO should retain its current trading fund status, but focusing further on leveraging the benefits of strategic relationships with other organisations. The site strategy has secured its future as a major employer in Taunton. In order to secure a sustainable future a transformation programme has been initiated and a full consultation with UKHO Trades Unions has begun; this will determine the appropriate size and shape of the organisation as it moves into the digital future. Wherever possible the new posts required will be filled by reskilling and retraining of existing staff.

## Further information

Further details on Trading Funds can be found in individual Trading Fund Annual Reports and Accounts at:

- UKHO – www.ukho.gov.uk
- Dstl – www.dstl.gov.uk;
- Met Office – www.met-office.gov.uk

# Annex F

## Government Standards

### Fraud

The Departmental emphasis on the deterrence and detection of irregularity, including fraud, theft and corruption, was reinforced in September 2007 when the Permanent Under Secretary of State and the Chief of the Defence Staff jointly endorsed and promulgated a revised and updated departmental 'zero tolerance' policy statement. The impact of this policy was strengthened during the year by the full development of the Defence Irregularity Reporting Cell which acts as the central point for the reporting and recording of all suspicions, the allocation of these to the appropriate investigative authorities, and the monitoring of progress on investigations. While not demonstrably certain, this simplification of reporting procedures, which involves whistleblowing disclosure, is likely to have contributed significantly to the identification of a record number of 664 suspicions with an estimated value of £14.61M. While this estimate is large compared to previous years it is mainly related to two procurement fraud investigations, one of which has been deemed to warrant no further action. The number of reported suspicions includes significant rises over the previous year in the volume of cases involving theft and in personnel management related cases such as abuse of flexi-time arrangements or Internet and computer facilities. A full programme of awareness training was undertaken by the department's Defence Fraud Analysis Unit during the year involving 97 presentations at 58 locations to 4355 departmental Crown Servants.

### Bill Payment

This was a very successful first year of operation for the Financial Management Shared Service Centre (FM SSC). One of the organisation's main

| | 2007-08 | | 2006-07 | |
|---|---|---|---|---|
| | **Target** | **Achieved** | **Target** | **Achieved** |
| ABRO | 100% | 95% 81,667 invoices representing £94.9M | 100% | 95% 74,237 invoices representing £80.6M |
| DARA | 100% | 96% 14,112 invoices representing £142.4M | 100% | 96% 14,305 invoices representing £146.4M |
| Financial Management Shared Service Centre | 99.9% (within 11 days) | 99.8% 4,785,227 invoices representing £22.69Bn | 99.9% (within 11 days) | 99.9 % 5,268,462 representing £20.79Bn |
| Defence Science and Technology Laboratory | 98% | 98.06% 26,355 invoices representing £301.67M | 98% | 98.23% 32,893 invoices representing £204.13M |
| Met Office | 99% | 99.2% 13,073 invoices representing £83.2M | 99% | 99.55% 12,722 invoices representing £68.774M |
| UK Hydrographic Office | 99% | 98.9% 19,507 invoices representing £57M | 100% | 98.8% 12,998 invoices representing £48.6M |

business objectives of paying 99.9% of correctly presented bills within elleven calendar days was narrowly missed by just 0.1%. This was a commendable performance given that we introduced Oracle Payables and we undertook a major change business change programme. Since September 2007, when Oracle was introduced, we achieved the 99.9% target.

# Open Government

## Freedom of Information

In 2007-08, the MoD again received more Freedom of Information requests than any other Central Government Department, totalling 2,954, or approximately 18% of all requests received by Whitehall; the next comparable number was 1,933 received by the Department for Transport. The MoD continues to provide performance statistics on a quarterly basis to the Ministry of Justice, the Department responsible for overseeing implementation of the FOI Act 2000. The MoD continues to have a good record on timeliness, and openness in respect to its responses to Freedom of Information requests, with 80% of requests being answered within the 20 working day statutory time limit and 70% of requests being answered in full. Comparable figures from the Ministry of Justice and Home Office were 67% and 76% of requests answered within 20 working days respectively; and 38% and 51% respectively answered in full. The MoD refused only 11% of requests in full, on the grounds that the

information was exempt from disclosure under provisions of the FOI Act 2000. The MoD's internal operating procedures for processing FOI requests continue to be improved as the Department's familiarity with the Act's stipulations increase. A formal training and seminar programme is fully established to demonstrable effect, in relevant branches, with newly-trained staff showing noticeable improvement in the accurate handling of requests. In-house guidance has been continuously improved and up-dated to reflect the evolving views of the Information Commissioner and the Information Tribunal, and policy developments issued by the Ministry of Justice. The Access to Information Toolkit, the MoD's database facility for tracking and monitoring requests across the Department, is undergoing a significant enhancement programme which will make it easier for those responding to FOI requests to reply appropriately. The improved system will also capture as standard, certain aspects of the MoD's FOI experience which have proven to be of Parliamentary interest, such as the source of requests for information, where identifiable.

The MoD has actively participated in a series of workshops run by the Information Commissioner's Office (ICO) in 2007 to develop new model Publication Schemes, under the umbrella of the Development and Maintenance Initiative. The approved scheme will be made available by the ICO to all public authorities

## Requests for information under the Freedom of Information Act in Financial year 2007-08

| Category | MoD Performance | Total for Central Government Departments |
|---|---|---|
| Number of requests received | 2,954 | 16,571 |
| Of these: | | |
| % of requests answered within 20 working days | 80% | 78% |
| % of requests answered 'in time'[1] | 86.4% | 88% |
| Total of 'resolvable requests'[2] | 2,607 | 12,677 |
| Of these: | | |
| % of resolvable requests answered in full | 70% | 58% |
| %of resolvable requests refused in full | 11%[3] | 21% |

Notes:
1. In time means that an extension to the timescale for response has been extended during the initial 20 working day period, under the terms of section 10 the FOI Act 2000.
2. Resolvable requests are those to which a substantive response can be given, and excludes lapsed or on hold requests, or those where the information is not held or where clarification was required.
3. The remainder of the requests for information (19% in the MoDs case) are normally answered by release of part of the information requested, with some information not provided because it is exempt under the FOI Act 2000.

from the end of April 2008 and is due to be adopted by 31st December 2008. The FOI website is in the process of being redeveloped to incorporate the new requirements arising from this process.

## Asbestos Contaminated Files

Work to re-establish access to the information contained in records affected by asbestos contamination in the Old War Office Building was completed in March 2008. Following successful scanning, the original files were destroyed in accordance with both security and health and safety regulations. FOI requests that have been frustrated because of the asbestos contamination are being answered in date-of-receipt order.

## Transfer of Files to The National Archives

In 2007-08 the routine review and transfer of records to The National Archives (TNA) resulted in around 14,000 files being reviewed and about 2,000 released for general access. In addition, MoD has continued to support TNA in dealing with FOI requests for files that are held by TNA but not available to the public.

## Ministerial Correspondence

Departmental and agency performance in replying to correspondence from Members of Parliament, Members of Devolved Legislatures, Members of the European Parliament, and Peers during 2007-08.

## Requests for information under the Freedom of Information Act between 1 April 2007 and 31 March 2008

| | Target set for dispatch (working days) | Number of letters received for answer | Percentage of replies within target |
|---|---|---|---|
| Ministry of Defence (excluding Defence Agencies) | 15 | 6,076 | 59 |
| **Defence Agencies** | | | |
| ABRO | 15 | 2 | 100 |
| Defence Analytical Services Agency | 15 | - | - |
| Defence Aviation Repair Agency[1] | 15 | 6 | 100 |
| Defence Medical Education and Training Agency[2] | 15 | - | - |
| Dstl | 15 | 20 | 100 |
| Defence Storage and Distribution Agency | 15 | - | - |
| Defence Vetting Agency | 7 | 2 | 100 |
| Ministry of Defence Police | 15 | 1 | 0 |
| People, Pay and Pensions Agency | 10 | 2 | 100 |
| Service Children's Education | 15 | - | - |
| The Met Office | 10 | 29 | 86 |
| UK Hydrographic Office | 15 | 2 | 100 |
| Service Personnel and Veterans Agency | 15 | 393 | 96 |

[1] On 31 March 2008, ABRO Trading Fund dis-established. ABRO merged with retained DARA businesses to create Defence Support Group on 1 April 2008. DARA TF Order revoked following sale of Rotary and Components businesses and retained businesses merged with ABRO.
[2] DMETA lost its Agency status on 1 April 2008.

# Sponsorship

The sponsorship return satisfies the Cabinet Office requirement to publish details of individual commercial sponsorship deals that are valued in excess of £5,000 ex VAT and where they supplement Government funding of any Departmental core business

| Activity | TLB | Individual Sponsors | Company Contribution £ EX VAT |
|---|---|---|---|
| HMS Albion | **Fleet** | Land Rover UK | 11,481 |
| HMS Ark Royal | | Land Rover/Jaguar | 11,950 |
| HMS Bulwark | | Land Rover UK | 11,481 |
| HMS Illustrious | | Land Rover UK | 9,369 |
| HMS Ocean | | Land Rover UK | 6,562 |
| Royal Navy Presentation Team | | Jaguar Cars Ltd | 8,302 |
| RNAS Culdrose Air Day 2007 | | Lockheed Martin Ltd | 29,788 |
| RNAS Yeovilton | | Jaguar Cars Ltd | 9,749 |
| RN Helicopter Display Team – The Black Cats | | Rolls Royce<br>Babcock | 10,000<br>10,855 |
| DAAvn Helicopter Display Team – The Blue Eagles | **Land** | Breitling UK<br>GM UK (SAAB) | 19,500<br>15,000 |
| D Inf Parachute Display Team – The Red Devils | | SEAT<br>Oakley | 60,000<br>5,000 |
| The Rheindahlen and Elmpt Bulletin | | Mitsubishi Motors Bruggen | 18,700 |
| Royal Regiment of Wales – Mascot's Vehicle | | Brains Brewery | 3,000 |
| Sixth Sense Newspaper – Germany | | Mitsubishi Motors Bruggen | 12,000 |
| RAF Aerobatic Display Team – The Red Arrows | **Air Cmd** | Serco<br>BAe Systems<br>Breitling<br>Hatched Brands<br>Leeds Commercial | 17,000<br>25,000<br>13,000<br>16,380<br>6,500 |
| RAF Falcons Parachute Display Team | | BAe Systems<br>Peli Products (UK) Ltd<br>Burton McCall Ltd | 5,000<br>44,000<br>9,000 |
| Red Arrows – Mid & Far East Tour | **Central** | BAe Systems<br>Rolls Royce | 900,000<br>150,000 |
| Falklands 25th Anniversary & Plymouth Veterans Weekend | **DE+S** | Babcock | 24,595 |
| **Total** | | | **1,463,212** |

# Advertising

Spending by the Royal Navy on advertising and public relations expenditure was £12.8M. This includes the costs of national and regional advertising, recruitment activities, publications, the website, and various other promotional activities, and was £2.5M more than 2006-07, primarily attributable to an additional autumn campaign. This expenditure supports recruiting, raises public awareness of the Naval Service and helps to spread a positive image of the Royal Navy and the Royal Marines. The Army's Recruiting Group national marketing spend in 2007-08 for both the Regular and Territorial Army, Officer and Soldier, was £26.1M. This encompassed television, press, radio and internet advertising, the production of DVDs and print media (brochures and pamphlets), response handling and fulfilment, the Camouflage youth information scheme, the ArmyJobs website, marketing research and tracking as well as overarching production and design work. In November 2007, the Army's Recruiting Group, along with their agency Euro RSG Biss Lancaster, won the 2007 PR Week Grand Prix Gold Award for Campaign of the year for the media campaign which accompanied the Army Everest West Ridge Expedition. The Army's Recruiting Group won several awards for it's work during 2007; the ArmyJobs website won 'Best Website' and 'Best Interactive Campaign' awards from the British Interactive Marketing Association, and the Camouflage youth information scheme won 'Best Customer Publication' from the Association of Publishing Agencies. Spending by the Inspectorate of Recruiting (RAF) on recruitment advertising and marketing totalled £12.9M. This comprised expenditure on a wide range of marketing activities for both the RAF and RAuxAF including all media and production for advertising campaigns, response handling, the RAF Careers and Youth websites, literature, films, exhibitions, events, sports, sponsorships, educational programmes, customer relationship marketing, promotional items and all marketing research. By 2009, when civilian HR is fully integrated as part of the People Programme, total costs of civilian advertising will also be available.

# Better regulation

The MoD is not currently supporting any primary legislation. Since 1 April 2007 the MoD has produced one consultation document and three Impact Assessments which are published on the MoD website. An Impact Assessment on the exclusion of complex weapons systems from competition law was signed by the Secretary of State on 4 April 2007. A consultation and Impact Assessment on the Submarine Enterprise Collaborative Agreement were published in February 2008. An Impact Assessment was also produced for the Home Office's amendment of the Rehabilitation of Offenders Act 1974 (Exceptions) Order in July 2007 which contained provisions for disclosing criminal records for personnel involved with military recruits under 18 years old.

## Civilian Recruitment

The MoD has a legal obligation to the Civil Service Commissioners to publish summary information about our recruitment processes and the use of permitted exceptions to the principles of fair and open competition and selection on merit. The information published in the table below also meets these requirements. The Department's recruitment figures for 2007-08 are at paragraph 323 of this report and include figures for permanent and temporary (casual) recruitment. The following information (in the table overleaf) on the use of permitted exceptions has been collated separately and does not include figures for temporary (casual) recruitment. It includes details of the number of individuals who were appointed and their appointment circumstances.

Use of temporary staff continues to be required in order to manage reductions and unit closures or to meet specialist skills shortages. Secondments are recognised as a beneficial development opportunity focused on the business needs. The transformation of the Civilian Human Resource as part of the People Programme will bring significant change to the recruitment flexibility offered to meet Government initiatives for the long term unemployment and those who require supported employment.

## Civilian Recruitment

| | 2007-08 | | 2006-07 | | 2005-06 | |
|---|---|---|---|---|---|---|
| | **Non-Industrial** | **Industrial** | **Non-Industrial** | **Industrial** | **Non-Industrial** | **Industrial** |
| Total number of staff recruited [1] | 2,470 | 1,120 | 2,860 | 1,070 | 3,510 | 1,130 |
| Number and percentage of women recruited | 1,140 (46.0%) | 220 (19.5%) | 1,250 (43.7%) | 250 (23.7%) | 1,510 (43.1%) | 290 (25.6%) |
| Number and percentage of ethnic minorities recruited [2] | 90 (5.5%) | 20 (3.7%) | 120 (6.5%) | 30 (4.2%) | 170 (7.2%) | 20 (3.00%) |
| Number and percentage of people with disabilities recruited [3] | 10 (0.6%) | - | 10 (0.4%) | - | 10 (0.3%) | - |
| Appointments of less than 12 months in respect of those posts specified in Annex A of the CSCRC. | 0 | 0 | 4 | 0 | 0 | 0 |
| Extensions up to a maximum of 24 months, of appointments originally made for a period of less than 12 months (with reasons). [4] | 5 | 7 | 14 | 0 | 28 | 2 |
| Recurrent short term appointments. | 0 | 0 | 2 | 30 | 2 | 27 |
| Short term appointments where highly specialised skills are required. [5] | 2 | 0 | 2 | 0 | 10 | 0 |
| Appointments under Government programmes to assist the long term unemployed. [6] | 0 | 0 | 0 | 0 | 0 | 0 |
| Secondments. [7] | 1 | 0 | 0 | 0 | 6 | 0 |
| Extensions to secondments (with reasons). [8] | 0 | 0 | 0 | 0 | 3 | 0 |
| Re-appointments of former civil servants. | 121 | 49 | 45 | 17 | 35 | 4 |
| Transfers of staff with their work (not under TUPE). | 0 | 92 | 9 | 2 | 2 | 3 |
| Transfers of staff from other public services without work (excluding public bodies staffed exclusively by civil servants). | 0 | 0 | 5 | 0 | 2 | 0 |
| Appointments of surplus acceptable candidates to shortage posts. | 0 | 0 | 0 | 0 | 3 | 0 |
| Appointments of disabled candidates under modified selection arrangements. | 0 | 0 | 1 | 0 | 3 | 1 |
| Supported employment appointments. | 0 | 0 | 0 | 0 | 0 | 0 |
| Number of exceptions reserved for the Commissioners' use. | 0 | 0 | 0 | 0 | 0 | 0 |
| Any appointments exceptionally approved by the Commissioners under the Orders in Council, outside the terms of the Code. | 0 | 0 | 0 | 0 | 0 | 0 |

Notes:
[1] The recruitment statistics shown are for all permanent and casual civilian personnel including Trading Fund staff. Figures for all years exclude Locally Engaged Civilian personnel and Royal Fleet Auxiliary. The exception categories reflect the information required to be published in the Civil Service Commissioners' Recruitment Code, and does not include figures for DSTL and Air Command this year due to data collection difficulties. Historical data is provided where possible.
[2] Percentage of staff recruitment is based on known declarations of ethnicity and excludes staff within unknown or undeclared ethnicity.
[3] Percentage of staff recruitment is based on known declarations of disability status and excludes staff with unknown or undeclared disability status.
[4] The majority of these extensions were to meet short-term requirements whilst permanent replacements were sought. Fair and open competition has been used wherever possible.
[5] This shows the number of staff recruited where the requirement was short term and required specialist skills and where holding an open competition would not have identified any further candidates.
[6] An exception approved by the Commissioners following the launch of the Governments Welfare to Work – New Deal Programme. Figures exclude those New Deal candidates recruited through normal open and fair competition.
[7] Excludes other Government departments, but includes for example, local authorities, hospitals, etc.
[8] Extension due to a requirement to utilise one individual's knowledge of PPP/PFI.

# Annex G

## Defence Equipment Programme

Major Projects are defined as the twenty largest equipment projects that have passed their main investment decision point (Main Gate), and the ten largest equipment projects that have passed their initial investment decision (Initial Gate), by value of forecast spend remaining. The Major Projects population was set at 1 April 2007, and the list below includes information for the end of the financial year, 31 March 2008. The data for each project is validated by the NAO. The following tables show key performance information of Major Projects that have passed Main Gate approval, broken down by capability area. The precise definition of In Service Date (ISD) varies with different equipment, although, in general terms, it can be taken to refer to the date on which the equipment is expected to be available and supportable in service in sufficient quantity to provide a useable operational capability. The dates quoted for ships and submarines are based on the acceptance date from the contractor of the First of Class, not the date by which the equipment (or a specified number of pieces of equipment) will contribute to the operational capability of the Royal Navy.

### Capability Manager Battlespace Manoeuvre Equipment Programme

| Post Main Gate Projects | | | | |
|---|---|---|---|---|
| **Equipment** | **Description** | **Current Forecast Cost (£millions)** | **Current Forecast ISD** | **Quantity Required Current** |
| **Air & Littoral Manoeuvre** | | | | |
| Future Lynx | Helicopter | 1911 | 2014 | 80 |
| Merlin Capability Sustainment Programme | Update of helicopter weapon system avionics | 832 | 2014 | 30 |
| Modernised Target Acquisition Designation Sight / Pilots Night Vision Sensor | Upgrade to Attack Helicopter sensor system | 228 | 2009 | 70 |
| **Expeditionary Logistics and Support** | | | | |
| A400M | Heavy transport aircraft | 2632 | 2011 | 25 |
| Support Vehicle | Cargo and recovery vehicles and trailers | 1272 | 2008 | 6928 Cargo; 288 Recovery; 69 Recovery Trailers |
| **Ground Manoeuvre** | | | | |
| Next Generation Light Anti-Armour Weapon | Short range anti-armour weapon | 310 | 2009 | 13699 |
| Terrier | Armoured engineering vehicle | 313 | 2011 | 65 |

| Post Main Gate Projects | | | | |
| --- | --- | --- | --- | --- |
| **Equipment** | **Description** | **Current Forecast Cost (£millions)** | **Current Forecast ISD** | **Quantity Required Current** |
| **Theatre Airspace** | | | | |
| Advanced Jet Trainer | Pre-operational flying Training system | 467 | 2009 | 28 |
| Beyond Visual Range Air To Air Missile | Air-to-air missile | 1279 | 2012 (Note 1) | Note 2 |
| Typhoon | Fighter aircraft | Note 3 | 2003 | 232 |
| Typhoon Future Capability Programme | Fighter aircraft enhancements | 436 | 2012 | n/a |

Notes:
(1) Beyond Visual Range Air To Air Missile ISD redefined following a review of the programme. ISD shown reflects missile ready for delivery and platform integration.
(2) Weapon Numbers are classified
(3) Current forecast cost for Typhoon is classified due to commercial sensitivities

## Capability Manager Information Superiority Equipment Programme

| Post Main Gate Projects | | | | |
| --- | --- | --- | --- | --- |
| **Equipment** | **Description** | **Current Forecast Cost (£millions)** | **Current Forecast ISD** | **Quantity Required Current** |
| **Command Control & Information Infrastructure** | | | | |
| Falcon | Deployable communication system | 291 | 2010 | n/a |
| Naval EHF/SHF Satellite Communications Terminals | Submarine satellite communications system | 200 | 2012 | 11 |
| **ISTAR** | | | | |
| Soothsayer | Integrated land electronic warfare system | 202 | 2009 | Note 1 |
| Watchkeeper | All weather/24 hour intelligence, surveillance and reconnaissance capability | 898 | 2010 | 54 |

Notes:
(1) Numbers are classified

## Capability Manager Precision Attack Equipment Programme

| Post Main Gate Projects | | | | |
| --- | --- | --- | --- | --- |
| Equipment | Description | Current Forecast Cost (£millions) | Current Forecast ISD | Quantity Required Current |
| **Above Water Effects** | | | | |
| T45 Destroyer | Anti-air warfare destroyer | 6464 | 2010 | 6 |
| **Deep Target Attack** | | | | |
| Joint Combat Aircraft | Fighter/attack aircraft | 1834 | Note 1 | Note 1 |
| **Under Water Effects** | | | | |
| Astute | Attack submarine | 3806 | 2009 | 3 |
| Nimrod Maritime Reconnaissance and Attack Mk4 | Reconnaissance and attack patrol aircraft | 3602 | 2010 | 12 |
| Sting Ray Life Extension & Capability Upgrade | Life extended and enhanced lightweight torpedo | 576 | 2006 | Note 2 |

Notes:
(1) Joint Combat Aircraft Main Gate Business Case was tailored for development only to match the US procurement cycle. Approval for ISD and Quantities required approval will be sought as part of Main Gate Production Business Case.
(2) Weapon Numbers are classified

# International Frameworks

## European Defence

The European Defence Agency (EDA) entered its third year working on a wide range of projects and initiatives in the areas of armaments and industry/markets. Key projects in which the UK took an active role included long-term work on establishing a European Defence Technological and Industrial Base, work on Security of Supply, Offsets and work to rationalise the European Defence Test and Evaluation Base. The UK has had a pivotal role in the development of the Code of Conduct on Defence Procurement and this year saw Spain and Hungary sign up to it, brining the total number of Subscribing Member States to 24. By 28 February 2008, 72 Government contracts at a value of €726M had been awarded of which 18 were cross-border contracts. Similarly 42 Defence companies had signed up to using the Electronic Bulletin Board to advertise Industry contracts and of these, eleven companies had advertised 27 sub-contract opportunities.

European Commission work on increasing competition and transparency within the European Defence Equipment Market continued with the publication of a Defence Package in December 2007. The package comprises a Communication and two draft Directives: one on Intra-Community Transfers of defence related products and another on Defence and Security Procurement. MoD has the lead on the Defence Directive, which aims to introduce specific procurement rules for the defence sector, reducing the need for member States to invoke Article 296, and is working closely with the Commission and other Member States in order to achieve a beneficial outcome.

## OCCAR (Organisation for Joint Armaments Co-operation)

OCCAR has reached a state of maturity, and attention has turned to sustainment of its future. This work has centred on the establishment of a formal working relationship with the European Defence Agency (building on the complementary nature of their roles) and also on continuing to deepen OCCAR's competences, with particular emphasis on in-service support.

## Letters of Intent (LoI) Frameowrk Agreement

During 2007-08 the six nations agreed to a dual approach of re-focussing the LoI on facilitating the restructuring of the European Defence Technological and Industrial Base, and developing the LoI Executive Committee into a more strategic forum able to initiate new ideas and produce outputs both for LoI and other organisations within the European framework such as the European Defence Agency.

## United States of America

Through a number of fora including the Bilateral Defence Acquisition Committee, we continued to work closely with the US Departments of Defense and State to press for improved information and technology exchange on a number of programmes, including the Joint Strike Fighter.

## France

In the Franco-British High Level Working Group, established at the 2006 Summit to explore the scope for enhancing cooperation between the two nations in defence acquisition, we have made significant progress in identifying and pursuing new avenues for bilateral cooperation in defence procurement, research and technology.

# Annex H

## Non Departmental Public Bodies

The Department sponsors five executive and eleven advisory Non-Departmental Public Bodies (NDPBs), two Public Corporations, a Stakeholder Advisory Board and an Independent Monitoring Board. Discussion is ongoing regarding the classification of a number of other bodies with links to the Department. A brief description of the Executive NDPBs and Public Corporations is set out below. Details of their funding from the Defence Budget and total gross expenditure can be found at page 248. More detailed information on these and the other bodies sponsored by the Department can be found at the MoD website at www.mod.uk.

## Executive NDPBs

The Principal Service Museums are the repositories of world-class collections of objects and artefacts relating to the heritage of the Armed Forces. In addition to raising public awareness of the history, traditions and achievements of the Armed Services and encouraging scholarship and research into their history, the museums directly support the strategic aims and policies of the Armed Forces and play an important role in service recruitment and education

The National Army Museum has worked to reinforce the Army's connection with society, and link the past with the present. The 86.5% growth in visitor numbers in 2006-07 was sustained, with a total again in excess of 200,000. Visits to the website grew by 99.9% on top of a 2006-07 increase of 368%. Page Hits rose, in comparison with the previous year, from some 13m to over 22m. The Museum's Special Exhibition programme was again successful in diversifying and expanding its audience through two original and innovative exhibitions – Faces of Battle, dealing with pioneer facial reconstruction during and after the First World War, and Helmand: The Soldiers' Story which

focuses on the operational tour of 16 Air Assault Brigade to Afghanistan in 2006. The latter Exhibition has been widely acclaimed and has been long-listed by The Art Fund for its prestigious prize for 2007.

The RAF Museum provides the world's only exhibition relating to the history of the Cold War. Since opening, the new exhibition in 2007 the Museum has welcomed a record number of visitors and has set a new standard in the display and interpretation of historic artefacts and material. Overall the Museum has noted a 17% increase in visitor numbers. The Museum's Access & Learning Development Division has introduced a range of interactive history and science classroom experiences where students and teachers may download the sessions and teaching materials for use within their own environment. New exhibits at the Museum include a prototype Typhoon aircraft.

Visitor numbers at the Royal Marine's Museum rose by 13.1% to 39,998, including serving members of the Corps. Successful fundraising made possible the complete refurbishment of the Museum's Medal Room, while the ornate ceiling of the Minstrels' Gallery has been restored prior to the re-display of the gallery's contents, which consist of fine portraits and exquisite pieces of silver. Other improvements to the Museum's public services included a re-designed website, better provision for schools and revitalised tearooms. The Museum's trading company has had an excellent year, mainly due to the success of its Corporate Hospitality operation. The Museum continues to be an Investor in People, a Quality Assured Visitor Attraction and an institution which has full accreditation status awarded by the Museums, Libraries and Archives Council.

The Royal Naval Museum mounted two very successful special exhibitions in 2007/8: *Chasing Freedom: The Royal Navy and the Suppression of the Atlantic Slave Trade* and *Task Force South! The Royal Navy and the Falklands War. Task Force South* which attracted over 70,000 visitors. The Museum continued to develop the *Sea Your History* website www.seayourhistory.org.uk, in collaboration with the other naval museums. Some 13,000 objects from the four naval collections have now been digitised and made available on the site, together with supporting research and a wide range of oral history interviews. The project, which has been made possible by a grant of £664,000 from the Heritage Lottery Fund, will be completed in the summer of 2008 and a special exhibition, based on the website, and featuring material from all four naval museums, opened to the public in April. The Museum's Learning programme continues to develop and expand and a total of 203 workshops were run in 2007/08 for over 6,000 children. The Museum received full accreditation from the Museums Libraries and Archives Council (MLA).

The Documentation Project at the Royal naval Submarine Museum that is dealing with the backlog of un-catalogued material in the archive and photographic archive has now been running for 12 months. Over 2000 catalogue entries have been created in the CALM computer system, which means over 6000 actual documents, and images now have a digital record that can be easily retrieved. The 'Fantastic Journey' temporary exhibition was opened by the Children's Laureate Michael Rosen in July 07 to universal approval. The exhibition is aimed particularly at families with early years children. A subsidised school bus scheme was run for a second year with the workshops and sessions receiving very high approval ratings from teachers and over 5000 children who visited the Museum site between October and March. Visitor figures were disappointing falling by 7% to 54,465 in 2008, approximately a 7% decline.

## Public Corporations

The Fleet Air Arm Museum experienced its best year for visitors in over ten years, seeing more than 115,000 people through the doors, up 17% on the previous year. The Education Team continued to deal with large numbers of school visits, with over 13,000 pupils of all ages attending structured presentations from the staff. A major exhibition to mark the 25th anniversary of the Falklands Campaign was opened by the BBC correspondent Brian Hanrahan. Planning is underway for a major gallery rework in 2009 to mark the Centenary of Naval Aviation, "Fly Navy100". The museum co-

operated with the Nautical Archaeology Society in commemorating the 75th anniversary of the loss of HMSM M2, the Royal Navy's only aircraft carrying submarine, which sank with all hands off Portland in 1932.

Oil and Pipeline Agency: The Government Pipelines and Storage System (GPSS) continued to play a significant role in supplying major civil airports during the year, as the ramifications of the Buncefield incident continue to have an impact on fuel delivery. The full military fuel movement requirement has also been delivered and as a result, fuels throughput achieved record levels. The Agency has completed a resilience study for the GPSS, which was carried out in conjunction with a review of the minimum military requirement. Major maintenance works on pipelines and storage facilities have been completed on time and to budget. A review of storage safety and control equipment has been conducted as a result of the Buncefield recommendations, which confirmed that the GPSS conforms to industry standards.

## Annual Public Appointment Plan

The Committee on Standards in Public Life recommended in its Tenth Report that departments produce annual plans setting out policy and practice relating to public appointments. The MoD's Annual Public Appointment Plan includes diversity figures and targets that previously included in the now discontinued Cabinet Office publication *Delivering Diversity in Public Appointments*.

## Policy

The MoD is committed to following the Code of Practice of the Commissioner for Public Appointments. All MoD Non-Departmental Public Bodies, Public Corporations and Independent Monitoring Boards are encouraged to follow the Code of Practice whether or not an appointment is Ministerial and therefore formally within the remit. In practice the majority of MoD public appointments are Ministerial. The Department is fully committed to improving diversity throughout its workforce and this is reflected in our approach to filling public appointments. Paragraphs 283 and 324 set out the initiatives and actions we have taken to improve diversity. MoD public appointments are made entirely on merit. Remuneration is based on the sum needed to attract suitably qualified candidates and to reflect the time commitment and regularity of work involved in the position.

# Report on Achievement of Objectives

The diversity targets for public appointments to MoD Non-Departmental Public Bodies, Public Corporation and Independent Monitoring Board to achieve during the period of this Annual Report and the actual figures achieved by our public appointees to Non-Departmental Public Bodies are shown below. We recently moved to a unified recruitment centre serving the whole Department. This could benefit our public appointments by widening the field of potential candidates, and particularly by identifying the best ways to communicate with minority groups.

Within the overriding principle of selection based on merit, we aim to improve the representation of women, people from minority ethnic backgrounds and people with disabilities within our public appointments to MoD NDPBs, Public Corporation and Independent Monitoring Boards. Our policy is in line with the Government's long-term objectives of equal representation of men and women, pro-rata representation of people from minority ethnic backgrounds the increased participation of people with disabilities. We also promote the benefits of diversity within their membership.

**Diversity Targets for public monitoring to the MoD Non-Departmental Public Bodies, Public Corporation and Independent Monitoring Board**

|  |  | 2007-08 | 2009 |
|---|---|---|---|
| **Women** | Target | 35% | 35% |
|  | Achieved | 16% |  |
| **Ethnic minorities** | Target | 4% | 4.5% |
|  | Achieved | 0.5% |  |
| **Disabled People** | Target | 5.5% | 6% |
|  | Achieved | 8.5% |  |

# Annex I – Further Sources of Information

## Purpose

### Current Operations

- *Ministry of Defence: Defence Plan 2007 and Defence Plan 2008-2012* at www.mod.uk/DefenceInternet/DefenceFor/Researchers/

- Quarterly Public Service Agreement reports, including Autumn and Spring Performance Reports, at www.mod.uk/DefenceInternet/DefenceFor/Researchers/

- Detailed Information on current operations at www.mod.uk

- *UK Defence Statistics 2008* at www.dasa.mod.uk (from September 2008)

- Defence White Paper *Delivering Security in a Changing World* (Cm 6041-1 in December 2003), at www.mod.uk/DefenceInternet/DefenceFor/Researchers/

- Defence White Paper *Delivering Security in a Changing World*: *Future Capabilities* (Cm 6269 in July 2004), at www.mod.uk/DefenceInternet/DefenceFor/Researchers/

- *The Future of the United Kingdom's Nuclear Deterrent* (Cm 6994 in December 2006) at www.mod.uk/DefenceInternet/DefenceFor/Researchers/

- Defence Committee Ninth Report of Session 2006-07: *The Future of the UK's Strategic Nuclear Deterrent: the White Paper* (HC 225) and Eleventh Special Report: *Government Response* (HC 551) at www.publications.parliament.uk/pa/cm/cmdfence.htm

- Defence Committee Eleventh Report of Session 2006-07: *Strategic Lift* (HC 462), and Fourteenth Special Report: *Government Response* (HC 1025) at www.publications.parliament.uk/pa/cm/cmdfence.htm

- Defence Committee Thirteenth Report of Session 2006-07: *UK Operations in Afghanistan (HC 408)*, and Thirteenth Special Report: *Government Response* (HC 1024) at www.publications.parliament.uk/pa/cm/cmdfence.htm

- Defence Committee First Report of Session 2007-08: *UK Land Operations in Iraq 2007* (HC 110), and Second Special Report: *Government Response* (HC 352) at www.publications.parliament.uk/pa/cm/cmdfence.htm

- *The Aitken Report. An Investigation into Cases of Deliberate Abuse and Unlawful Killing in Iraq in 2003 and 2004 (January 2008)* at www.mod.uk/DefenceInternet/DefenceFor/Researchers/

- Defence Committee Fourth Report of Session 2007-08: *The Iran hostages incident: the lessons learned* (HC 181), and Fourth Special Report: *Government Response* (HC 399) at www.publications.parliament.uk/pa/cm/cmdfence.htm

- Defence Committee Fifth Report of Session 2007-08: *Ministry of Defence Annual Report and Accounts* (HC 61) and Fifth Special Report: *Government Response* (HC 468) at www.publications.parliament.uk/pa/cm/cmdfence.htm

- Defence Committee Seventh Report of Session 2007-08: *Medical Care for the Armed Forces* (HC 327) and Sixth Special Report: *Government Response* (HC 500) at www.publications.parliament.uk/pa/cm/cmdfence.htm

- Defence Committee Ninth Report of Session 2007-08: *The Future of NATO and European Defence* (HC 111) and Eighth Special Report: *Government Response* (HC 660) at www.publications.parliament.uk/pa/cm/cmdfence.htm

- *Central Government Supply Estimates 2007-08: Winter Supplementary Estimates* (HC 29) at www.hm-treasury.gov.uk/documents/public_spending_reporting/

- Defence Committee Second Report of Session 2007-08 on *Costs of operations in Iraq and Afghanistan: Winter Supplementary Estimate 2007-08* (HC 138) at www.publications.parliament.uk/pa/cm/cmdfence.htm

- *Central Government Supply Estimates 2007-08: Spring Supplementary Estimates* (HC 273) at www.hm-treasury.gov.uk/documents/public_spending_reporting/

- Defence Committee Eighth Report of Session 2007-08: *Operational costs in Afghanistan and Iraq: Spring Supplementary Estimate 2007-08* (HC 400) at www.publications.parliament.uk/pa/cm/cmdfence.htm

- Defence Committee Eleventh Report of Session 2007-08: *Ministry of Defence Main Estimates 2008-09* (HC 885), including the Government Response to the Defence Committee Eighth Report on the *Spring Supplementary Estimate*, at www.publications.parliament.uk/pa/cm/cmdfence.htm

- National Audit Office Report *Hercules C-130 Tactical Fixed Wing Airlift Capability* (HC 627 Session 2007-08) at www.nao.org.uk/publications/nao_reports/

- Analysis of the cost of operations 2007-08 at Note 2 to the Accounts on page 290.

- National Audit Office *Third Validation Compendium Report* on PSA data systems (HC 127 Session 2006-07) at www.nao.org.uk/publications/nao_reports/

## Readiness

- *Ministry of Defence: Defence Plan 2007* and *Defence Plan 2008-2012* at www.mod.uk/DefenceInternet/DefenceFor/Researchers/

- Quarterly Public Service Agreement reports, including Autumn and Spring Performance Reports, at www.mod.uk/DefenceInternet/DefenceFor/Researchers/

- Defence White Paper *Delivering Security in a Changing World* (Cm 6041-1 in December 2003), at www.mod.uk/DefenceInternet/DefenceFor/Researchers/

- MoD Annual Report and Accounts 2004-05 (HC 464 dated 28 October 2005), essay on *Measuring and Reporting Readiness* at www.mod.uk/DefenceInternet/DefenceFor/Researchers/

- MoD Annual Report and Accounts 2005-06 (HC 1394 dated 14 July 2006), essay on *Delivering Readiness at the Front Line* at www.mod.uk/DefenceInternet/DefenceFor/Researchers/

- MoD Annual Report and Accounts 2006-07 (HC 697 dated 23 July 2007), essay on *Supporting current operations and the impact on readiness* at www.mod.uk/DefenceInternet/DefenceFor/Researchers/

- National Audit Office Report *Assessing and Reporting Military Readiness* (HC 72 dated 15 June 2005) at www.nao.org.uk/publications/nao_reports/

- Public Accounts Committee Report on *Assessing and reporting military readiness* (HC 667 dated 28 February 2006) and the Treasury Minute containing the Government Response (Cm 6775 dated 26 April 2006) at www.publications.parliament.uk/pa/cm200506/cmselect/cmpubacc/cmpubacc.htm

- National Audit Office *Third Validation Compendium Report* on PSA data systems (HC 127 Session 2006-07) at www.nao.org.uk/publications/nao_reports/

- Defence Committee Fifth Report of Session 2007-08: *Ministry of Defence Annual Report and Accounts* (HC 61) and Fifth Special Report: *Government Response* (HC 468) at www.publications.parliament.uk/pa/cm/cmdfence.htm

## Policy

- *Ministry of Defence: Defence Plan 2007* and *Defence Plan 2008-2012* at www.mod.uk/DefenceInternet/DefenceFor/Researchers/

- Quarterly Public Service Agreement reports, including Autumn and Spring Performance Reports, at www.mod.uk/DefenceInternet/DefenceFor/Researchers/

- Defence White Paper *Delivering Security in a Changing World* (Cm 6041-1 in December 2003), at www.mod.uk/DefenceInternet/DefenceFor/Researchers/

- *The Future of the United Kingdom's Nuclear Deterrent* (Cm 6994 in December 2006) at www.mod.uk/DefenceInternet/DefenceFor/Researchers/

- The Secretary of State for Defence's February 2008 speech to the Conference on Disarmament on *Laying the Foundations for Multilateral Disarmament* at www.mod.uk/DefenceInternet/AboutDefence/People/Speeches/

- *The National Security Strategy of the United Kingdom* (Cm 7291 in March 2008) at www.cabinetoffice.gov.uk/reports/

- Memorandum of Understanding – UK US Defence Trade Cooperation Treaty at www.mod.uk/DefenceInternet/MicroSite/DES/

- UK Global Threat Reduction Programme Annual Report at www.berr.gov.uk/energy/non-proliferation/global-threat-reduction/index.html

- Annual Report on UK Strategic Export Controls at www.fco.gov.uk/en/fco-in-action/counter-terrorism/weapons/export-weapons/

- 2007 Review of Export Control legislation at www.berr.gov.uk/europeandtrade/strategic-export-control

- Conflict Prevention Pools at www.fco.gov.uk/en/about-the-fco/what-we-do/funding-programmes/conflict-prevention-pools/

- Proliferation Security Initiative at www.fco.gov.uk

- Stabilisation Unit at www.stabilisationunit.gov.uk

- Defence Committee Ninth Report of Session 2006-07: *The Future of the UK's Strategic Nuclear Deterrent: the White Paper* (HC 225) and Eleventh Special Report: *Government Response* (HC 551) at www.publications.parliament.uk/pa/cm/cmdfence.htm

- Defence Committee Fourteenth Report of Session 2006-07: *Strategic Export Controls: 2007 Review* (HC 117) at www.publications.parliament.uk/pa/cm/cmdfence.htm

- Defence Committee's Third Report of Session 2007-08: *UK/US Defence Trade Cooperation Treaty* (HC 107) and Third Special Report: *Government Response* (HC 375) at www.publications.parliament.uk/pa/cm/cmdfence.htm

- Defence Committee Fifth Report of Session 2007-08: *Ministry of Defence Annual Report and Accounts* (HC 61) and Fifth Special Report: *Government Response* (HC 468) at www.publications.parliament.uk/pa/cm/cmdfence.htm

- Defence Committee Ninth Report of Session 2007-08: *The Future of NATO and European Defence* (HC 111) and Eighth Special Report: *Government Response* (HC 660) at www.publications.parliament.uk/pa/cm/cmdfence.htm

- Intelligence and Security Committee *Annual Report 2006-07* (Cm 7299) at
  www.cabinetoffice.gov.uk/reports

- NATO reference publications and ministerial communiqués, including Comprehensive Political
  Guidance, at www.nato.int

- EU reference publications and ministerial communiqués at www.consilium.europa.eu

- United Nations Security Council and General Assembly publications at www.un.org

- Convention on Cluster Munitions at www.clustermunitionsdublin.ie/

- National Audit Office *Third Validation Compendium Report* on PSA data systems (HC 127 Session
  2006-07) at www.nao.org.uk/publications/nao_reports/

## Defence in the Wider Community

- *Ministry of Defence: Defence Plan 2007* and *Defence Plan 2008-2012* at
  www.mod.uk/DefenceInternet/DefenceFor/Researchers/

- *Securing the Future – UK Government sustainable development strategy* (Cm 6467 of March 2005) at
  www.sustainable-development.gov.uk;

- *'Procuring the Future' – The Sustainable Procurement Task Force National Action Plan'* , June 2006, at
  www.sustainable-development.gov.uk;

- *UK Government Sustainable Procurement Action Plan (incorporating the Government Response to the
  Sustainable Procurement Task Force)*, March 2007 at www.sustainable-development.gov.uk;

- *Sustainable Development in Government 2007*: Annual Report by the Sustainable Development
  Commission on central Government performance, March 2007, at
  http://www.sd-commission.org.uk/sdig2007/

- Defence Committee Fifth Report of Session 2007-08: *Ministry of Defence Annual Report and
  Accounts (HC 61)* and Fifth Special Report: *Government Response* (HC 468) at
  www.publications.parliament.uk/pa/cm/cmdfence.htm

- Defence Committee's Fifteenth Report of Session 2006-07: *The Work of Defence Estates* (HC 535)
  and First Special Report of Session 2007-08: *Government Response* (HC 109) at
  www.publications.parliament.uk/pa/cm/cmdfence.htm

- NAO Report on *Managing the Defence Estate: Quality and Sustainability* (HC 154 of 23 March 2007)
  available at www.nao.org.uk/publications/nao_reports/

- Public Accounts Committee Report on *Managing the Defence Estate: Quality and Sustainability*
  (HC 537 dated 27 November 2007) and the Treasury Minute containing the Government Response
  (Cm 7322 dated 21 February 2008) at
  www.publications.parliament.uk/pa/cm200607/cmselect/cmpubacc/cmpubacc.htm

- NAO Report on *Building for the future: Sustainable construction and refurbishment on the government
  estate* (HC 324 of 20 April 2007) available at www.nao.org.uk/publications/nao_reports/

- Public Accounts Committee Report on *Building for the future: Sustainable construction and
  refurbishment on the government estate* (HC 174 dated 15 January 2008) and the Treasury Minute
  containing the Government Response (Cm 7323 dated 27 March 2008) at
  www.publications.parliament.uk/pa/cm/cmpubacc.htm

- MoD Sustainable Development Action Plans, Annual Reports and detailed strategies
  at www.mod.uk/DefenceInternet/AboutDefence/WhatWeDo/ HealthandSafety/DSC/
  DsandcEnvironmentSustainableDevelopmentDocumentLibrary.htm

- *Stewardship Reports on the Defence Estate* at
  www.defence-estates.mod.uk/ publications/corporate/corporate.php

- MoD Art Collection at
  www.mod.uk/DefenceInternet/AboutDefence/WhatWeDo/ DefenceEstateandEnvironment/

- *MOD Heritage Report 2005-2007* at
  www.defence-estates.mod.uk/publications/ corporate/corporate.php

- Information on Government Skills at www.government-skills.gov.uk;

- NAO Report on *Leaving the Services* (HC 618 of 27 July 2007) available at
  www.nao.org.uk/publications/nao_reports/

- Evidence given to the Public Accounts Committee on 18 February 2008 on *Leaving the Services* (HC 351-i) at www.publications.parliament.uk/pa/cm/cmpubacc.htm

- Commemorative booklets, *Veterans WORLD* Service Personnel and Veterans Agency Annual Report and Accounts at www.veterans-uk.info;

- Homelessness research *Improving the Delivery of Cross Departmental Support and Services for Veterans* at www.mod.uk/DefenceInternet/AboutDefence/CorporatePublications

- York University study *The Experiences of Homeless Ex-Service Personnel in London* at
  www.veterans-aid.net/pdf/yorkstudy.pdf

- UK Gulf Veterans Mortality Data at www.dasa.mod.uk;

- *The 1990/1991 Gulf Conflict: Health and Personnel Related Lessons Identified* at

- www.mod.uk/DefenceInternet/AboutDefence/CorporatePublications

- Kings College research papers published in The Lancet *'The Health of UK Military Personnel Who Deployed To The 2003 Iraq War'* and *'Is there an Iraq syndrome?'* available at
  www.thelancet.com (registration required)

- Armed Forces Pension Scheme resource accounts at www.official-documents.gov.uk

# Future

## Future Capabilities

- *Ministry of Defence: Defence Plan 2007* and *Defence Plan 2008-2012* at
  www.mod.uk/DefenceInternet/DefenceFor/Researchers/

- 2004 Spending Review: *Stability, security and opportunity for all: investing for Britain's long-term future: New Public Spending Plans 2005-2008* (Cm 6237) at www.hm-treasury.gov.uk;

- Defence White Paper *Delivering Security in a Changing World*: *Future Capabilities* (Cm 6269 in July 2004), at www.mod.uk/DefenceInternet/DefenceFor/Researchers/

- The Defence Committee Fourth Report of Session 2004-05 *Future Capabilities* (HC 45) at
  www.publications.parliament.uk/pa/cm/cmdfence.htm and the Government Response (Cm 6616, July 2005) at www.mod.uk/DefenceInternet/DefenceFor/Researchers/

- Defence Committee's Seventh Report of Session 2006-07: *The Army's requirement for armoured vehicles: the FRES programme* (HC 159) and Ninth Special Report of Session 2006-07: *Government Response* (HC 511) at www.publications.parliament.uk/pa/cm/cmdfence.htm

- Defence Committee's Eleventh Report of Session 2006-07: *Strategic Lift* (HC 462) and
  Fourteenth Special Report of Session 2006-07: *Government Response* (HC 1025) at
  www.publications.parliament.uk/pa/cm/cmdfence.htm

- National Audit Office Report on *Progress in Combat Identification* (HC 936 of 3 March 2006) at
  www.nao.org.uk/publications/nao_reports/

- Public Accounts Committee Report on *Progress in Combat Identification* (HC 486 dated 1 May 2007) and the Treasury Minute containing the Government Response (Cm 7151 dated 5 July 20087 at www.publications.parliament.uk/pa/cm200607/cmselect/cmpubacc/cmpubacc.htm

- National Audit Office Report on *Chinook Mk3 Helicopters* (HC 512 of 4 June 2008) at www.nao.org.uk/publications/nao_reports/

- Evidence given to the Public Accounts Committee on 18 June 2008 on *Chinook Mk3 Helicopters* (HC 747-i) at www.publications.parliament.uk/pa/cm/cmpubacc.htm

- National Audit Office Report on *Hercules C-130 Tactical Fixed Wing Airlift Capability* (HC 627 of 27 June 2008) at www.nao.org.uk/publications/nao_reports/

- National Audit Office Report on *The Defence Information Infrastructure* (HC 788 of 4 July 2008) at www.nao.org.uk/publications/nao_reports/

- *UK Defence Statistics* at www.dasa.mod.uk;

- *Defence Industrial Strategy* at www.mod.uk/DefenceInternet/DefenceFor/Researchers/

- *Defence Technology Strategy* at www.mod.uk/DefenceInternet/DefenceFor/Researchers/

- *Maximising Benefit from Defence Research* at www.mod.uk/DefenceInternet/DefenceFor/Researchers/

- *Maximising Defence Capability Through Research and Development* at www.mod.uk/DefenceInternet/DefenceFor/Researchers/

- Information on Competition of Ideas at www.science.mod.uk/Engagement/enterprise.aspx

- Information on Grand Challenge at www.Challenge.mod.uk;

- Information on The MoD Counter Terrorism Science & Technology Centre at www.ctcentre.mod.uk;

- Information on Science Innovation Technology at www.science.mod.uk;

- Defence Science and Technology Laboratory *Annual Report and Accounts* at www.mod.uk/DefenceInternet/DefenceFor/Researchers/

- Defence Committee's Eight Report of Session 2006-07: *The Work of the Defence Science and Technology Laboratory and the funding of Defence Research* (HC 84) and Tenth Special Report of Session 2006-07: *Government Response* (HC 512) at www.publications.parliament.uk/pa/cm/cmdfence.htm

- *Innovation Nation* (Cm 7345), at www.dius.gov.uk/policy/innovation.html

- Sainsbury Review: *The Race to the Top*: *A Review of Government's Science and Innovation Policies* at www.hm-treasury.gov.uk/media/5/E/sainsbury_review051007.pdf and *Implementing "The Race to the Top"* at www.dius.gov.uk/publications/index.html

- *Enterprise: unlocking the UK's talent* at www.berr.gov.uk/files/file44992.pdf

## Change

- *Ministry of Defence: Defence Plan 2007* and *Defence Plan 2008-2012* at www.mod.uk/DefenceInternet/DefenceFor/Researchers/

- 2004 Spending Review: *Stability, security and opportunity for all: investing for Britain's long-term future: New Public Spending Plans 2005-2008* (Cm 6237) at www.hm-treasury.gov.uk;

- MoD Capability Review and the Department's Response at www.civilservice.gov.uk/reform/capability_reviews/reports.asp

- *Defence Industrial Strategy* at www.mod.uk/DefenceInternet/DefenceFor/Researchers/

- *Enabling Acquisition Change: An examination of the Ministry of Defence's ability to undertake Through Life Capability Management* at www.mod.uk/DefenceInternet/DefenceFor/Researchers/

- *Defence Equipment and Support Blueprint: The Future Operating Model* at www.mod.uk/DefenceInternet/MicroSite/DES/

- *Acquisition Operating Framework* at www.aof.mod.uk/index.htmDefence

- Defence Committee Fifth Report of Session 2007-08: *Ministry of Defence Annual Report and Accounts* (HC 61) and Fifth Special Report: *Government Response* (HC 468) at www.publications.parliament.uk/pa/cm/cmdfence.htm

## Future Personnel

- *Ministry of Defence: Defence Plan 2007* and *Defence Plan 2008-2012* at www.mod.uk/DefenceInternet/DefenceFor/Researchers/

- Armed Forces Continuous Attitude Survey at www.mod.uk/DefenceInternet/FreedomOfInformation/PublicationScheme

- Service Personnel and Veterans Agency corporate publications at www.mod.uk/DefenceInternet/AboutDefence/WhatWeDo/Personnel/SPVA/

- Civilian Workforce Strategy at www.pppaservices.qinetiq-tim.com/pppain~1uk/people~1/doc_st~1/doc_pr~6.htm

- People Pay and Pensions Agency corporate publications at www.mod.uk/DefenceInternet/MicroSite/PPPA/

- *UK Defence Statistics* at www.dasa.mod.uk

- Defence Committee Fifth Report of Session 2007-08: *Ministry of Defence Annual Report and Accounts* (HC 61) and Fifth Special Report: *Government Response* (HC 468) at www.publications.parliament.uk/pa/cm/cmdfence.htm

# Enabling Process

## Equipment and Support

- *Ministry of Defence: Defence Plan 2007* and *Defence Plan 2008-2012* at www.mod.uk/DefenceInternet/DefenceFor/Researchers/

- Quarterly Public Service Agreement reports, including Autumn and Spring Performance Reports, at www.mod.uk/DefenceInternet/DefenceFor/Researchers/

- *Defence Industrial Strategy* at www.mod.uk/DefenceInternet/DefenceFor/Researchers/

- *Acquisition Operating Framework* at www.aof.mod.uk

- *Defence Equipment and Support Business Strategy April 2007* at http://www.mod.uk/NR/rdonlyres/8717D017-0EF5-4101-9A98-05142AA9B0E5/0/200704DES_Business_Strategy.pdf

- *Defence Equipment and Support Business Strategy 2008-12* at www.mod.uk/DefenceInternet/MicroSite/DES/

- *Defence Equipment and Support Blueprint: The Future Operating Model* at www.mod.uk/DefenceInternet/MicroSite/DES/

- Memorandum of Understanding – UK US Defence Trade Cooperation Treaty at www.mod.uk/DefenceInternet/MicroSite/DES/

- Annual *UK Defence Statistics* available at www.dasa.mod.uk

- Defence Committee's Seventh Report of Session 2006-07: *The Army's requirement for armoured vehicles: the FRES programme* (HC 159) and Ninth Special Report of Session 2006-07: *Government Response* (HC 511) at www.publications.parliament.uk/pa/cm/cmdfence.htm

- Defence Committee's Eleventh Report of Session 2006-07: *Strategic Lift* (HC 462) and Fourteenth Special Report of Session 2006-07: *Government Response* (HC 1025) at www.publications.parliament.uk/pa/cm/cmdfence.htm

- Defence Committee Fourteenth Report of Session 2006-07: *Strategic Export Controls: 2007 Review* (HC 117) at www.publications.parliament.uk/pa/cm/cmdfence.htm

- Defence Committee's Third Report of Session 2007-08: *UK/US Defence Trade Cooperation Treaty* (HC 107) and Third Special Report: *Government Response* (HC 375) at www.publications.parliament.uk/pa/cm/cmdfence.htm

- Defence Committee Fifth Report of Session 2007-08: *Ministry of Defence Annual Report and Accounts* (HC 61) and Fifth Special Report: *Government Response* (HC 468) at www.publications.parliament.uk/pa/cm/cmdfence.htm

- Defence Committee Tenth Report of Session 2007-08: *Defence Equipment 2008* (HC 295) and Seventh Special Report: *Government Response* (HC 555) at www.publications.parliament.uk/pa/cm/cmdfence.htm

- National Audit Office Report *Assessing and Reporting Military Readiness* (HC 72 dated 15 June 2005) at www.nao.org.uk/publications/nao_reports/

- Public Accounts Committee Report on *Assessing and reporting military readiness* (HC 667 dated 28 February 2006) and the Treasury Minute containing the Government Response (Cm 6775 dated 26 April 2006) at www.publications.parliament.uk/pa/cm200506/cmselect/cmpubacc/cmpubacc.htm

- National Audit Office Report on *Progress in Combat Identification* (HC 936 of 3 March 2006) at www.nao.org.uk/publications/nao_reports/

- Public Accounts Committee Report on *Progress in Combat Identification* (HC 486 dated 1 May 2007) and the Treasury Minute containing the Government Response (Cm 7151 dated 5 July 2007) at www.publications.parliament.uk/pa/cm200607/cmselect/cmpubacc/cmpubacc.htm

- National Audit Office Report *Major Projects Report 2006* (HC 23 of 24 November 2006) at www.nao.org.uk/publications/nao_reports/

- Public Accounts Committee Report on *Ministry of Defence: Major Projects Report 2006* (HC 295 dated 11 September 2007) and the Treasury Minute containing the Government Response (Cm 7275 dated 29 November 2007) at www.publications.parliament.uk/pa/cm200607/cmselect/cmpubacc/cmpubacc.htm

- National Audit Office Report on *The Efficiency Programme: A Second Review of Progress* (HC 156 of 8 February 2007)

- Public Accounts Committee Report on *The Efficiency Programme: A Second Review of Progress* (HC 349 dated 11 October 2007) and the Treasury Minute containing the Government Response (Cm 7276 dated 18 December 2007) at www.publications.parliament.uk/pa/cm200607/cmselect/cmpubacc/cmpubacc.htm

- National Audit Office Report *Transforming Logistics Support for Fast Jets* (HC 825 of 17 July 2007) at www.nao.org.uk/publications/nao_reports/

- National Audit Office Report *Major Projects Report 2007* (HC 98 of 30 November 2007) at www.nao.org.uk/publications/nao_reports/

- Evidence given to the Public Accounts Committee on 17 March 2008 on *Major Projects Report 2007* (HC 433-i) at www.publications.parliament.uk/pa/cm/cmpubacc.htm

- National Audit Office Report on *Chinook Mk3 Helicopters* (HC 512 of 4 June 2008) at www.nao.org.uk/publications/nao_reports/

- Evidence given to the Public Accounts Committee on 18 June 2008 on *Chinook Mk3 Helicopters* (HC 747-i) at www.publications.parliament.uk/pa/cm/cmpubacc.htm

- National Audit Office Report on *Hercules C-130 Tactical Fixed Wing Airlift Capability* (HC 627 of 27 June 2008) at www.nao.org.uk/publications/nao_reports/

- National Audit Office *Third Validation Compendium Report* on PSA data systems (HC 127 Session 2006-07) at www.nao.org.uk/publications/nao_reports/

## Safety, Security and Business Continuity

- *Ministry of Defence: Defence Plan 2007* and *Defence Plan 2008-2012* at www.mod.uk/DefenceInternet/DefenceFor/Researchers/

- Annual *UK Defence Statistics* available at www.dasa.mod.uk

- *Revitalising Health and Safety* at www.hse.gov.uk

- Secretary of State's Policy Statement on Safety, Health, Environmental Protection and Sustainable Development at www.mod.uk/DefenceInternet/AboutDefence/CorporatePublications/

- Defence Health and Safety publications at www.mod.uk/DefenceInternet/AboutDefence/CorporatePublications/

- Air Safety and Aviation publications at www.mod.uk/DefenceInternet/AboutDefence/CorporatePublications/

- Boards of Inquiry Reports at www.mod.uk/DefenceInternet/AboutDefence/CorporatePublications/

- Report into the Loss of MoD Personal Data – Sir Edmund Burton Review and MoD's action plan in response to the Burton Report at www.mod.uk/DefenceInternet/AboutDefence/CorporatePublications/

## Reputation

- *Ministry of Defence: Defence Plan 2007* and *Defence Plan 2008-2012* at www.mod.uk/DefenceInternet/DefenceFor/Researchers/

- MoD Freedom of Information at www.mod.uk/DefenceInternet/FreedomOfInformation/

- Public Opinion Surveys at www.mod.uk/DefenceInternet/FreedomOfInformation/

- *Report of Inquiry into National Recognition of our Armed Forces* at www.mod.uk/DefenceInternet/AboutDefence/CorporatePublications/

# Resources

## People

- *Ministry of Defence: Defence Plan 2007* and *Defence Plan 2008-2012* at www.mod.uk/DefenceInternet/DefenceFor/Researchers/

- Quarterly Public Service Agreement reports, including Autumn and Spring Performance Reports, at www.mod.uk/DefenceInternet/DefenceFor/Researchers/

- Annual *UK Defence Statistics* available at www.dasa.mod.uk

- Armed Forces Continuous Attitude Survey at www.mod.uk/DefenceInternet/FreedomOfInformation/PublicationScheme

- Defence civilian continuous attitude surveys at
  www.mod.uk/DefenceInternet/FreedomOfInformation/

- The Demography in the MoD at www.mod.uk/DefenceInternet/FreedomOfInformation/

- Armed Forces Pay Review Body Reports at
  www.mod.uk/DefenceInternet/AboutDefence/CorporatePublications/

- Senior Staff Review Body Reports at
  www.official-documents.gov.uk

- Equality and Diversity publications at
  www.mod.uk/DefenceInternet/AboutDefence/WhatWeDo/Personnel/EqualityAndDiversity/

- Duty of Care publications at www.mod.uk/DefenceInternet/AboutDefence/
  CorporatePublications/PersonnelPublications/DutyofCare/

- Adult Learning Inspectorate report: *Better training* at
  www.mod.uk/DefenceInternet/AboutDefence/CorporatePublications/

- An overview of the Military Criminal Justice System and the Armed Forces Act 2006 at
  www.mod.uk/DefenceInternet/AboutDefence/CorporatePublications/

- Annual *Analysis of Sickness Absence in the Civil Service* at www.civilservice.gov.uk

- CBI AXA Absence Surveys at hwww.cbi.org.uk/

- CIPD Absence Management Survey at www.cipd.co.uk/

- Defence Committee Fifth Report of Session 2007-08: *Ministry of Defence Annual Report
  and Accounts* (HC 61) and Fifth Special Report: *Government Response* (HC 468) at
  www.publications.parliament.uk/pa/cm/cmdfence.htm

- Defence Committee Seventh Report of Session 2007-08: *Medical Care for the Armed Forces* (HC 327)
  and Sixth Special Report: *Government Response* (HC 500) at
  www.publications.parliament.uk/pa/cm/cmdfence.htm

- Memoranda on *Recruitment and Retention in the Armed Forces*, and Evidence given to the Defence
  Committee on 22 April and 20 May 2008, at
  www.publications.parliament.uk/pa/cm/cmdfence.htm

- National Audit Office Report on *Recruitment and retention in the armed forces* (HC 1633 of 3
  November 2006) at www.nao.org.uk/publications/nao_reports/

- Public Accounts Committee Report on *Recruitment and Retention in the Armed Forces* (HC 43 dated 3
  July 2007) and the Treasury Minute containing the Government Response (Cm 7216 dated 11 October
  2007) at www.publications.parliament.uk/pa/cm200607/cmselect/cmpubacc/cmpubacc.htm

- National Audit Office Report on *Ministry of Defence: Reserve Forces* (HC 964 of 31 March 2006) at
  www.nao.org.uk/publications/nao_reports/

- Public Accounts Committee Report on *Reserve Forces* (HC 729 dated 12 July 2007) and the Treasury
  Minute containing the Government Response (Cm 7216 dated 11 October 2007) at
  www.publications.parliament.uk/pa/cm200607/cmselect/cmpubacc/cmpubacc.htm

- National Audit Office *Third Validation Compendium Report* on PSA data systems
  (HC 127 Session 2006-07) at www.nao.org.uk/publications/nao_reports/

## Finance and Efficiency

- *Ministry of Defence: Defence Plan 2007* and *Defence Plan 2008-2012* at www.mod.uk/DefenceInternet/DefenceFor/Researchers/

- *The Government's Expenditure Plans 2007-2008* at http://www.mod.uk/NR/rdonlyres/95BBA015-22B9-43EF-B2DC-DFF14482A590/0/gep_200708.pdf

- Quarterly Public Service Agreement reports, including Autumn and Spring Performance Reports, at www.mod.uk/DefenceInternet/DefenceFor/Researchers/

- Annual *UK Defence Statistics* available at www.dasa.mod.uk

- 2004 Spending Review: *Stability, Security and Opportunity for all: Investing in Britain's long-term future: New Public Spending Plans 2005-2008* at www.hm-treasury.gov.uk

- *Releasing resources to the front line: Independent Review of Public Sector Efficiency* at www.hm-treasury.gov.uk;

- *The Lyons Review: Independent Review of public sector relocation* at www.hm-treasury.gov.uk

- 2007 Pre-Budget Report and Comprehensive Spending Review: *Meeting the Aspirations of the British People* at www.hm-treasury.gov.uk

- National Asset Register at www.hm-treasury.gov.uk

- MoD Asset Management Strategy at www.mod.uk/DefenceInternet/AboutDefence/CorporatePublications/

- Defence Committee Fifth Report of Session 2007-08: *Ministry of Defence Annual Report and Accounts* (HC 61) and Fifth Special Report: *Government Response* (HC 468) at www.publications.parliament.uk/pa/cm/cmdfence.htm

- Public Accounts Committee Report on *Excess Votes 2006-07* (HC 299 dated 1 February 2008) at www.publications.parliament.uk/pa/cm/cmpubacc.htm

- *Central Government Supply Estimates 2007-08: Main Supply Estimates* (HC 438) at www.hm-treasury.gov.uk

- *Central Government Supply Estimates 2007-08: Supplementary Budgetary Information* (Cm 7079) at www.hm-treasury.gov.uk

- Defence Committee Twelfth Report of Session 2006-07: *Ministry of Defence Main Estimates 2007-08* (HC 835) and Fifteenth Special Report: *Government Response* (HC 1026) at www.publications.parliament.uk/pa/cm/cmdfence.htm

- *Central Government Supply Estimates 2007-08: Winter Supplementary Estimates* (HC 29) at www.hm-treasury.gov.uk/documents/public_spending_reporting/

- Defence Committee Second Report of Session 2007-08 on *Costs of operations in Iraq and Afghanistan: Winter Supplementary Estimate 2007-08* (HC 138) at www.publications.parliament.uk/pa/cm/cmdfence.htm

- *Central Government Supply Estimates 2007-08: Spring Supplementary Estimates* (HC 273) at www.hm-treasury.gov.uk/documents/public_spending_reporting/

- Defence Committee Eighth Report of Session 2007-08: *Operational costs in Afghanistan and Iraq: Spring Supplementary Estimate 2007-08* (HC 400) at www.publications.parliament.uk/pa/cm/cmdfence.htm

- *Public Expenditure Statistical Analyses 2008* (HC 489) at www.hm-treasury.gov.uk

- National Audit Office Report on *The Efficiency Programme: A Second Review of Progress* (HC 156 of 8 February 2007) at www.nao.org.uk/publications/nao_reports/

- Public Accounts Committee Report on *The Efficiency Programme: A Second Review of Progress* (HC 349 dated 11 October 2007) and the Treasury Minute containing the Government Response (Cm 7276 dated 18 December 2007) at www.publications.parliament.uk/pa/cm200607/cmselect/cmpubacc/cmpubacc.htm

- National Audit Office Report on *The privatisation of QinetiQ* (HC 52 of 23 November 2007) at www.nao.org.uk/publications/nao_reports/

- Public Accounts Committee Report on *The privatisation of QinetiQ* (HC 151 dated 10 June 2008) at www.publications.parliament.uk/pa/cm/cmpubacc.htm

- National Audit Office Report on *Managing financial resources to deliver better public services* (HC 240 dated 20 February 2008) at www.nao.org.uk/publications/nao_reports/

## Estate

- *Ministry of Defence: Defence Plan 2007* and *Defence Plan 2008-2012* at www.mod.uk/DefenceInternet/DefenceFor/Researchers/

- *The Defence Estate Strategy 2006: In Trust and On Trust* at www.defence-estates.mod.uk/publications/corporate/corporate.php

- Defence Estates Annual Stewardship Reports at www.defence-estates.mod.uk/publications/corporate/corporate.php

- *The DE Corporate Plan 2007-2012* at www.defence-estates.mod.uk/publications/corporate/corporate.php

- *Defence Estates Development Plan 2008* at www.defence-estates.mod.uk/publications/dedp08.php

- Information on Service Families Accommodation and Defence Estates major projects at www.defence-estates.mod.uk/

- *The Lyons Review: Independent Review of public sector relocation* at www.hm-treasury.gov.uk

- Housing Green Paper: *Homes for the future: more affordable, more sustainable* at www.communities.gov.uk/publications/housing/homesforfuture

- Defence Committee Fifteenth Report of Session 2006-07: *The Work of Defence Estates* (HC 1024) and First Special Report of Session 2007-08: *Government Response* (HC 109) at www.publications.parliament.uk/pa/cm/cmdfence.htm

- National Audit Office Report on *Managing the Defence Estate: Quality and Sustainability* (HC 154 of 23 March 2007) at www.nao.org.uk/publications/nao_reports/

- Public Accounts Committee Report on *Managing the Defence Estate: Quality and Sustainability* (HC 537 dated 29 November 2007) and the Treasury Minute containing the Government Response (Cm 7322 dated 21 February 2008) at www.publications.parliament.uk/pa/cm200607/cmselect/cmpubacc/cmpubacc.htm

- NAO Report on *Building for the future: Sustainable construction and refurbishment on the government estate* (HC 324 of 20 April 2007) available at www.nao.org.uk/publications/nao_reports/

- Public Accounts Committee Report on *Building for the future: Sustainable construction and refurbishment on the government estate* (HC 174 dated 15 January 2008) and the Treasury Minute containing the Government Response (Cm 7323 dated 27 March 2008) at www.publications.parliament.uk/pa/cm/cmpubacc.htm

# Glossary

**1SL/CNS. First Sea Lord and Chief of the Naval Staff:** Professional head of the Navy. Member of the Defence Board, the Admiralty Board and the Chiefs of Staff Committee and the Chair of the Navy Board. Currently held by an officer of the rank of Admiral.

**1 Star, 2 Star, 3 Star and 4 Star:** Gradings of the Senior Civil Service.

**2nd PUS. 2nd Permanent Under Secretary.** The Deputy to the Permanent Under Secretary. Member of the Defence Council and Defence Board, the Admiralty, Army and Air Force boards and their executive committees, the Acquisition Policy Board, the Investment Approvals Board, official chair of the Defence Environment and Safety Board, and joint head, with the Vice Chief of the Defence Staff, of the Central Top Level Budget organisation.

**2SL/CNH. Second Sea Lord and Commander-in-Chief Naval Home Command.** The Royal Navy's Principal Personnel Officer of the rank of Vice Admiral, and a member of the Admiralty and Navy Boards. Also known as the Chief of Naval Personnel. He has responsibility for maintaining operational capability by providing correctly trained manpower through recruitment into the Royal Navy and Royal Marines and individual training.

**ABRO.** A Trading Fund Agency of the MoD formally known as Army Base Repair Organisation. ABRO provides engineering support (including complex repair and servicing, re-manufacture and assembly) and fleet management services to the MoD, the defence industry and other commercial businesses for land based equipment ranging from radios to battle tanks.

**ACPP: Africa Conflict Prevention Pool.** The arrangements run jointly by the MoD, FCO and DfID to deliver the Government's conflict prevention objectives in Africa. The ACPP has an annual budget of £31M.

**Activity Levels.** The proportion of regular military personnel deployed on operations and other military tasks.

**Admiralty Board.** The Admiralty Board is chaired by the Secretary of State for Defence and is delegated by the Defence Council to administer the activities and personnel of the Royal Navy.

**AFB: Air Force board.** The Air Force Board is chaired by the Secretary of State for Defence and is delegated by the Defence Council to administer the activities and personnel of the Royal Air Force.

**AFBSC Air Force Board Standing Committee.** The AFBSC conducts the day-to-day business of managing the Royal Air Force on behalf of the Air Force board. It brings together, under the Chief of the Air Staff (CAS), the RAF operational and personnel commanders, and supports the CAS in his executive role, his management and operational advisory roles, and as the professional head of the RAF.

**AFCS: Armed Forces Compensation Scheme.** A scheme, introduced from 6 April 2005, for members and ex-members of the Regular Armed Forces (including Gurkhas) and Reserve Forces, to pay compensation for injuries, illnesses or deaths which are caused by service on or after 6 April 2005. In the event of a Service person's death caused by service, benefits are payable to eligible dependants.

**AFPS: Armed Forces Pension Scheme.** The non-contributory defined benefits pension scheme covering all members of the Armed Forces.

**AG: Adjutant General.**

    a)    The Army's Principal Personnel Officer, of the rank of Lieutenant General, and a member of the Army Board and the Executive Committee of the Army Board. He has responsibility for providing trained army officers and other ranks through recruitment into the Army and individual training. He also provides education services to children of all members of the Services on long-term foreign postings.

    b)    The Top Level Budget (TLB) organisation managed by the Adjutant General.

**ALI: Adult Learning Inspectorate.** The ALI is a statutory non-departmental public body that inspects and reports on the quality of education and training for adults and young people funded by public money.

**AME: Annually Managed Expenditure.** Spending included in Total Managed Expenditure that does not fall within Departmental Expenditure Limits (DELs), such as nuclear provisions and War Pension Benefits. Expenditure in AME is generally less predictable and/or controllable than expenditure within DELs.

**AMP: Air Member for Personnel.** The RAF's Principal Personnel Officer, of the rank of Air Marshall, a member of the Air Force Board and Air Force Standing Committee. He is responsible for providing trained RAF officers and other ranks through recruitment into the RAF, individual training and subsequent management.

**Anti-surface weapons.** Weapons designed to attack targets on the surface of the land or sea.

**AFPAA: Armed Forces Personnel Administration Agency**. Responsible for provision of personnel services, including administration of pay and pensions, for the Armed Forces. Merged with the Veterans Agency from April 2007 to form the Service Personnel and Veterans Agency.

**APB: Acquisition Policy Board.** The MoD's top level board, chaired by the Minister for Defence Procurement or, in his absence, the PUS. It overseas the development of defence acquisition policy and processes and defence industrial policy, and reviewing and monitoring the coherence of acquisition performance targets.

**Apprentices.** New entrants to the Armed Forces undertaking training in particular skilled trades.

**Appropriations-in-aid (A-in-A).** Receipts used to offset expenditure. They generally arise from the provision of repayment services, the sale of surplus goods or of equipment purchased on behalf of the Defence Sales Organisation. Excess A-in-A are subject to Consolidated Fund Extra Receipt (CFER).

**Army Board.** The Army Board is chaired by the Secretary of State for Defence and is delegated by the Defence Council to administer the activities and personnel of the Army.

**Army Reserve** See **Regular Reserves.**

**Assessment Centre.** The formal process used by the MoD to assess suitability of civil servants for promotion into junior management (Band D) and middle management (Band B) grades.

**Assets.** Can be either financial or non-financial. Financial assets include monetary gold, bank deposits, IMF Special Drawing Rights, loans granted bonds, shares, accounts receivable, and the value of the government's stake in public corporations. Non-financial assets consist of fixed capital (such as buildings and vehicles); stock, land and valuables.

**ASTA: Aircrew Synthetic Training Aids.** A Full Mission simulator that replicates all aspects of a real flying mission, allowing pilots to match the aircraft and its weapons against interactive attacks, whilst experiencing the pressures and demands of high speed jet flight. A cockpit trainer, a lower level device, is primarily used to introduce the pilot to the cockpit environment and procedures.

**ASTOR: Airborne Stand Off Radar.** A new capability which will provide a long range all weather theatre surveillance and target acquisition system capable of detecting moving, fixed and static targets.

**AWE: Atomic Weapons Establishment.** One of the largest high technology research, design development and production facilities in the UK. Its primary task is to produce and maintain the warheads for the UK's independent nuclear deterrent.

**BAE Systems:** An international company engaged in the development, delivery and support of advanced defence and aerospace systems in the air, on land, at sea and in space. It designs, manufactures and supports military aircraft, surface ships, submarines, fighting vehicles, radar, avionics, communications and guided weapons systems.

**Balance Sheet.** A financial statement showing the assets, liabilities, and net worth of a business on a specified date.

**Band B.** A grade in the civilian rank structure immediately below the Senior Civil Service. Previously know as Unified Grades 6 and 7.

**Battalion.** An Army fighting unit, usually comprising between 400 – 800 personnel, commanded by a Lieutenant Colonel. See **Regiment.**

**Berlin Plus Arrangements.** Arrangements negotiated between the European Union and NATO to allow for the EU to have access to NATO's assets and capabilities so that NATO can support the EU, so that there's full transparency between the two organisations and so that we cooperate with the most efficient, the most effective mechanisms possible so that resources are used in the most efficient way.

**BOWMAN.** A tri-Service tactical communications and information system.

**BNFL: British Nuclear Fuel plc.** An international nuclear energy business, involved in fuel manufacture, reactor design and services, as well as decommissioning and environmental services; cleaning up the legacy of the Cold War.

**Brigade.** An Army Brigade is a collection of units that have been formally grouped together for a specific purpose, commanded by a Brigadier. A fighting Brigade will contain a mix of infantry, Reconnaissance, Armoured, Engineer, Artillery and Logistic units together with supporting specialist capabilities. The composition of a Brigade will differ depending on its responsibility but usually contains about 5,000 soldiers.

**BTEC. Business and Technology Education Council.** Vocational qualifications to prepare students for employment or for progression to higher education, often taken as an alternative to A-levels.

**BVRAAM: Beyond Visual Range Air-to-Air Missile.** The next generation air-to-air weapon, also known as Meteor, which will provide Typhoon with the capacity to combat projected air-to-air threats throughout the life of the aircraft and contribute to the superiority requirements of UK and NATO operations.

**Capability Reviews.** A Cabinet Office initiative, launched in early 2006, aimed at improving the capability of the Civil Service to meet today's delivery challenges and be ready for tomorrow's. The reviews will help departments to identify where they need to improve and what support they need to do so. The reports on these reviews will be published, with clear assessments of current performance and key actions to be taken to improve. Capability Reviews supersede Performance partnership Agreements.

**CAS: Chief of the Air Staff.** Professional head of the Royal Air Force, member of the Defence Council and Defence Board, the Air Force Board and the Chiefs of Staff Committee, and Chair of the Air Force Board Standing Committee. Currently held by an officer of the rank of Air Chief Marshal.

**CBRN: Chemical, Biological, Radiological and Nuclear materials.** Unconventional materials potentially capable of use in weapons of wide area impact, often collectively known as Weapons of Mass Destruction.

**CBW: Chemical and Biological Warfare.** The use of chemical and biological weapons in conflict. Possession and use of Chemical and biological Warfare is illegal under the Chemical Weapons Convention and the Biological and Toxin Weapons Convention.

**CDL: Chief of Defence Logistics.** Head of the Defence Logistics Organisation TLB. Member of the Defence Council and Defence Board, Acquisition Policy Board and Investment Approvals Board. The post was disestablished on creation of the DE&S organisation headed by the CDM on 2 April 2007.

**CDP: Chief of Defence Procurement.** Head of the Defence Procurement Agency TLB and member of the Defence Council and Defence Board, Acquisition Policy Board and Investment Approvals Board. The post was disestablished on creation of the DE&S organisation headed by the CDM on 2 April 2007.

**CDM:** Chief of Defence Materiel. The head of Defence Equipment and Support, launched on 2 April 2007 as a result of merging the Defence Procurement Agency and Defence Logistics Organisation. Member of the Defence Council and Defence Board, Investment Approvals Board and Acquisition Policy Board.

**CDS: Chief of Defence Staff.** The professional head of the UK Armed Forces and principal military adviser to the Secretary of State for Defence and the Government. Member of the Defence Council and Defence Board, and Chairman of the Chiefs of Staff Committee.

**CFE: Treaty on Conventional Armed Forces in Europe.** A treaty which established comprehensive limits on conventional military equipment in Europe (from the Atlantic to the Urals) mandated the destruction of excess weaponry and provided for verification and inspection.

**CFER: Consolidated Fund Extra Receipt.** Receipts realised in excess of amounts authorised as Appropriations in Aid of the supply Estimates, or of kinds which HM Treasury does not allow Departments to use in aid of expenditure. Such receipts are surrendered to the Consolidated Fund as Extra Receipts.

**CGS: Chief of the General Staff.** Professional head of the Army, member of the Defence Council and Defence Board, the Army Board and Chiefs of Staff Committee, and the Chair of the Executive Committee of the Army Board. Currently held by an officer of the rank of General.

**CJO: Chief of joint Operations.**

  a) the senior joint military operational commander, of the rank of Vice Admiral, Lieutenant General or Air Marshall, responsible for running all military operations other than those so large that a more senior officer is required, or those undertaken predominantly by one

Service such that it makes sense for the operation to be commanded by the operational TLB led by that Service (CINCFLEET, Land Command, or Strike Command). Military assets are assigned to CJO only for the duration of the operation.

b) The Top Level Budget organisation managed by CJO, including the Permanent joint Headquarters, the Sovereign Base Areas in Cyprus and British forces in Gibraltar and the Falkland Islands.

**CINCFLEET: Commander-in-Chief Fleet.** The Royal Navy's principal operational commander, of the rank of Admiral, and a member of the Admiralty and Navy Boards.

**CINCLAND: Commander-in-Chief Land.**

a) The Army's principal operational commander, of the rank of General, and a member of the Army Board and Executive Committee of the Army Board.

b) Top Level budget organisation managed by CINCLAND responsible for the delivery of trained expeditionary armed forced to CJO at agreed readiness rates.

**CINCAIR: Commander-in-Chief Air Command.**

a) The Royal Air Force's principal operational commander, of the rank of Air Chief Marshall, and a member of the Air Force Board and Air Force Board Standing Committee.

b) Top Level Budget organisation managed by Air Command responsible for the deliver of trained expeditionary air power to CJO at agreed readiness levels.

**CIS: Communication and Information systems.**

**Civil Contingencies Act.** The Act, and accompanying non-legislative measures, will deliver a single framework for civil protection in the United Kingdom capable of meeting the challenges of the twenty-first century. The Act is separated into two substantive parts: local arrangements for civil protection and emergency powers. It Received Royal Assent in November 2004.

**CMS: Common Military Skills.** Core military skills in which recruits are trained in the first stages of their training.

**COBRA: Counter-Battery Radar.** A 3-D phased radar system designed to locate enemy artillery at very long ranges.

**Combat I.D.:** The process of combining situational awareness, target identification and specific tactics, techniques and procedures to increase operational effectiveness of weapons systems and reduce the incidence of casualties caused by friendly fire.

**Commission.** The legal authority of an Officer's appointment to the Armed Forces. Precise terms vary according to Service and specialisation within each Service.

**Conflict Prevention.** Early warning, crisis management, conflict resolution, peacemaking, peacekeeping, and peace-building activity and an associated strengthening of international and regional systems and capacity.

**Corps:**

a) An organised collection of Regiments or groupings of soldiers that share a common area of specialist expertise to ensure common practice and that common interests can be catered for efficiently.

b) An Army fighting unit comprising two or more divisions with associated specialist supporting units, commanded by a Lieutenant General.

**COS: Chiefs of Staff Committee.** The Chiefs of Staff Committee is chaired by the Chief of the Defence Staff. It is the main forum in which the collective military advice of the Chiefs of Staff is obtained on operational issues. The PUS attends the COS Committee.

**Cost of Capital Charge.** An annual non-cash charge applied to each department's budget. It is 3.5% of the net assets of the department and is used to make departments aware of the full cost of holding assets.

**CSA:**

a) **Chief Scientific Adviser.** The MoD's senior expert scientific advisor, recruited externally, Head of Science Innovation and Technology TLB, member of the Defence Council and Defence Board and Chair of the Investment Approvals Board.

b) **Customer Supplier Agreement.** An agreement, usually between TLBs, detailing in terms of quality, quantity and timeliness the outputs required from the supplier to enable the customer to meet its defence outputs.

**CSPS: Civil Service Pension Scheme.**

**CTLB: Central TLB.** The Central Top Level Budget organisation has responsibility for the MoD Head Office, covering Defence policy as well as Departmental policy on the equipment programme, resources, finance, personnel and security, as well as a range of non-Head Office functions. The Central TLB provides a diverse range of corporate services for the MoD as a whole. These include pay, bill payment, consultancy services, accountancy, some training, statistical analysis, central IT systems, public relations, defence exports and policing. The Central TLBs remit also encompasses provision of medical services.

**CTP: Career Transition Partnership.** A partnering arrangement between Right Management Consultants and the MoD to deliver improved resettlement services to all ranks from the Armed Forces.

**Current expenditure** on goods and services is the sum of expenditure on pay, and related staff costs, plus spending on goods and services. It is net of receipts from sales. It excludes capital expenditure, but includes expenditure on equipment that can only be used for military purposed since that is counted as current expenditure. It differs from final consumption in that capital consumption is not included.

**Current prices.** Prices prevailing at the time.

**CVR(T): Combat Vehicle Reconnaissance (Tracked).** A light tank used for reconnaissance.

**DAC: Defence Audit Committee.** The Defence Audit Committee is a subcommittee of the Defence Board, chaired by an independent non-executive member of the DB. It reviews and constructively challenges the adequacy of internal controls, risk management and assurance processes within the MoD. In particular it reviews the Department's assurance arrangements and Statement on Internal Control contained within the Departmental Resource Accounts (the DRAc) annually and reports on these to the Accounting Officer.

**DACP: Defence Acquisition Change Programme.** The Defence Acquisition Change Programme is a single coherent acquisition reform programme that has been initiated to deliver aspects of the cultural, behavioural, procedural and organisational change identified in the Defence Industrial Strategy and the recommendations from the Enabling Acquisition Change report.

**DARA: Defence Aviation Repair Agency.** In 1999, DARA brought together the RAF maintenance Group Defence Agency (MGDA) and the Naval Aircraft Repair Organisation (NARO). It is the largest Government owned aerospace repair facility within Europe, delivering one-stop-shop aerospace support to the MoD, overseas governments and Industry. DARA became a Trading Agency of the MoD in April 2001. Following changes in provision of aviation support, the Government announced in MAY 2007 that DARA's residual functions will be merged with ABRO from April 2008.

**DASA: Defence Analytical Services Agency.** DASA was created in July 1992 and provides National Statistics on Defence and other corporate information, forecasting and planning and consultancy, advice and research services to the MoD.

**DBA: Defence Bills Agency.** Primarily responsible for paying bills submitted to the MoD by defence contractors.

**DCSA: Defence Communication Services Agency.** Provided telecommunications and related services to the MoD and was part of the DLO. Disestablished from 1 April 2007 on creation of DE&S.

**DE: Defence Estates.** The Top Level Budget organisation that manages and maintains the defence estate. DE ceased to be an Agency in April 2007.

**DE&S: Defence Equipment & Support.** DE&S is the single organisation (formed on 2 April 2007 from merging the Defence Procurement Agency and Defence Logistics Organisation) responsible for the procurement and support of equipment used by the Armed Forces.

**Defence Aim.** The Defence Aim is set out in the MoD's Public Service Agreement. It is to deliver security for the people of the UK and Overseas territories by defending them, including against terrorism, and act as a force for good by strengthening international peace and security.

**Defence Balanced Scorecard.** The Defence Balanced Scorecard is a framework that helps the DB to translate strategy into operational objectives that drive both behaviour and performance. This strategy is articulated in the Departmental Plan, which sets out the department's top level strategic objectives, including our Public Service Agreement (PSA) targets. The Defence Balanced Scorecard tells the DB how well Defence is doing in terms of the objectives that underpin the plan. Ultimately this assessment tells the DB whether Defence is 'succeeding' and gives them an insight into the department's ability to achieve the Defence vision.

**Defence Budget.** Under Cash Accounting, the amount of money planned to be spent during a financial year. Under Resource Accounting and Budgeting (RAB), the sum of resources planned to be consumed during a financial year. See Resource budgeting.

**Defence Council.** The Defence Council is chaired by the Secretary of State for Defence and provides the formal legal basis for the command and administration of the Armed Forces under a range of powers vested in it by statute and Letters Patent.

**Defence Estate.** The built facilities and rural land required to deliver defence output.

**Defence Mission.** The objectives of the Ministry of Defence are to provide the capabilities needed: to ensure the security and defence of the United Kingdom and Overseas Territories, including against terrorism; to support the Government's foreign policy objectives particularly in promoting international peace and security.

**DTC: Defence Technology Centre.** Centres of excellence for conducting innovative, cutting edge research for enhanced UK Defence capability. They are exemplars for research collaboration between Government, UK Defence, Small-Medium Sized Enterprises, and Universities.

**Defence Vision.** The Defence Vision set out by the Defence Board, is: Defending the UK and its interests; Strengthening international peace and stability; A Force for good in the world. We achieve this aim by working together on our core task to produce battle-winning people and equipment that are: Fit for the challenge of today; Ready for the tasks of tomorrow; Capable of building for the future.

**DEFRA: Department for Environment, Food and Rural Affairs.** DEFRA is the Government Department responsible for all aspects of the environment, rural matters, farming and food production.

**DEL: Departmental Expenditure Limit.** DELs are firm plans for three years for a specific part of a department's expenditure. In general the DEL will cover all running costs and all programme expenditure except, in certain cases, spending is included in departmental AME because it cannot be reasonably be subject to close control over a three year period. DELs are divided into current and capital budgets.

**Depreciation.** Also termed capital consumption. The measure of the wearing out, consumption or other loss of value of a fixed asset whether arising from use, passage of time or obsolescence through technological and market changes.

**DERA: Defence Evaluation and Research Agency.** On 2 July 2001 DERA was split into two parts: QinetiQ, and the Defence Science and Technology Laboratory (Dstl).

**DESB: Defence Environment and Safety Board.** Chaired by the Under Secretary of State or, in his absence, the 2nd PUS, provides direction, sets objectives, monitors, reviews and reports on performance with regard to the environment and safety in defence.

**Devolved Administrations.** The devolved administrations of Scotland, Wales and Northern Ireland have responsibility for certain defined areas of domestic Government in their parts of the UK.

**DFAU: Defence Fraud Analysis Unit.** A dedicated unit within the Defence Internal Audit organisation to evaluate suspected irregularities, support police authorities, promote risk awareness, record reported fraud and theft, liaise with the Treasury and provide advice on procedures and policy.

**DfES: Department for Education and Skills.** Government Department responsible for setting education and skills policy in England.

**DfID: Department for International Development.** Government Department responsible for the UK's development aid and work to get rid of extreme poverty.

**DH: Department of Health.** Government Department responsible for setting health and social care policy in England, and sets standards and drives Modernisation across all areas of the NHS, social care and public health.

**DIA: Defence Internal Audit.** The MoD's principal Internal Auditing body, whose primary role is the provision of independent and objective advice on the economy, efficiency and effectiveness of systems and controls at all levels of the Department. It reports directly to the Defence Audit Committee.

**DII: Defence Information Infrastructure.** A fully networked and managed information system being acquired to support Defence worldwide, underpinning much of the defence Change Programme.

**Direct Entry Officers.** Army officers (previously called Mainstream officers) who either come direct from civilian life or from the ranks of the Army, commissioned on completion of the 11 month Royal Military Academy Sandhurst (RMAS) Commissioning Course. They will normally be under the age of 29 on entry to RMAS.

**DIS:**

    a)   **Defence Industrial Strategy.** Announced on 15 December 2005, the Defence Industrial Strategy is aimed at ensuring that our Armed Forces are provided with the equipment that they require, on time, and at best value for money. It aims to identify the sustainable industrial base required to retain within the UK those industrial capabilities (including infrastructure, skills, intellectual property and capacity).

    b)   **Defence Intelligence Staff.** Organisation that provides timely, all-source intelligence assessments to: guide Departmental decision making on the formulation of Defence policy and the commitment and employment of the UK's military forces; inform decisions on the generation and maintenance of operational military capability, including through the Equipment Programme; and contribute to wider national intelligence collection and assessment.

**Division.** An Army Division made up of two or more Brigades depending on the specific role it is to undertake and is configured in a similar fashion to a Brigade but on a larger scale, commanded by a Major General. 1 (UK) Division and 3 (UK) Division are fighting Divisions. 2, 4 and 5 Division are responsible for administrative support of specific geographical areas within the UK.

**DLO: Defence Logistics Organisation.** The Top Level Budget organisation formed on 1 April 1999 to bring together the logistics support organisations in the Royal Navy, Army and Royal Air Force and Centre staff. It contains a number of specialist Defence Agencies. With effect from 2nd April 2007, Defence Logistic and Defence Procurement Agency have merged to form the new Defence Equipment & Support TLB.

**DLTP: Defence Logistics Transformation Programme.** A single coherent programme of work incorporating all logistic transformation activities across Defence to achieve improved operational effectiveness, efficiency and flexibility.

**DB: Defence Board.** The Defence Board (DB) is the highest, non-ministerial committee in the MoD. Chaired by PUS, it is essentially the main corporate board of the MoD, providing senior level leadership and strategic management of Defence. Its role is to deliver the Defence Aim set out in the Public Service Agreement. It comprises the non-ministerial members of the Defence Council and a number of non-executive members. It is responsible for the role of Defence, providing strategic direction, vision and values; for Objectives and targets, establishing the key priorities and defence capabilities necessary to deliver the MoD's Departmental objectives; for Resource allocation and strategic balance of investment to match Defence priorities and objectives; and for Performance management, managing and driving corporate performance.

**DMS: Defence Medical Services.** Comprises the Defence Medical Services Department and the three single Service medical directorates.

**DOC: Directorate of Operational Capability.** DOC provides an independent source of evaluation and audit within the Armed Forces on a range of issues, including operational lessons learnt studies and appraising the care and welfare of

Armed Forces initial training establishments.

**DPA: Defence Procurement Agency.** The DPA was the Top Level Budget Organisation responsible for the procurement of equipment to meet new requirements. It is also a Defence Agency. It is located mainly at Abbey Wood, Bristol. With effect from 2nd April 2007, Defence Logistic and Defence Procurement Agency have merged to form the new Defence Equipment & Support TLB.

**DRDL: Devonport Royal Dockyards Ltd.** A company which runs and owns the Devonport Royal Dockyards in Plymouth.

**DSDA: Defence Storage and Distribution Agency.** The Defence Agency that provides the Armed Forces with storage and distribution services.

**DSL: Debut Services Ltd.** A joint venture between Bovis Lend lease Ltd and Babcock Infrastructure Services to provide property maintenance and capital works projects across Defence.

**DSTL: Defence Science and Technology Laboratory.** An agency and trading fund of the MoD created from part of DERA on 2 July 2001. It provides specialist scientific and technical support to the MoD.

**DTC: Defence Technology Centre.** A formal collaborative arrangement between industry and academic experts in a particular technology, funded jointly by participants and the MoD, who work together to generate and enhance the technology vital to the delivery of future UK Defence capabilities.

**DU: Depleted Uranium.** Uranium is a natural element found in soil, water and mineral deposits. It is a heavy metal, nearly twice as dense as lead, is radioactive and chemically toxic. DU is a waste product, (what is left after the removal of some of the more radioactive parts of natural uranium for use in the nuclear industry) and being a very dense and hard metal is an ideal core for tank shells designed to pierce armoured vehicles.

**DUOB: Depleted Uranium Oversight Board.** An independent panel of scientists and veterans' representatives appointed to oversee the MoD's depleted uranium (DU) screening programme.

**DWR: Deep Waste Repository.** A facility for the storage of nuclear waste deep underground.

**EAC: Enabling Acquisition Change.** An internal study established to examine the MoD's ability to conduct Through Life Capability Management. The study team report was published on 3 July 2006.

**ECAB: Executive Committee of the Army Board.** ECAB conducts the day-to-day business of managing the Army on behalf of the Army Board. It brings together, under the Chief of the General Staff, the Army operational and personnel commanders, and supports the CGS in his executive role, his management and operational advisory roles, and as the professional head of the Army.

**Environment Agency.** The environmental regulator for England and Wales.

**ERW: Explosive Remnants of War.** Unexploded ordnance (such as bombs, missiles and artillery shells), which may be primed, fused, armed or prepared for use, and may have been abandoned.

**ESDP: European Security and Defence Policy.** The European Union has agreed on the establishment of a European Security and Defence Policy to ensure it has the tools to undertake crisis management operations, where NATO as a whole is not engaged, in support of its Common Foreign and Security Policy.

**Ethnic Minority.** A group within a community which differs ethnically from the main population.

**EU: European Union.** The framework for economic and political co-operation between 25 European countries. It began as a post-war initiative between six countries pooling control over coal and steel to guarantee a more peaceful future for Europe. It now manages co-operation on issues as wide-ranging as the environment, transport and employment, and has increasing influence in defence and foreign policy.

**EUFOR.** The EU-led peacekeeping force responsible for security in Bosnia-Herzegovina.

**FCO: Foreign and Commonwealth Office.** The Government department responsible for UK foreign and security policy.

**Finance Director.** The MoD's senior finance officer, responsible for all aspects of the Department's financial performance and a member of the Defence Board.

**Fleet.** The Top Level Budget (TLB) organisation managed by Commander-in-Chief Fleet which was formed on 1 April 2006 from the CINC Fleet TLB and Chief of Naval Personnel TLB.

**FOI: Freedom of Information.** An Act giving a right of public access to recorded information held by public authorities subject to certain defined exemptions.

**FRES: Future Rapid Effects System.** A project to enhance the deployability of UK Land Forces by delivering a family of medium weight, network capable armoured vehicles, such as armoured personnel carriers, reconnaissance, command and control, and or ambulance vehicles. The project is currently in the Assessment Phase.

**FE: Force Element.** An Armed Force grouping used for the measurement of readiness. This may be an armoured brigade in the Army, an individual ship in the Royal Navy or an individual aircraft or squadron of aircraft in the Royal Air Force.

**Full-Time Equivalent.** A measure of the size of the workforce that takes account of the fact that some people work part-time.

**Full-Time Reserve Service.** Individuals on FTRS fill Service posts on a full-time basis while being a member of one of the reserve services, either as an ex-regular or as a volunteer. In the case of the Army and the Naval Service, these will be posts that would ordinarily have been filled by regular service personnel, in the case of the RAF, FTRS personnel also fill posts designated solely for them.

**GDP: Gross Domestic Product.** The sum of all output (or income or expenditure) in the economy, excluding net property income from abroad.

**GOCNI: General Officer Commanding Northern Ireland.**

a) The senior military officer in command of the Armed Forces in Northern Ireland, of the rank of Lieutenant General. He is responsible for military aid to the civil power and counter terrorist operations in Northern Ireland;

b) The joint-Service Top Level Budget organisation managed by GOCNI. With effect from April 2007, The General Officer Commanding Northern Ireland has been incorporated into Command-in-Chief Land Command TLB.

**Global Conflict Prevention Pool.** Global Pool Conflict Prevention Pool (GCPP) consists of geographical and thematic strategies focused on conflict prevention, conflict resolution and / or post-conflict reestablishment throughout the world.

**Gurkhas.** Citizens of Nepal recruited and employed in the Army under the terms of the 1947 Tri-Partite Agreement. They remain Nepalese citizens but in all other respects are full members of HM Forces.

**GWMB: Guided Weapons, Missiles and Bombs.** Explodable munitions which incorporate guidance mechanisms.

**HCDC: House of Commons Defence Select Committee.** The Defence Committee is appointed to examine on behalf of the House of Commons the expenditure, administration and policy of the Ministry of Defence and any associated public bodies.

**Headline Goal 2010.** The aim, adopted by the European Union at the Helsinki European Council in December 1999, to be able to deploying 50-60,000 troops, capable of conducting the full range of crisis management tasks, within 60 days, sustainable for up to a year, with air and naval support as necessary, before the end of 2003.

**Heavy Equipment Transporter.** A 120 tonne tractor and trailer unit tank transporter, capable of carrying battle tanks and fighting vehicles straight to the front line at speeds of up to 50 mph on road or off road over harsh terrain.

**HMG:** Her Majesty's Government.

**HNBS:** Harrier Night Bombing System.

**HOME: Head Office Modern Environment.** The HOME programme was a comprehensive Modernisation package using the redevelopment of MoD's Main Building as a catalyst for organisational and cultural change to make the MoD Head Office a better, more streamlined, organisation in which to work and enable it to provide more effective support and leadership for UK Defence capability.

**HQ: Headquarters.**

**HR: Human Resources.** Civilian personnel management, organisation and arrangements.

**HSE: Health and Safety Executive.** The Health and Safety Executive is responsible for regulation of risks to health and safety arising from work activity in Britain.

**Hydrographic Office.** See **UK Hydrographic Office.**

**IAB: Investment Approvals Board.** The Investment Approvals Board (IAB) is responsible for central scrutiny of equipment requirements, major capital works and Information Technology projects. It makes recommendations to Ministers on the procurement of major defence equipment. The IAB is chaired by the Chief Scientific Adviser and includes the Vice Chief of the Defence Staff, the 2nd Permanent Under Secretary, the Chief of Defence Materiel, and the Defence Commercial Director.

**ICT: Information and Communications Technology.**

**ICT FS: Information and Communications Technology Fundamental Skills.**

**Industrial staff.** Civilian staff in certain pay bands often performing manual work.

**Insensitive munitions.** Munitions incorporating design features to reduce the risk of inadvertent reaction to specified stimuli, such as heat, shock and impact.

**In-Service Date.** The date on which equipment being procured is expected to be available and supportable in service in sufficient quantity to provide a valuable operational capability.

**ISAF: International Security Assistance Force.** The NATO controlled peacekeeping force providing security in Kabul since the fall of the Taliban in 2001. More than 30 countries contribute troops.

**IS: Information Systems.**

**ISO 9001:** is the internationally recognised standard for an organisation's internal Quality Management. The term 'quality' refers to all those features of a product or service which are required by the customer.

**Intake.** Those entering the Armed Forces or Civilian workforce.

**IT: Information Technology.**

**JPA: Joint Personnel Administration.** A modern commercial information system enabling provision of pay, pensions and administration services for military personnel, JPA was introduced to the RAF from April 2006, the RN in December 2006 and the Army in April 2007.

**JRRF: Joint Rapid Reaction Forces.** A substantial pool of capabilities, composed of all readily available forces, from which tailored force packages of up to Brigade level or equivalent for operations on land, sea and air can be assembled and deployed quickly.

**KFOR: NATO Kosovo Force.** The International NATO led peacekeeping force whose main role is maintaining a secure civilian environment.

**LAN: Local Area Network.** Two or more connected computers in a room or building.

**Land Command.** See CINCLAND.

**Locally Entered/Engaged Personnel.** Civilian personnel working for one of the Armed Forces or directly for the Ministry of Defence who are recruited at overseas MoD locations normally for work at those locations. Also includes Gurkhas.

**LS: Large Scale.** Operational deployments of division size or equivalent for warfighting or other operations.

**Main Gate.** The main investment point for a procurement project, comprising In-depth review timed to coincide with the most critical point of the project – the point at which the "Assessment" phase ends and user requirements, system requirements, time and cost can be set with confidence.

**MAMBA weapon locating radar.** Mobile Artillery Monitoring Battlefield Radar, a radar system that can instantly track incoming mortars, shells and rockets and will help troops pinpoint the enemy's position for rapid counter attacks.

**MANPADS: Man Portable Air Defence Systems.** Systems designed for military air defence use, and are surface to air missiles, usually shoulder launched and fired by an individual or more than one individual acting as crew.

**MDP: Ministry of Defence Police.** The non-regional, national police force headed by a Chief Constable, responsible for providing effective policing of the Defence Estate.

**Memorandum of Understanding.** A formal signed agreement between partners setting out how they will work together in a process to achieve agreed goals.

**MIDIT: Means of Identifying and Developing Internal Talent.** The MoD's internal corporate development scheme for civilian personnel.

**Military Aid to the Civil Authorities: MACA.** The provision of military assistance: in time of emergency such as natural disasters and major emergencies; to provide more routine assistance for special projects or events of significant social value to the civil community in the creation and development of local community projects; of individual assistance by full-time attachment to social service or similar organisations; or for the maintenance of law, order and public safety using specialist capabilities or equipment, in situations beyond the capability of the Civil Power.

**Military Tasks.** The framework on which the MoD bases its detailed planning for the size, shape and capabilities of the Armed Forces, reflecting the broad types of tasks and operations in which they are likely to be involved.

**MoD: Ministry of Defence.**

**MS: Medium Scale.** Operational deployments of brigade size or equivalent for warfighting or other operations.

**MND(SE): Multi National Division (South East).** The UK led element of the Multinational Forces in Iraq responsible for the four southern provinces of Al Basrah, Al Muthanna, Dhi Qar, and Maysan.

**NAAFI: Navy, Army and Air Force Institutes.** Official trading organisation of HM Forces, providing retail and leisure services to the Services and their families.

**NAO: National Audit Office.** The independent organisation responsible for scrutinising public spending on behalf of Parliament, reporting to the Public Accounts Committee. It audits the accounts of all government departments and agencies as well as a wide range of other public bodies, and reports on the economy, efficiency and effectiveness with which government bodies have used public money.

**NATO: North Atlantic Treaty Organisation.** A regional defence alliance formed in 1949 under the Washington Treaty. Its general aim is to "safeguard the freedom, common heritage and civilisation" of its members by promoting "stability and well-being in the North Atlantic area". Members agree that an armed attack against one shall be considered an attack against them all, and that they will come to the aid of each other. Currently there are 26 member countries with the headquarters in Brussels.

**Naval Manning Agency.** Created on 1 July 1996 and dissolved as an agency 1 April 2004. Its mission was: to ensure that sufficient manpower is available on the trained strength and deployed effectively in peace, transition to war or war.

**Naval Service.** The Royal Navy (including QARNNS) and the Royal Marines together.

**Navy Board.** The Navy Board conducts the day-to-day business of managing the Royal Navy on behalf of the Admiralty Board. It brings together, under the Chief of the Naval Staff, the Royal Navy's operational and personnel commanders, and supports the CNS in his executive role, his management and operational advisory roles, and as the professional head of the Royal Navy.

**NCO: Non-commissioned officer.** Ratings of Leading Hand and above in the Royal Navy, other ranks of lance corporal and above in the Army and other ranks of corporal and above in the Royal Marines and Royal Air Force.

**NDA: Nuclear Decommissioning Authority.** The body sponsored by the DTI responsible for nuclear clean-up issues.

**NDPB: Non-Departmental Public Bodies.** Public bodies carry out a wide range of functions on behalf of government. As part of the commitment to transparency and accountability, the Cabinet Office collects and publishes annually information about public bodies as a whole, to supplement information about individual bodies already contained in departmental annual reports.

**NEC: Network Enabled Capability.** A programme to enhance military capability through the exploitation of information. Implemented through the coherent and progressive development of Defence equipment, software, processes, structures and individual and collective training, NEC will enable the MoD to operate more effectively in the future strategic environment by more efficient sharing and exploitation of information within the UK Armed Forces and with our coalition partners.

**NED: Non Executive Director.** Non Executive Directors serve on various boards and audit committees within the Ministry of Defence, providing independent scrutiny and advice on defence business from their experience in Industry.

**Net Cash Requirement.** The amount of actual money that MoD requires from the government in order to fund its activities. The NCR takes account of the movements in working capital levels (debtors, creditors and stocks) but not non-cash costs.

**NHS: National Health Service.** Set up on 5th July 1948, the NHS provides healthcare for all citizens, based on need, not the ability to pay, and is funded by the tax payer and managed by the Department of Health, which has the responsibility to provide healthcare to the general public through the NHS.

**Non-cash items.** Non cash items include various notional transactions such as depreciation, impairments and cost of capital that appear in the operating cost statement under RAB.

**Non-industrial staff.** All Civil servants who are not Industrial staff.

**NPT: Treaty on the Non-Proliferation of Nuclear Weapons.** An international treaty to limit the spread of nuclear weapons and the foundation of the international nuclear disarmament and non-proliferation system.

**NRA: Net Recoverable Amount.**

**NRF: NATO Response Force.** Giving NATO a significant crisis response capability, the NRF is a powerful multi national military force with land, air, maritime and command elements, designed to stand alone for up to 30 days. It is not a permanent or standing force.

**NRV: Net Realisable Value.** The estimated disposal sale value of an item of materiel not expected to be used or sold in the ordinary course of business. The estimated disposal sale value may be nil or scrap in appropriate circumstances, and will be net of any costs incidental to the sale, e.g. agent's fees, to the extent that these are identifiable to individual items or sales contracts and are deducted from the sales proceeds on a net receipt basis.

**Nursing Services.** Queen Alexandra's Royal Naval Nursing Service, Queen Alexandra's Royal Army Nursing Corps, and Princess Mary's Royal Air Force Nursing Service.

**OCCAR: Organisation Conjoint de Cooperation en matièrs d'ARmement.** An Administrative Arrangement established on 12th November 1996 by the Defence Ministers of France, Germany, Italy and the UK. Its aim is to provide more effective and efficient arrangements for the management of certain existing and future collaborative armament programmes.

**OECD: Organisation for Economic Co-operation and Development.** The OECD comprises 30 countries sharing a commitment to democratic government and the market economy. Its work covers economic and social issues from macroeconomics, to trade, education, development and science and innovation.

**Officer.** A member of the Armed Forces holding the Queen's Commission. Includes ranks from Sub-Lt/2nd Lt/Pilot Officer up to Admiral of the Fleet/Field Marshal/Marshal of the Royal Air Force. Excludes NCO's.

**Officer cadet.** An entrant from civil life to the officer corps of the Armed Forces.

**OGC: Office of Government Commerce.** An independent Office of the Treasury which aims to work with the public sector as a catalyst to achieve efficiency, value for money in commercial activities and improved success in the delivery of programmes and projects.

**Operating Cost Statement.** The statement in departmental resource accounts that shows the current income and expenditure on an accrual basis. It is similar to the profit and loss statement on commercial accounts. This is the Public Sector's equivalent of a commercial organisation's Profit and Loss Account.

**Operational TLBs.** The TLBs directly responsible for the planning and management of military operations and the delivery of front-line capability. Operational personnel are those working in these TLBs plus some other small groups.

**OPG: Office of HM Paymaster General.** The Office of HM Paymaster General is part of HM Treasury. It is responsible for holding the working balances of Government Departments and other public bodies in accounts at the Bank of England and making them available to the National Loans Fund overnight to reduce the government's borrowing costs, and provides cash flow information to the Treasury.

**OSCE: Organisation for Security and Co-operation in Europe.** With 55 States drawn from Europe, Central Asia and America, the OSCE is the world's largest regional security organisation, bringing comprehensive and cooperative security to a region that stretches from Vancouver to Vladivostok. It offers a forum for political negotiations and decision-making in the fields of early warning, conflict prevention, crisis management and post-conflict rehabilitation, and puts the political will of the participating States into practice through its unique network of field missions.

**Other Ranks.** Members of the Royal Marines, Army and Royal Air Force who are not officers. The equivalent group in the Royal Navy is known as "Ratings".

**Outflow** Those leaving the Armed Forces or Civil Service for any reason. Those who rejoin and then leave again will be counted twice if the time period includes both exit dates.

**Outturn** and **estimated outturn** describe expenditure actually incurred, or estimated on the basis of actual expenditure to date.

**Part-time.** Civil servants working fewer than 37 hours a week (36 hours in London), excluding meal breaks.

**PCPF: Parliamentary Contributory Pension Fund.** The fund of the parliamentary pension scheme.

**People Programme:** A programme to enable MoD civilians to make the best contribution to the Defence capability. This will be achieved by: maximising our pool of talent and skills; matching people and their skills to the jobs that need to be done, now and in the future; and by raising our collective performance by improving management, training and development throughout the Department.

**PPPA: People, Pay & Pensions Agency.** The organisation providing civilian pay and personnel services, including the administration of pensions, the payment of salaries of MoD civilian staff and the payment of fees. Launched on 7 April 2006.

**PCRU: Post Conflict Reconstruction Unit.** An organisation set up to enhance the Government's ability to plan, develop and deliver effective and co-ordinated post conflict stabilisation activity. The organisation is interdepartmental.

**PFI: Private Finance Initiative.** A system for providing capital assets for the provision of public services. Typically, the private sector designs, builds and maintains infrastructure and other capital assets and then operates those assets to sell services to the public sector. In most cases, the capital assets are accounted for on the balance sheet of the private sector operator.

**PPP: Public Private Partnership.** An initiative through which the private sector is involved in the delivery of public services by providing management and service delivery expertise and sometimes the provision of assets. Improved value for money is the essential prerequisite, with better quality of service provision a highly desirable addition. It is delivered through several mechanisms including Private Finance Initiative, Partnering, Wider Markets Initiative and Contractor Logistic Support.

**PSA: Public Service Agreement.** An agreement between HM Treasury and each Government Department setting out each department's aim, objectives and key outcome-based targets. They form an integral part of the spending plans set out in Spending Reviews. Progress against the PSA targets is assessed and reported via the Defence Balanced Scorecard.

**PSI: Proliferation Security Initiative.** The Proliferation Security Initiative is a global effort that aims to stop shipments of weapons of mass destruction, their delivery systems, and related materials worldwide. It was announced by President Bush on May 31, 2003.

**PSG: Professional Skills for Government.** Professional Skills for Government is a key part of the Government's Delivery and Reform agenda. It is a major, long-term change programme designed to ensure that civil servants, wherever they work, have the right mix of skills and expertise to enable their Departments or agencies to deliver effective services.

**PTC: RAF Personnel and Training Command.** The Top Level Budget organisation managed by the RAF's Principal; Personnel Officer, the Air Member for Personnel. PTC provides trained personnel to Strike Command and other TLBs. PTC merged with STC from April 2007 to form Air Command.

**PUS: Permanent Under Secretary.** PUS is the Government's principal Civilian advisor on Defence and has the primary responsibility for Policy, Finance, Management and Administration in the department. He is the MoD Accounting Officer reflecting his responsibility to the Secretary of State for the overall organisation, management and staffing of the department and financial procedures and other matters. He is personally accountable to Parliament for the expenditure of all public money voted for defence purposes, chairs the Defence Board and is Secretary of the Defence Council.

**PVR: Premature Voluntary Release.** Those who leave the Armed Forces voluntarily before the end of their agreed engagement or commission period. Now known as voluntary outflow.

**PRT: Provincial Reconstruction Team.** A combination of international military and civilian personnel based in one of Afghanistan's provinces with the aim of extending the authority of the Afghan central government and helping to facilitate development and reconstruction by contributing to an improved security environment. PRTs also aim to support the reform of the Afghan security sector – disarmament and demobilisation of militias; building an accountable national army and national police force under government control; stamping out the drugs trade; and helping build a

legal system.

**QARNNS: Queen Alexandra's Royal Naval Nursing Service.** The Royal Navy's internal nursing service.

**QinetiQ Group plc.** A defence technology and security company, formerly part of DERA, partially owned by the MoD. QinetiQ was floated in March 2006 to become QinetiQ Group plc, but still retains a shareholding.

**Quick Impact Projects.** Programmes aimed at kick-starting local economies and creating employment opportunities in immediate post-conflict environments. Projects are identified and implemented by local groups with international assistance. Examples include the reconstruction and refurbishment of schools in Iraq.

**RAB.** Resource Accounting and Budgeting.

**RAF:** The Royal Air Force.

**Rank.** Grade within the Military structure.

**Ratings.** Junior military personnel in the Royal Navy.

**Real terms** figures are amounts adjusted for the effect of general price inflation relative to a base year, as measured by the GDP market price deflator.

**Regiment.** A formed unit of personnel sharing a common identity and area of expertise, carrying the spirit of the people who have gone before.

**Regular Reserves.** Former members of the UK regular forces who have a liability for service with the Reserve forces. Includes the Royal Fleet Reserve, Army Reserve and Royal Air Force Reserve as well as other individuals liable to recall.

**RES: Race Equality Scheme.** The MoD Race Equality Scheme sets out how the Department is fulfilling its obligations under the Race Relations (Amendment) Act 2000.

**Resource Accounting.** The accounting methodology used to record expenditure in the departmental accounts which replaced cash accounting. It applies UK generally accepted accounting practice (UK GAAP) used in private industry and other Government Departments to departmental transactions. Spending is measured on an accruals basis.

**Resource Budget.** The sum of a department's resource Departmental Expenditure Limit and resource Annually Managed Expenditure. It is the budget for current expenditure on an accruals basis.

**Resource budgeting.** The budgeting regime adopted for the spending plans set in the 2000 Spending Review. It is derived from resource accounting rules, but there are several differences in treatment between resource accounts and resource budgets.

**RFA: Royal Fleet Auxiliary Service.** The civilian manned fleet, owned by the Ministry of Defence. Its main task is to supply warships of the Royal Navy at sea with fuel, food, stores and ammunition which they need to remain operational while away from base. It also provides aviation support for the Royal Navy, together with amphibious support and secure sea transport for Army units and their equipment. Its employees are full-time civil servants, but who come under the Naval Discipline Act when deployed to sea under naval command.

**RfR: Request for Resources.** An accruals-based measure of current expenditure which forms part of a Resource Estimate. It represents the basic unit of Parliamentary control.

**RM: Royal Marines.** Sea-going soldiers who are part of the Naval Service.

**RMR: Royal Marines Reserve.** The volunteer reserve service of the Royal Marines. See **Volunteer Reserves.**

**RN: Royal Navy.** The sea-going defence forces of the UK, including ships, submarines, Naval aircraft and their personnel, and Queen Alexandra's Royal Naval Nursing Service, but excluding the Royal Marines and the Royal Fleet Auxiliary Service (RFA).

**RNAS: Royal Naval Air Station.** An air base operated by the Fleet Air Arm.

**RNR: Royal Naval Reserve.** The volunteer reserve service of the Royal Navy. See Volunteer Reserves.

**RO-RO Shipping.** Ships designed to allow cargo, such as vehicles, to be loaded by being rolled instead of lifted, often with a drive-through concept with bow and stern doors. It is commonly used in the in the ferry trades to transport cars and goods vehicles, but also used to transport military vehicles.

**RPC: Regional Prime Contracts.** Five regionally-based contracts for the provision of construction and maintenance services on the Defence Estate across Great Britain, where stand-alone arrangements are not appropriate. The objective of Regional Prime Contracting is to achieve better long-term value for money through improved Supply Chain Management, incentivised payment mechanisms, continuous improvement, economies of scale, and partnering.

**RRUs: Regional Rehabilitation Units.** Facilities located around the UK and in Germany containing doctors, physiotherapists and Remedial Instructors providing assessment and rehabilitation for physical injuries sustained by Service personnel.

**SALW: Small Arms and Light Weapons.** Personal weapons, such as pistols, rifles and light machine guns.

**SBAC: Society of British Aerospace Companies**. A trade association representing the UK aerospace and defence industry

**SC: Supply Chain.**

**SCAPE:** An estimate of the cost of providing future superannuation protection for all personnel currently in pensionable employment.

**SCS: Senior Civil Service.** The senior management of the Civil Service.

**SDR: Strategic Defence Review.** The Defence Review conducted in 1997-98 which reassessed Britain's security interests and Defence needs and set out objectives designed to enhance the Armed Forces.

**SEC: Service Executive Committees.** The three committees that conduct the day-to-day business of managing the Services on behalf of the Admiralty, Army and Air Force Boards. They bring together, under the Chief of Staff, the Service's operational and personnel commanders, to support the Chief of Staff in his executive role, his management and operational advisory roles, and as the professional head of his Service. See Navy Board, The Executive Committee of the Army Board; and The Air Force Board Standing Committee.

**Senior Non-commissioned officer.** Senior members of the Ratings/Other Ranks, including Warrant Officer (all classes), Charge Chief Petty Officer, Chief Petty Officer, Colour sergeant, Staff Sergeant, Flight Sergeant/Chief Technician, Petty Officer, Sergeant.

**SFA: Service Family Accommodation.** Housing for service personnel with families.

**SFOR: NATO Stabilisation Force.** The International NATO led peacekeeping force, responsible for security in the Balkans, before handing over to EUFOR in December 2004.

**SIC: Statement of Internal Control.** The formal statement in the resource Accounts by the Accounting Officer, that effective systems are in place for managing the organisation.

**SIT: Science Innovation and Technology.** The Top Level Budget organisation managed by the Chief Scientific Advisor providing science and technology advice and solutions.

**SLAM: Single Living Accommodation Modernisation.** A project to raise the standard of single living accommodation for service personnel by delivering over 30,000 new or refurbished bed-spaces from 2003-2013.

**Smart Acquisition.** Smart Acquisition is a policy which aims to acquire Defence capability faster, cheaper, better and more effectively integrated. The objectives of Smart Acquisition are to deliver and sustain defence capabilities within the performance, time and cost parameters approved at the time the major investment decisions are taken; to acquire defence capabilities progressively, at lower risk; to optimise trade-offs between military effectiveness, time and whole life cost are maximised; and to cut the time for (key) new technologies to be introduced into the frontline, where needed to secure military advantage and industrial competitiveness.

**SNM: Special Nuclear Materials.** Plutonium, uranium-233, or uranium enriched in the isotopes uranium-233 or uranium-235.

**Sovereign Base Areas.** The UK Overseas Territory in Cyprus, which is the joint responsibility of the Foreign and Commonwealth Office and the Ministry of Defence.

**SS: Small Scale.** Operational deployment of battalion size or equivalent.

**SSR: Security Sector Reform.** This aims to help developing and transitional countries manage their security functions in a democratically accountable, efficient and effective way by initiating and supporting reform and providing appropriate education and training.

**SSRB: Senior Salaries Review Body.** The independent body advising the Government on Senior Civil Service pay.

**SSSI: Sites of Special Scientific Interest.** Protected sites of particular environmental and scientific importance, including wetlands, rivers, heathlands, meadows, beaches, moorland and peat bog. The Defence Estate contains 289 SSSIs.

**STC: Strike Command.** The RAF's operational Top Level Budget organisation, providing aircraft and trained aircrews to CJO. STC merged with PTC from April 2007 to form Air Command.

**SCAPE: Superannuation Contributions Adjusted for Past Experience.**

**TLB: Top Level Budget.** The major organisational grouping of the MoD. There are three types: "Operational", "Military Support" and "HQ and other support".

**TLCM: Through Life Capability Management.** An approach to the acquisition and in-service management of military capability in which every aspect of new and existing military capability is planned and managed coherently across all Defence Lines of Development from cradle to grave.

**TNA: The National Archives** is responsible for looking after the records of central government and the courts of law, and making sure everyone can look at them.

**Trading Fund.** Trading Funds were introduced by the Government under the Trading Funds Act 1973 as a 'means of financing trading operations of a government department which, hitherto, have been carried out on Vote'. They are self-accounting units that have greater freedom, than other government departments, in managing their own financial and management activities. They are also free to negotiate their own terms and conditions with their staff and for this reason their grading structures do not always match that of the rest of the Ministry, and this is reflected in some of the tables. MoD Trading Funds are ABRO, DARA, DSTL, the Met Office, and the UK Hydrographic Office.

**UAV: Unmanned Aerial Vehicle.** An unmanned aerial vehicle (UAV) is an aircraft with no onboard pilot. UAV can be remote controlled or fly autonomously based on pre-programmed flight plans or more complex dynamic automation systems. UAV are currently used in a number of military operations, including reconnaissance and attack.

**UKAEA: United Kingdom Atomic Energy Authority.** A non-departmental public body, responsible to the Department of Trade and Industry. Its primary task today is managing the decommissioning of its nuclear reactors and other radioactive facilities used for the UK's nuclear research and development programme in a safe and environmentally responsible manner and to restore its sites for conventional use.

**UKHO: UK Hydrographic Office.** A trading fund agency of the MoD responsible for the supply of marine navigational information and services to the Royal Navy, and in support of UK Safety of Life at Sea (SOLAS) obligations and to the commercial mariner.

**UOR: Urgent Operational Requirement.** Additional capability requirements for specific operations met using a streamlined version of the Department's normal procurement procedures. This provides speedy and flexible procurement of capabilities.

**UNFICYP.** The United Nations Force in Cyprus, which polices the line separating the Greek and Turkish Cypriot communities.

**VAT: Value Added Tax.**

**VAW: Veterans Awareness Week.** A week to raise the profile of veterans. The first took place in July 2005.

**VCDS: Vice Chief of the Defence Staff.** The deputy to the Chief of the Defence Staff. Joint head of the Central Top Level Budget organisation with the 2nd PUS, and a member of the Defence Council, Defence Board, Chiefs of Staff Committee and Investment Approvals Board.

**Veterans Agency.** Formerly the War Pensions Agency. Responsible for veterans' affairs, including war and service pensions, service records, military graves, medals and welfare issues. The Veterans Agency merged with the Armed Forces Personnel Administration Agency from April 2007 to become the Service Personnel and Veterans Agency.

**VFM: Value for Money.** Value for Money (VfM) is HM Treasury's terminology to assess whether or not an organisation has obtained the maximum benefit from the goods and services it acquires and/or provides, within the resources available to it. It not only measures the cost of goods and services, but also takes account of the mix of quality, cost, resource use, fitness for purpose, timeliness and convenience to judge whether or not, when taken together, they constitute good value.

**Voluntary Outflow.** Those who leave the Armed Forces voluntarily before the end of their agreed engagement or commission period. Previously known as voluntary release or premature voluntary release (PVR).

**Voluntary Release.** See **Premature Voluntary Release.**

**Volunteer Reserves and Auxiliary Forces.** Civilian volunteers who undertake to give a certain amount of their time to train in support of the Regular Forces. Includes the Royal Naval Reserve, the Royal Marines Reserve, Territorial Army and the Royal Auxiliary Air Force. Does not include Royal Fleet Auxiliary Service (RFA). Some Volunteer Reservists undertake (paid) Full-Time Reserve Service.

**VOP: Variation of Price.** A contractual provision providing for variation in contract prices if inflation over the period of the contract falls outside defined bands.

**Vote.** An individual Supply Estimate by Parliament. Replaced by Requests for Resources since the introduction of Resource Budgeting in 2001, except for Votes A setting maximum numbers of personnel to be maintained by the Armed Forces.

**WAN: Wide Area Network.** A computer network covering a large geographic area, such as the internet or a network of bank cash dispensers.

**War Pensions Agency. See Veterans Agency.**

**WEAG: Western European Armaments Group.** A group of European countries established in 1993 with the objective of more efficient use of resources through, inter alia, increased harmonization of requirements; the opening up of national defence markets to cross-border competition; to strengthen the European defence technological and industrial base; and cooperation in research and development. The group closed in May 2005 with many of its activities now undertaken by the European Defence Agency.

**WPB: War Pensions benefits.** A non-contributory financial benefit paid to people who have been disabled as a result of conflict, or to dependants of those killed in conflict.

# Index

Printed in the UK for The Stationery Office Limited
on behalf of the Controller of Her Majesty's Stationery Office
ID5810778  07/08

Printed on Paper containing 75% recycled fibre content minimum.